D1257977

The New Asian Corporation

Michael Alan Hamlin

The New Asian Corporation

Managing for the Future in Post-Crisis Asia

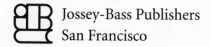
Jossey-Bass Publishers
San Francisco

Substantial discounts on bulk quantities of Jossey-Bass books are available to
corporations, professional associations, and other organizations. For details and
discount information, contact the special sales department at Jossey-Bass Inc.,
Publishers (415) 433–1740; Fax (800) 605–2665.

For sales outside the United States, please contact your local Simon & Schuster International
Office.

 Manufactured in the United States of America on Lyons Falls Pathfinder
Tradebook. This paper is acid-free and 100 percent totally chlorine-free.

Library of Congress Cataloging-in-Publication Data

Hamlin, Michael A.
    The new Asian corporation / by Michael Alan Hamlin—1st ed.
        p.   cm.—(The Jossey-Bass business & management series)
    Includes bibliographical references and index.
    ISBN 0-7879-4606-0 (alk. paper)
    1. Corporations—Asia.   2. Corporations—Asia—Finance.   3.
Industrial management—Asia.   I. Title.   II. Series.
    HD2891.85 .H36   1999
    658'-0095—dc21   99-6602

FIRST EDITION
HB Printing   10 9 8 7 6 5 4 3 2 1

The Jossey-Bass Business &
Management Series

Contents

Acknowledgments xiii

The Author xvii

Introduction: Emerging from Crisis 1

Part One: The New Asia 17

1 Transition to Excellence 19

2 The New Asia: What's Different and What's Not 45

Part Two: The New Asian Corporation 79

3 Rising from the Ashes 81

4 *Guanxi*, Mergers and Acquisitions, and the
New Asian Corporation 103

5 Building Corporate Identity and Influence 125

Part Three: A Shift to Strategy 153

6 The Shift to Strategy: Betting the Company 155

7 The First Source of Competitiveness:
Productivity and Innovation 176

8 The Second Source of Competitiveness: Market Intimacy 198

Part Four: Pressing Asian Realities 221

9 Training and Education: The Innovation Factor 223

10 The New Transparency: Managing Global Equity Flows 246

Part Five: What Comes Next?   261

11 Asia in the Next Century   263

    References   273

    Index   281

To Monette, whom I don't deserve. You are my life. And to Kazuma, Melissa, Chris, Michael, Bea, Cara, and Niccolo. I treasure you all.

—ᵥᵥ— Acknowledgements

Three things have happened that are making Asia a recurring miracle. The first is the Asian financial crisis. Its surprise, intensity, and aftermath are tempering Asian corporations, making them tougher, more focused, and strategically innovative. The second is liberalization. Liberalization is making Asian enterprise more competitive, and Asian companies are learning to put profit ahead of revenue and market share. The third is globalization, Asia's challenge to rise to world-class standards of efficiency, productivity, and quality. The impact of globalization extends beyond management practice to lifestyle and values. That means that the Asian continent will not only be a recurring enterprise miracle, but that it will have the most democratically elected governments serving the largest and most demanding group of consumers on earth.

The opportunity to write about Asia's transition has been made possible by many people. My previous publisher, Stephen Troth of Prentice Hall Asia, introduced me to Cedric Crocker at Jossey-Bass in the United States. At the time of the introduction, Stephen and Cedric were on the same team. By the time I finished the final manuscript—late, as usual—Viacom's restructuring had left them parts of two different organizations.

But Stephen had already given me up. By introducing me to Cedric, he had presented me with the opportunity for wider distribution of my work in the United States than was possible under the Prentice Hall Asia umbrella. I'm not sure how profound that sacrifice will prove to be, but it was a truly selfless act by a respected publisher who has stood by me and encouraged me for a good many years. I'm very grateful, Stephen.

Cedric inspired me with his enthusiasm for the project, which evolved from a United States edition of my first book, *Asia's Best: The Myth & Reality of Asia's Most Successful Companies,* into an entirely new venture. His guidance in developing the initial concept and outline for the book was especially important in focusing my energy on issues that are relevant and important to management practitioners in the United States and Europe. His deputy, Byron Schneider, like Stephen before him, has been a paragon of patience, a dedicated guide and counselor, and a tested taskmaster.

Veronica Oliva was my persevering permissions editor. She kept me out of trouble and offered her own welcome inspiration. Julianna Gustafson put all the pieces together professionally to produce the final product, despite the spotty quality of my cooperation, especially when it came to preparing the final electronic files. Forgive me, Julianna, and thanks to both you and Veronica.

Top executives throughout Asia struggling to contain the crisis and set directions for their companies kindly gave of their extremely valuable time to talk with me, answer my questions, and respond to my researchers. They were eager to share their experiences and saw the value of communicating what they had learned to other managers and aspiring managers. These successful executives understand the critical importance of disseminating management technology in a region where competent management is its most strategic resource.

As in the past, I benefitted greatly from the counsel of some of the world's most respected management authorities who responded to my requests to review my work. Fred Wiersema, co-author of *The Discipline of Market Leaders* and author of *Customer Intimacy,* reviewed several chapters a number of times and read through the entire manuscript prior to its final revision. Thank you, Fred, for your patience and invaluable advice. I feel that this book is as much yours as it is mine.

Philip Kotler, S. C. Johnson & Son Distinguished Professor of International Marketing at the Kellogg Graduate School of Management at Northwestern University, and Adrian Slywotzky, principal of Mercer Management Consulting and co-author of *The Profit Zone,* likewise read the entire manuscript. Both of these renowned authors and teachers were encouraging throughout, and their counsel proved to be insightful and inspiring. Peter S. Cohan, author of *Net Profit,* spent much time with several chapters as well as the final manuscript. He consistently provided comprehensive and detailed feedback that kept me focused as well as organized. My sincere gratitude to you all.

In my office in Manila, a number of associates assisted me with research for the project. They included Kathy David, Harvey Calim, and Arnold Aguirre.

Others at TeamAsia patiently took on more work over the year while I spent time on the book. At the same time, our business grew dramatically, despite the effects of the crisis. This patience was especially true of the president of TeamAsia, my wife Monette Iturralde-Hamlin, who also put up with my absence from family outings and evenings with the children. She was, and is, my greatest inspiration. She is also an Asian manager to be reckoned with: Monette has done a truly remarkable job building our firm and our reputation under often very difficult circumstances.

Finally, I want to thank the people who read my columns in *BusinessWorld, Manila Bulletin,* and the *Far Eastern Economic Review* and listen to my presentations and react to them. Your feedback, criticism, and advice has been of great value in my attempt to put together a book that provides a practical perspective of management in Asia, and how Asian companies and governments have responded to crisis, liberalization, and globalization.

Where the book falls short of my readers' expectations, or may be in error, I accept full responsibility for these transgressions, as well as any failures of omission.

Asia is a wonderful place to be. I'm extremely grateful to have the privilege of living in what I consider to be the most exciting environment in the global economy. I'm equally grateful to have this chance to share my enthusiasm and love for Asia with you in this new book. Thank you for allowing me this opportunity.

September 1999   Michael Alan Hamlin
Manila, The Philippines

—ᨑ— The Author

Michael Alan Hamlin is the managing director of TeamAsia and its Philippine and Singapore affiliates, Hamlin-Iturralde Corporation, where he is responsible for strategic planning and development. Key clients include Intel, SAP, Canon, Cisco, IBM, Smart Communications, Philippine Long Distance Telephone Company, San Miguel Corporation, Smart Communications, and Globe Telecom. Previously, Hamlin was vice president for external affairs and a faculty member of the Asian Institute of Management (AIM).

A talented speech writer and public policy analyst, Hamlin has written speeches for a number of popular public figures throughout Asia. He has authored many articles for international and Asian publications on business and management. He is also a weekly columnist for *BusinessWorld,* the Philippines' leading business newspaper, and the *Manila Bulletin,* a major daily newspaper, and he is a regular contributor to "Rethinking Asia," a column which appears in the *Far Eastern Economic Review.* Hamlin is the author of *Asia's Best: The Myth & Reality of Asia's Most Successful Companies,* published in 1998.

—∿— Introduction
Emerging from Crisis

It was its great weaknesses that inspired Asia's greatest triumphs; and, its greatest strengths that account for its most profound failures. The Asian financial crisis refocused Asia on its weaknesses, and the need to overcome them.

About the time Massachusetts Institute of Technology economist Paul Krugman dramatically called for currency controls in *Fortune* magazine and in a series of meetings and interviews in Asia in August 1998, the world was already witnessing the beginnings of a New Asian Corporation. Its emergence would ultimately have much more to do with Asia's salvation than would artificial controls, International Monetary Fund (IMF) prescriptions, or intervention (as in the Hong Kong government's surprising decision to punish speculators by intervening in the stock market).

While Krugman argued that Asia's malaise was nowhere near its end, innovative, well-managed Asian firms were at work seeking out new sources of profit, tightening their focus, and reengineering processes to boost productivity and quality. While other economists, analysts, and policymakers fretted over bankrupt banks, inefficient conglomerates, and restructuring economies, many companies weren't waiting around for someone to announce the end of the crisis. They were taking advantage of it.

The argument for the emergence of what shall be called here the New Asian Corporation and, indeed, the New Asia, is built around two premises. First, the Asian financial crisis, as it will hereafter be referred to, was not an event with a beginning and an end. This was not a storm that Asian corporations could ride out until things returned to "normal." Normal instead took on a whole new meaning. The Asian financial crisis was a process of change—profound and necessary change—that in all likelihood could only have been provoked by financial calamity on a scale never before seen. Every fundamental of doing business in Asia was rocked.

There will be no return to traditional ways of doing business characterized by close private sector–government relationships and direction, although vested interests in Indonesia, Malaysia, and Thailand have tried hard to slow the pace of change. And for a time, they succeeded. In Indonesia, bank reform was stalled and the banks worsened. In Malaysia, corporations with close government ties were bailed out of their problems, further alienating foreign investors and minority shareholders severely frightened by Prime Minister Mahathir Mohamad's racist rhetoric. In Thailand, a gentrified senate struggled to hold back banking and regulatory reforms.

But as Asia began to emerge from crisis, it was clear that in the same way a particular management style is appropriate for small corporations and an entirely new set of skills is necessary for larger, more complex corporations, the New Asia—a much more complex Asia than its precursor—demanded a new way of being managed.

The second related premise is that the Asian financial crisis was not the only powerful force buffeting Asian economies and their companies, although it overshadowed other forces because of its suddenness and severity. There were actually three forces: the Asian financial crisis, globalization, and liberalization. The crisis accelerated the inevitable restructuring of economies, industries, and corporations. Globalization brought to bear international standards of profitability, quality, efficiency, and productivity. The pressure was to perform according to globally accepted standards. Liberalization introduced bonafide competition and a new mindset: Growth had to be value driven, not opportunity driven. Companies that understood this quickly showed that they could be real competition for some of the world's most respected multinational firms. Many others would enter new strategic relationships with multinationals to survive.

THE ASIAN FINANCIAL CRISIS

With the Asian financial crisis winding down through the last year of the twentieth century, the region was suddenly swamped by incredibly lucid analyses purporting to explain why the crisis occurred and who was responsible. Foremost among the finger pointers was Harvard University economist Jeffrey Sachs, who has argued long and hard that the crisis would be more accurately referred to as the Asian financial panic. Sachs believes it was started by private bankers who—as they appear to on a regular, cyclical basis—suddenly realized their Southeast Asian clients had overextended themselves. An obvious sign was the huge inventories of empty buildings in Thailand.

It's interesting to note that the private bankers in this case were mostly Europeans and Japanese. The Americans resisted the temptation, for the most part, to recreate their unsavory South American problem in Southeast Asia. But that doesn't mean they didn't contribute to the panic, as we'll see. Southeast Asia, meanwhile, relied happily on the notion of Asian values to convince itself that the inevitable correction wouldn't—even couldn't—happen.

International currency traders and stock brokers thought otherwise. After encouraging clients to borrow heavily—US$360 trillion in derivatives were traded in 1997, a value more than a dozen times the entire global economy—Thailand's increasingly beleaguered real estate sector and overextended banks presented the opportunity to short both stocks and currency to reap huge windfall profits. At the same time, Japan (Thailand's principal investor and trading partner after the United States), was contracting by 11 percent, pushing the economy into deep recession and significantly denting demand from Thailand's overbuilt manufacturing and export sector.

As a result, local banks, real estate developers, and exporters began buying dollars amidst speculation that the local currency would devalue, meeting the expectations of short sellers, who upped their bets against the baht, the monetary unit of Thailand. Writing in the *New York Times*, Nicholas D. Kristof and Edward Wyatt asked, "Who were these speculators? They were mostly American, and the hedge funds were prominent among them. But they also included major United States banks, trading for themselves to make a profit. J. P. Morgan said in a court document that it had traded US$1 billion worth of baht in the fall of 1996" (Kristof, 1999). American banks saw the crisis coming thanks to their South American experience and were ready to help it along.

Thailand and the rest of financially panicked Asia actually set themselves up for the speculators, according to most observers, including Paul Krugman, Hong Kong fund manager Marc Faber, and bank analyst Philippe F. Delhaise, along with Sachs. But unlike Sachs, Faber and Delhaise take credit for seeing the crisis coming. Krugman denies direct insight, but nevertheless receives credit for predicting the crisis in an infamous 1994 *Foreign Affairs* article "The Myth of Asia's Miracle." None of them, however, believe that the crisis should have been as bad as it ultimately was.

Krugman emerged during the crisis as its chief expert and most noteworthy pundit, despite some very public waffling from remedy to remedy—ranging from capital controls to the exercise of good horse sense. Marc Faber is the subject of a book by *Far Eastern Economic Review* columnist Nury Vittachi entitled *Doctor Doom: Riding the Millennial Storm*. Faber is an obvious contrarian who looks for wicked opportunity. He searches for situations that can't imaginably get any worse, and he encourages investors to get involved. In the meantime, he talks down strong market performers and encourages investors to short their stock.

Philippe Delhaise is the author of *Asia in Crisis: The Implosion of the Banking and Financial Systems*. He is a strident critic of Asian banking practices and argues that "the figures and ratios published by banks across Asia—with very few exceptions—are totally misleading. Crudely said, the banks have been cooking the books for years. Dozens of banks are bankrupt, but nobody knows about it" (1998, p. 8).

Actually, everybody knew, but was afraid to admit it because of the clout the banking sector wielded during the miracle years. That everyone did know it encouraged them to assume the worst when the attacks began on the Thai baht. For Faber, the crisis was inevitable because, like economist John Mayward Keynes, he believes "the inevitable never happens. It is the unexpected always. Except for those who always expect the unexpected, apparently.

"To illustrate this, Faber asks his clients to visualize themselves as a powerful person wishing to invest in Asia in the year 1800. Your most logical choices would have been Calcutta, which was the administrative center of the British Empire, or Batavia, the capital of the Dutch East Indies. Today, Calcutta has lost all its luster; and Batavia, now called Jakarta, is one of the region's poor performers" (Vittachi, 1998, p. 47). Unlike Faber, Vittachi is given to serious understatement.

"Imagine if you were making the same decision a century or so later, say in 1920," Vittachi continues. "The most important city in Asia was Shanghai, a lively, bustling place known as 'the Paris of the East'. Other places which looked set to boom were Canton (now Guangzhou), Macao, Saigon, Rangoon, and Manila—none of which survived." For Faber, the crisis was a matter of fate overtaking complacent expectation.

But what of our two international economists, Sachs and Krugman, and our analysis of who's ultimately to blame for the Asian financial panic? In Sachs's opinion, the IMF did the most damage, reacting radically to the speculative attacks against the baht and its ultimate release from the dollar peg. "When the IMF panicked—ostentatiously declaring that Asia needed drastic financial surgery such as immediate and widespread bank closures, astronomical interest rates, and drastic fiscal cuts—the investors panicked right alongside" (Sachs, 1999, pp. 70–71).

By early 1999, Krugman appeared to have adopted the same view. While the private sector was irresponsible in its borrowing, international and local banks reckless in their lending, governments oblivious to the need to provide appropriate regulatory frameworks, and local and international investors' unmerciful, it was the collective panic exacerbated by the IMF that was the catalyst that turned a significant problem into a full-scale, historic rout. Krugman wrote again in

Foreign Affairs, "The idea that economies are being punished for their weaknesses is ultimately unconvincing on at least two grounds. For one thing, the scale of the punishment is wholly disproportionate to the crime. Furthermore, if the fault lies with the countries, why have so many of them gotten into trouble at the same time?" (1999, pp. 70–71).

Still, Krugman continued to hedge his bets and came up short of outright subscribing to Sachs's thesis because, as he frequently said himself, he just did not know. Perhaps it is because Southeast Asia is not perceived as a bunch of countries by most international investors, and that prior to the crisis, the economies of Southeast Asia had become so increasingly intertwined that they suffered universally. Perhaps it was the wretched hedge funds that went unsatiated by the carnage in Thailand and that thirsted for more. Or, maybe it was just time for Southeast Asia to grow up and get real.

However, much of the Asian miracle was idyllic. This was a time when corporations were able to grow almost exclusively through debt financing, yet report returns on investment that were absurdly low in the absence of real competition. In Thailand, lending to the private sector exceeded 140 percent of gross domestic product just prior to the crisis. In Malaysia, it was more than 160 percent, and in South Korea and Indonesia, greater than 70 and 60 percent, respectively.

It was also a time when businessmen could throw money at opportunity and stay viable with their eyes closed. Opportunity was a function of privilege bestowed by benevolent politicians. The product of these excesses took two forms. First, there was overcapacity. Asian corporations were no longer able to generate revenues to cover their obligations. Second, the capacity was characterized by aging technology, inefficient use of financial resources, and lagging productivity. In short, prosperity had made Asia uncompetitive by eroding its low-cost labor advantage. Asian corporations failed to compensate for this eroding advantage by improving operations and increasing the value-added of output. The financial crisis, then, was the result of trying to sustain gross inefficiency in a coddled corporate sector.

But whatever the complete answer is, and whether it is ever completely understood, it is important to acknowledge that investors who understand Asia best remained almost universally steadfast. A survey conducted by the Asia Society and the *Asian Wall Street Journal* in January 1999 among almost 1,500 senior executives in Asia showed that 88 percent of corporations with headquarters in the United States had either expanded or left unchanged plans for direct investment since the Asian financial crisis began in 1997. Forty-one percent had expanded their plans.

Likewise, 86 percent of companies with headquarters in Asia had expanded or left plans unchanged. A slightly lower number, 35 percent, had expanded their investments. Perhaps direct investors have little other choice, given the long-term quality of their investments. But the same survey also showed that 75 percent of companies with U.S. headquarters had expanded or maintained their level of portfolio investment in Asia. Sixty-one percent of firms headquartered in Asia had expanded or maintained their level of portfolio investment as well.

All this brings us to suggest this: Asia's development cycles are going to be as rapid as its development over the last half of the twentieth century. Downturns will be more severe although relatively short-lived and with reforms not as severe in their unpleasantness. But that's another story. In the meantime, let the new prosperity begin.

WHAT IS THE NEW ASIAN CORPORATION?

The New Asian Corporation is a phrase that describes a corporate community and management practice in transition (Table I.1). Observation of Asian enterprise shows that management practice in excellent organizations demonstrates the application of universal principles of sound and enlightened management. Not all Asian organizations

Corporate Strategy	Focus on key business processes and the development of new business models
Management and Corporate Culture	Premium on management expertise and strategic thinking
Opportunity	Market and customer centric

Table I.1. Characteristics of the New Asian Corporation.

demonstrate this quality, only the best. This is also true in the United States as well as in Europe, where we see major corporations increasingly resembling American corporations as world economies globalize, and accepted standards to gauge management performance become universal.

Yet none of our argument suggests that there is a perfect organization, or even a conceptually perfect corporate image to work toward. Rather, it is to say that in strategically successful companies, certain basic principles stand out: relentless cost efficiency, high operational productivity, and innovation-inspired, value-driven strategic growth. And there is creative chaos, a natural product of the evolution of companies that are effectively managing organizational change in response to dramatically new conditions.

What distinguishes excellent corporations in the United States, Asia, and Europe is where they are in their respective transitions. In Europe and Asia, resistance to change is pronounced for a variety of reasons, some cultural, some personal (i.e., the desperate desire to hold on to family heirlooms), and some historical—while many American corporations have learned the hard way not to resist the pressure for change. But despite these barriers, strategic success invariably hinges on the capacity of organizations to accept the need for change and to successfully maneuver through increasingly frequent and profound transitions.

Companies that have difficulty doing this are likely to go the way of companies like Ford Motor Company. Henry Ford stubbornly refused to play by the new industry rules General Motors was forcing on the marketplace. Another example is American electrical appliances manufacturers that refused to acknowledge that Japanese competitors actually knew what they were doing. A more recent example is the retailers who insisted to analysts that the Internet is a fad, not a business tool.

Of course, there are worldwide examples of companies and industries that have failed to accept change, the pace of change, and the need to change. We see this in Asia—as we continue to see elsewhere, too—in instances where inefficient, protected industries cry out for government protection against better-run regional and multinational corporations. But we also see it more commonly in domestic corporations that just cannot bring themselves to set aside business models that appeared to work for generations in favor of new ways of doing business.

In response to these observations, the question is frequently asked about the unique qualities and operating styles of Japanese, Korean, and Chinese family organizations. These companies, in many obvious and well-documented ways, demonstrated certain unique characteristics during the Asian miracle years. And this was the result of unique circumstances. But because world economies are globalizing and integrating, those circumstances are fading away. The driver is liberalization. Governments cannot preserve conditions that gave rise to unique business practices if they want reciprocal access to the global economy.

This is particularly true for Japanese and Korean corporations, although there is a great deal of resistance to "reality-shifts" among the *chaebols* (conglomerates) in Korea now. The Japanese seem finally resigned to the idea that the old must give way to the new, particularly now that younger managers are assuming top positions in business, government bureaucracy, and political leadership.

The Chinese family corporation is of course a different and oft romanticized story. The family corporation was an amazingly successful aberration that benefitted by capitalizing on opportunity amid social and development chaos. It is a feudal organization. Hong Kong's Li & Fung and Gold Peak companies provide the best examples of what will happen to formerly family-run Chinese companies that have a strategic future. Both are now professionally run, no longer predominately owned by family members, and the next generation of leaders is likely to come from among a pool of professional managers.

One of the most powerful indicators of the growing impact of market economics on Asian economies is the diminishing returns of *guanxi,* or connections, throughout Asia. Taking the place of connections is reputation for performing consistently according to internationally accepted standards of growth in revenues, profitability, and shareholder value. If you can't perform, you are simply out of the game.

A few other observations. We frequently argue that excellent companies are driven by strategy, not opportunity. It is important to distinguish between market opportunity within a focused, strategic framework versus undisciplined expansionary opportunity across highly unrelated industries. Arguments for strategy-driven growth over opportunity-driven growth do not mean that recognizing opportunity is no longer important. In fact, it is more important than ever. The difference is that opportunity optimization is dependent on two things: 1) disciplined focus on core businesses and business processes and 2) strategic anticipation of shifts in industry rules and consumer behavior which render old sources of profit unreliable, but generate new profit opportunities.

Change—and the pressure for change—is not new. The pace of change we see in the global economy is new. Change is faster, more profound, and increasingly dramatic. And that is the only constant in Asia's new corporate landscape. As Faber argues, the unexpected is inevitable. And it's happening faster than ever.

There is no unique Asian management style; certainly none has emerged as a result of the impact of the three forces. In fact, Asian corporations have shifted perceptibly toward increasing Westernization in management practice, strategic focus, and accountability to stakeholders. As we also argued in the past, application of what we prefer to call universal principles of management excellence demonstrated fascinating instances of impressive levels of innovation and creativity in meeting the challenges of crisis, globalization, and liberalization.

But it would be inaccurate to suggest that the West has nothing to learn from Asia. In fact, Asia and its managers have been on the front lines of the most profound financial conflagration ever seen either in scope or severity. The three forces driving change in Asia have provoked a dramatic shift in priorities away from asset and market-share building toward increased productivity, innovation, and strategic thinking. This is a shift as significant as the forces driving it. And it would be a serious mistake to dismiss the tempering Asian organizations are undergoing as a result.

PART ONE: THE NEW ASIA

The three forces—crisis, globalization, liberalization—quickly rendered rusty, old Asian business models irrelevant and provoked a new way of thinking about managing in Asia. Chapter One: Transition to Excellence provides a summary of the powerful impact of these three forces on companies in Asia, and the product of their effect: new leaders, the passing of old corporate icons, and innovative application of what is called global best practices.

Corporate restructuring both drove and was driven by changes in Asian economies. Competition for intellectual and financial resources, the new regulatory role of governments, the eclipse of the privileged banking sector, and the convergence of national development strategies created a whole new business environment. We examine this more closely in Chapter Two: The New Asia: What's Different and What's Not.

PART TWO: THE NEW ASIAN CORPORATION

Part Two provides our first in-depth look at the New Asian Corporation. Chapter Three: Rising from the Ashes, focuses on the key resources managers in Asia must maximize to survive and thrive in the New Asia. Thriving is determined less by economic circumstances than by the organization's—and its leadership's—capacity to adapt quickly to vastly different business realities and to capitalize on them with persistent regularity.

While networking will continue to be important in Asia, as it is everywhere else, that famous esoteric notion of powerful connections is no longer pervasive. With the gold rush days over in Asia, both long-term investor and business decision-making is focused on quality of assets, management, and products, not political influence. Solid management, introduced in Chapter Four: *Guanxi*, Mergers and Acquisitions, and the New Asian Corporation, is the key to success in Asia.

In the heady days of the Asian miracle years, outside of multinational corporations, brand building and corporate identity was low on the list of strategic priorities, especially for Asian firms enjoying the benefits of protected marketplaces. For the New Asian Corporation, building goodwill goes much further than political connections. The prosperity of the corporation relies on the goodwill of all key publics. In increasingly democratic, constituent-sensitive Asian economies, corporations can no longer count on political and business relationships to bail them out in times of trouble. That means corporate image becomes a tool for controlling events, and not just reacting when bad things happen to good companies. That's the focus of Chapter Five: Building Corporate Identity and Influence.

PART THREE: A SHIFT TO STRATEGY

Part Three is concerned with the fundamental requisites of doing business for the New Asian Corporation. The first of these is a shift to strategy. But to understand the shift, we must first look at what we mean by strategy, especially in the economic and business context prevailing in Asia. Chapter Six: The Shift to Strategy: Betting the Company examines what strategy means to some of Asia's most resourceful corporations.

Next, we consider productivity and innovation in the New Asian Corporation. The three forces of change have collectively forced a sense of urgency in the introduction of productivity-enhancing measures and innovation-inspiring management. Chapter Seven: The First Source of Competitiveness: Productivity and Innovation examines the unrelenting pressure to think faster than the competition.

In Chapter Eight: The Second Source of Competitiveness: Market Intimacy, we examine how the New Asian Corporation is relying on hard, scientific information to show it how to be soft— or market intimate—with the customers who count: those who are the most profitable. Keeping those customers satisfied and coming back for more requires that the New Asian Corporation continually look for new ways to build share of customer and change industry rules. We argue that profitability depends more on increasing the amount of business a firm does with profitable customers rather than market share.

PART FOUR: PRESSING ASIAN REALITIES

It's not all good news for the New Asian Corporation. The key resource—appropriately trained and educated people—is in short supply on the world's most populous continent. During the miracle years of the 1980s and 1990s, most Southeast Asian governments neglected investment in educational infrastructure; the existing infrastructure is capable of producing far fewer managers, engineers, and scientists than are required to help the continent make the transition to high value-added manufacturing and service delivery. Worse yet, developed economies are relentlessly competing for Asia's best brains and talent. Addressing this most serious of resource shortfalls is the focus of Chapter Nine: Training and Education: The Innovation Factor.

There has been a lot of loose talk about the evils of global private fund flows and their contribution to the Asian financial crisis. But it was not the funds that caused the crisis. Their outflow was a symptom of the real causes: bankrupt banking practices, inefficient corporations protected by government benefactors, and irrational euphoria leading to phantom growth and profits. Because these fund flows far exceeded the value of foreign direct investment, recovery from the financial crisis in many respects hinged on restoring investor confidence in Asian enterprise and financial institutions. Confidence meant acceptance of global standards of transparency and accountability to shareholders.

The idea of shareholder accountability was far-fetched during the Asian miracle years. That is all changing. Increasingly stringent regulatory frameworks are being put in place to safeguard against the excesses that helped bring about the Asian financial crisis. Strategic, institutional, and small investors alike are looking for complete transparency and management accountability before providing the financial resources most Asian firms require. How these new imperatives are changing corporate Asia and its related cultures is the focus of Chapter Ten: The New Transparency: Managing Global Equity Flows.

PART FIVE: WHAT COMES NEXT?

MIT professor Lester Thurow proclaimed in his book *Head to Head* (1992) that the future belonged not to the Asia Pacific—specifically Japan and the United States—but to Europe. The Asian financial crisis provided new credibility to Thurow's argument. Indeed, Paul Krugman argues, "Compared with Asia's debacle, the tequila crisis of 1995 now looks like a minor wobble; and the once terrifying debt crisis of the 1980s, a positively placid affair" (1998, p. 33). Krugman catapulted to infamy by warning that Asia's growth was the product of straightforward resource mobilization, rather than productivity gains. And that should have been an argument that Asia listened to instead of reacted against.

But for all the wonder of the vaunted Asian miracle years, there have always been informed voices that sought to temper the enthusiasm for what was the world's fastest-growing group of economies, even when practically everyone else concluded the owners of those voices were, well, nuts. In mid-1998 with the European economy strong and growing—before the Russian blowout—there was good reason to think that Thurow was right after all.

However unhealthy and dangerous the untempered enthusiasm of the nature that characterized the Asian miracle years may have been, the resources that initially suggested Asia's great potential are still very much present. This issue is debated in Chapter Eleven: Asia in the Next Century.

Asia lost a good deal of luster during the time this book was being written. The continent's incredible fall has been every bit as breathtaking as its spectacular growth. But the crisis provided a tempering of Asia with the ultimate result that its economies and companies will emerge stronger and better fit for the long-term. Make no mistake, recalcitrant holdouts among national leaderships in some instances delayed the emergence of their economies and their corporate sector from the debilitating financial chaos, but they could not hold back the pace of change nor their people for long.

SOME PRACTICAL CLARIFICATIONS

When we say that this book is about Asia, we refer most particularly to Southeast Asia and more exclusively to the original members of the Association of Southeast Asian Nations (ASEAN), plus Hong Kong. From time-to-time, Japan, South Korea, Taiwan, and China are discussed mainly in a very peripheral way. As for ASEAN, readers won't find much about Indonesia. Aside from the obvious reasons—given that the first draft of this manuscript was completed in September 1998 at the height of Asia's financial crisis—and as we have argued elsewhere, Indonesia's economy has been so artificially manipulated that it is next to impossible to find truly innovative instances of management excellence.

This is also frequently the case in Malaysia, although there are some obvious exceptions. It's clear that in an environment in which opportunity is so closely linked to political favoritism and connections, it isn't necessary to be better than the competition at much more than being the first in line to shake someone's hand. But again, we would hasten to add that these conditions merely hide rather than reduce the potential of a nation's people. Once conditions are created in which competent, responsible management is allowed to compete and flourish, so will Malaysia. There will always be the need for government to provide a reasonable and effective regulatory framework, but government should foster competition, not decide who will reign over its industries. Tragically, Malaysia's stubborn resistance to corporate restructuring has left many of its largest companies ill-prepared for competition on a level playing field.

We believe that anyone who is interested in management excellence and innovative leadership in the world's most populous marketplace will find value in spending some time reading this book. The instances of excellence profiled here are valuable for at least two reasons. First, they present reliable trends for management and strategic development of corporations in Asia. Second, all managers can learn valuable lessons from these instances of innovation in response to the most debilitating financial and enterprise crisis that not just Asia but the world has ever seen. Companies that withstood the effects of the crisis and learned how to survive amidst its chaos are companies to watch and from which to learn. It can be said, to editorialize on an old theme, Asian companies have been where no company has been before. And now they're back.

PART ONE

The New Asia

CHAPTER ONE

Transition to Excellence

I
t's a new Asia.

In his nineteenth floor office along Bangkok's Sukhumvit Road, act-ing chief executive Robert Mollerstuen is struggling to revive Alphatec Electronics from financial ruin after high-flying founder and former chief executive Charn Uswachoke diverted loans taken out by the company to related but separately incorporated real estate and high-tech ventures. Auditors announced that Alphatec had falsified financial reports over a three-year period. The company went from being one of Asia's most admired entrepreneurial technology firms, and the darling of media and the Thai government, to being the epitomization of the excesses of crony capitalism and loose corporate and banking regulations.

Thailand's new bankruptcy law may be Alphatec's salvation, ac-cording to Mollerstuen, providing the means for new capital infusion after Charn blocked efforts to recapitalize that would dilute his interest. Meanwhile, Mollerstuen, thanks to his personal reputa-tion and the quality of Alphatec output, has managed to retain his high-technology client base and even envisions expanding into higher value-added production.

Across town, Thai Farmers Bank president Banthoon Lamsam has recently completed a recapitalization exercise with the infusion of US$857 million from international institutional investors. "The placement expanded foreign ownership in Thai Farmers shares to 49 percent," yet raised less money than expected. Still the placement makes it possible "to avoid the fate of many other Thai banks, which have been forced into often-difficult searches for cash-rich foreign partners" (Hilsenrath, 1998, p. 3).

But Banthoon believes that's not the principal reason Thai Farmers will survive the Asian crisis and continue to be among the nation's top banks. "It's the companies that have made the investment in people and technology that will survive. Getting your best people in the right place with the right technology is critical." So, too, is quality in three areas: products and services, governance, and supervision. In that sense, the Asian crisis was actually a good thing, Banthoon says. "A major shift in behavior in organizations is being forced by this crisis. This shift would not come about otherwise. That's what I do most everyday—shift culture" (Interview with author, June 3, 1998).

The Shangri-La Hotel in Singapore is undergoing a major facelift. General manager John Segreti is a tough, bottom-line-focused hotelier from New York. He is ripping out the Shangri-La's lobby and coffee shop with the ultimate result intended to be an airier, lighter, and imposingly grander entrance to one of Asia's best-known hotels. He also plans to build a large central kitchen—satellite kitchens were previously scattered throughout the complex—that will be used for baking pastries and other items for two other Kuok Group hotels, too, sharply lowering capital requirements and operations and personnel costs.

That's not all Segreti is centralizing. "All three hotels will operate on a common technology platform," he says, "and we are likewise centralizing purchasing, human resource, and financial control" (Interview with author, June 25, 1998). Big changes. But the biggest change is a shift in leadership and people management style. Compensation is no longer based on seniority and loyalty, but on results.

At precision machine and tool manufacturer Excel, Executive Vice President Wee Yue Chew is enthusiastic about the future (Interview with the author, June 25, 1998). Investment in a Hungarian company in 1995 has paid off in the acquisition of technology that would have taken years and a significantly larger investment to develop in Singapore. As a result, Excel is able to meet a broader range of its clients' needs.

Lower labor costs had nothing to do with Excel's acquisition of the Hungarian manufacturer. "Cheap labor is no use to me," Wee says. "Productive labor is important. I believe that money walks on two legs. Motivated people can do a third more, so if I need four people, I hire three." But neither the expanded offerings nor high productivity are the most important reason for Excel's success in a highly competitive industry.

Founded by three friends with a few thousand dollars, Excel quickly developed a reputation for quality but soon realized that quality was a basic requisite of business, not a competitive advantage. The company started telling prospects that it would design the factories' floors and specify the best equipment—including that of its competitors—in return for their business. It also services competitors' equipment. That extra value-added paid off. And with the Hungarian acquisition, Excel provides even more of the equipment it designs for clients.

The Asian crisis has provoked more innovation expanding the company's "total customer solution" approach to business. With their own credit tight, Excel worked with clients' bankers on the basis of their bonafide letters of credit to provide funds for the acquisition of equipment required to fill orders. The company even helped clients sell old equipment. But foresight has also paid off in reducing the company's dependence on Asian markets to 20 percent of total revenues.

Fast food entrepreneur Michael Chan Yue Kwong enjoyed a windfall when the Asian crisis struck and Hong Kong's bustling, hustling executives began "eating down," which put his stock into play in a dramatically depressed market. Sudden and precipitous falls in real estate and stock values had returned the Special Autonomous Region's employed millionaires to the status of simple employees. And many were lucky to be employed.

But Chan knows that it would be dangerous to become complacent. Expanding his successful Café de Coral franchise had shown that while market share was increasing, returns on investment in new stores was decreasing. Like Excel, Chan began thinking how he could increase the amount of business he did with existing customers. And he decided he could best do that by doing more business with existing customers, rather than investing in additional marketing to attract new customers.

So, Chan created a more diverse menu—one that he could rotate so that his mainstay company employee and student customers would visit more than once a week and have a different selection to choose from each time.

Like Chan, Tony Tan Caktiong's Philippine fast food chains are setting new records. Jollibee first grabbed international attention by drubbing McDonald's in the local market. In 1998, Greenwich Pizza—like Jollibee, set up to appeal to local tastes—became the second-largest fast food chain in the country, in terms of market share. Consequently, McDonald's dropped to third place. Tan also increased his share of business with loyal clients, but unlike Chan, he gave them a whole new pizza chain.

That doesn't mean that Tan isn't intent on growing the number of stores he operates as company-owned or franchised outlets. In fact, he's growing far afield. When the first Jollibee opened in the United States—in Daly City, California, which boasts a large Filipino population—customers waited for up to two hours for a ten-minute meal. And that's not the company's first overseas store. It has thriving operations in China, Vietnam, and Saudi Arabia.

After its 1994 partial privatization, Petron Corporation's directors and top management knew that transforming a government bureaucracy into a market-oriented company would be a huge task. Today, more than five years later, the company has a new identity and a new orientation. Concerned about its capacity to compete in the Philippines' deregulated market, the company has launched a strategic scenario planning program to take it into the next century.

The truly fascinating aspect of Petron, however, is not its sexy, new identity, but its preoccupation with becoming "customer intimate." Not many will accuse the world's monolithic petroleum companies of knowing much about getting close to customers. But to Petron's way of thinking, petroleum is a service industry. The company has devised an organizational transformation program anchored on seven principles that support its drive for customer intimacy: entrepreneurial spirit, critical thinking, commitment to excellence, team orientation, empowerment, adaptability, and ethics. Petron is setting a new standard for service excellence in its industry.

It could be said that TA Enterprises was saved by the bell. Like many firms in the heyday of the Asian miracle, this Malaysian brokerage, flush with cash, decided to diversify into the unknown but seductive real estate development industry. Lucky for TA, its ambitions were thwarted by delays in bureaucratic approvals.

Another investment, however, has provided insights into how the company should restructure itself to strengthen its capacity to withstand future crises. Botly, a brokerage headquarter in the city of Ipoh, is one-third the size of its giant parent, but has extremely low overhead. Wong Hong Meng, TA's executive director, says, "[C]osts are 25 percent of Kuala Lumpur prices, and the brokerage is making good money in the crisis.

"We believe the Botly model is good, and so we are realigning other businesses to this model." That means no more monuments, like TA's gleaming new headquarters, which are now major drags on revenue. Wong believes that the Asian recovery will dawn with new rules, and maybe even new players. TA's founder Tony Tiah Thee Kian has decided that he wants younger managers to take over the operations of the firm because the New Asia requires "managers with new ideas, new drive, new energy" (Interview with author, June 23, 1998).

Indeed, "everyone wanted to be in property development," says Dató Mohamed Haji Said, managing director of Sime UEP Properties, a subsidiary of Asia's best-known, homegrown conglomerate, Malaysia's Sime Darby. "Smaller people getting on the bandwagon got caught in the downswing because it takes time to prepare to enter the industry [properly]" (Interview with author, June 22, 1998), Mohamed says. He believes that many of these firms are technically bankrupt, and that it didn't have to be that way. Sime UEP has no debt, and a large land bank that continues to exhibit attractive values.

Unlike unrelated competitors who strayed into the property markets, Sime UEP steadfastly maintained its focus. "There were temptations," Mohamed reveals. "For example, construction—that we resisted. We don't do architecture either, or engineering, surveying, or even our own legal work." As a result, Sime UEP is completely debt-free and sitting on a massive land bank whose value remains higher than its acquisition cost. Mohamed believes that the principal cause of Malaysia's crisis after nine historic boom years was "euphoria," which provoked unrealistic assumptions and opportunity-driven business decisions.

But Mohamed also believes that the downturn demonstrates "symptoms and signs that are very close to those not too long ago. The property industry now is reminiscent of the 1970s and 1980s. Then, after recession, stronger developers were in the market almost immediately." Likewise, Mohamed is sitting back for the moment—content to dabble in low-margin, low-income housing—secure in the knowledge that the economy will turn the corner in time, and ultimately prove to be better than ever. And he'll be there when it does.

UNDERSTANDING THE NEW ASIAN CORPORATION

These companies provide important insights into what we call the New Asian Corporation. Like all fundamental change, the transformation of corporate Asia is profound, yet eminently understandable. These changes are not distinguished by their "uniqueness," but by their universality. While the New Asian Corporation is much more "Western" in management practice, it uses proven management technology in innovative ways in unique circumstances to produce surprising results.

The New Asian Corporation emerged not just from history's most significant instance of rapid and substantial growth, but, probably even more important, from the fiercest, most debilitating financial crisis that has ever occurred. The crisis was made worse by the fact that no one really, or entirely, understood why it happened, or how to make it go away. Having withstood calamity of historic proportion, and now adapted to new realities, these new corporations are tough competitors. From the examples of these individual companies we can identify at least eleven important ways the New Asian Corporation is better than its predecessor. (See Table 1.1.)

MANAGEMENT AND CORPORATE CULTURE

Consider the ways management and corporate culture are changing.

Rising From the Ashes

Excellence is found in the strangest places. Alphatec, run by Western managers yet set up to lead Thailand's charge into high technology,

Management and Corporate Culture: Premium on management expertise and strategic thinking

1. Rising from the Ashes—Excellence is found in surprising places
2. Ownership and Accountability—Shareholders become cosmopolitan, and demanding
3. Wrenching Cultural Change—Seniority is out, productivity is in
4. New Social Contract—Tenure is based on contribution
5. End of Affirmative Action—Competence, not ethnic background or citizenship, is the priority
6. Changing of the Old Guard—New blood and fresh ideas

Corporate Strategy: Focus on key business processes and the development of new business models

7. Strategy and Focus—Developing foresight and consolidating strengths
8. Shifting Profit Zones—New sources of profitability fuel strategy-led growth

Opportunity: Market and customer centric

9. Revitalization—A sense of urgency and innovation pervades across industry boundaries
10. Expansion to New Markets—Liberalization works both ways
11. Tuning Into the Customer—Identifying who customers should be

Table 1.1. Eleven Ways the New Asian Corporation is Different.

has never fit the mold of a typical Asian company. Although a good many observers forecast its demise in the early days of the Asian financial crisis, the bankrupt Alphatec's endurance is testimony to the contribution of corporate reform. Thailand's new bankruptcy law provides for the company's recapitalization by international investors despite the founder's clinging opposition, and therefore offers good prospects for the future. While Alphatec is an extreme case, it is certainly not the only endangered company to ultimately withstand and emerge stronger from the forces of crisis, liberalization, and globalization on Asian enterprise.

Ownership and Accountability

The fact that Alphatec will survive is not the only important issue. The fact that it will survive by doing the right thing—trading new equity for the original shareholders' interests rather than being bailed out with public money—is what's fundamentally important. The family-owned, paternal character of most Asian corporations is under intense pressure to change. Troubled firms and illiquid banks are easy targets for investors, but even healthy firms have a new perspective on ownership and accountability.

In a liberalized environment, for many of these companies fresh equity and strategic partnerships are the only viable alternatives for sustaining industry leadership and growth. Debt financing is not viable for companies that need to achieve global standards of operations quickly. Equity financing provides the prospect of rapid growth. Ideally, taking on a strategic partner also provides new technology that contributes to improved efficiency, productivity, and quality. These changes reflect a new pragmatism that sees the role of families in well-run Asian firms on the wane.

As the role of equity financing in Asian development builds, so too does transparency and accountability of management. This happens for three reasons. First, risk management and credit analysis by lenders is now more than window dressing, in part because banks and financial institutions realize they need to protect themselves, and in part as a result of a new regulatory environment. Second, strategic partners' require meaningful due-diligence before undertaking new partnerships, and complete transparency in the management of the merger and allocation of resources. This includes regular reporting of bottom line results, as in the United States. Third, portfolio managers can no longer manage their Asian investments by riding the wave of enthusiasm. They must know which companies are best-managed and therefore represent the best potential return.

Wrenching Cultural Change

In a competitive and transparent world, where stockholder interests come before those of founders, competitiveness reflects the determination of the company's leadership to champion fundamental change in corporate practices and cultural values. This includes a transition from seniority-based promotion that rewards loyalty, to performance-based appraisal that celebrates exemplary performance characterized by high productivity and innovation, like the transition taking place at the Singapore Shangri-La Hotel. Workers must adapt to the reality that they will never know the security of tenure their predecessors did. And, they must accept the fact that a janitor, whether he's worked a year or twenty years, will always be paid a janitor's salary. Janitors—and managers—who want to improve will have to perform better, assume more responsibility, and be willing to take risks.

New Social Contract

Management is under increased pressure to inspire exemplary performance and to recruit the best minds. But employees—skilled labor, knowledge workers, and even senior management—understand that the relationship is now contractual in very practical terms, rather than cultural, and based on specific conditions. If the terms of the contract are not met—or conditions change—all bets are off. As a result, high-flyers are demanding more from their employers than ever to offset the pressure to perform. The uneasy dichotomy that top management must juggle is the critical need for the best minds versus constant and unrelenting evaluation of results. It's a process not unlike wooing the lion trainer into the lion's cage for an extended performance.

End of Affirmative Action

Because seasoned managers will always be in short supply, top posts will no longer automatically go to Asian nationals or particular ethnic groups, in the same way that multinational posts frequently do go to local managers. Management appointment and tenure will go to the man or woman who gets the job done best. That's why hotelier Segreti and high-tech executive Mollerstuen are leading two of Asia's most high-profile enterprises. Asia will fast become extremely cosmopolitan and an even richer melting pot.

Changing of the (Old) Guard

The pace of change is too dizzying for many old-time entrepreneurs and founders of Asian companies to keep pace. Those that can't keep pace—if they want their organizations to survive—are demonstrating the courage to turn over responsibility to a younger generation of managers prepared to do battle in an unpredictable marketplace. Enlightened firms like TA Securities started this transition early and are feeling their way into a new corporate culture.

CORPORATE STRATEGY

How has corporate strategy evolved?

Strategy and Focus

While opportunities will remain plentiful in Asia, opportunity-driven growth—a product of developing, protected markets—will no longer provide reasonable prospects for growth and success. There will be great pressure to apply corporate resources efficiently and in an effective, focused manner to capitalize on distinct competencies. Top managers like Chan and Tan are spending increasing amounts of their time thinking about vision and strategy. A 1998 survey by PriceWaterhouseCoopers showed that 61 percent of nearly three hundred big-name CEOs and other top managers spend most of their time "setting corporate strategy and vision" ("CEOs in Asia . . . ," 1998).

Shifting Profit Zones

Old development models no longer work. Neither do old corporate models. Traditional sources of profitability are drying up as quality and high productivity increasingly become requisites of doing business rather than providers of competitive advantage. Competitive advantage will be a product of innovation in addressing the needs and desires of a demanding client base notable for its constantly changing preferences. Excel shows how companies respond to shifting profit zones in a competitive technology sector, while Café de Coral and Jollibee stake out divergent strategies to sustain growth in crowded marketplaces.

OPPORTUNITY

What do we mean when we say the notion of opportunity is different?

Constant Revitalization

Innovation isn't limited to high-profile technology industries and exporters. Rather, consistent innovation is a requisite in every industry as the competition to capitalize on shifting profit zones heats up and the traditional cachet accruing to market share evaporates. From food processing to business services, management excellence will be characterized by the capacity to think differently, like another company we will look at, ABS-CBN Broadcasting in Manila, which is producing world-class entertainment for all Asian audiences, not just Filipinos, by fostering internal competition.

Tuning In to the Consumer

The Asian consumer has finally come into her own. After decades of lording it over a captive marketplace, lumbering private-sector bureaucracies are learning to be customer intimate. This is a truly dramatic development that will gain momentum as prosperity increases in Asia and consumers become comfortable "throwing around their weight." According to the PriceWaterhouseCoopers survey, the second priority of Asian decision makers is staying in contact with customers.

Expansion to New Markets

Liberalization is not a one-way street. While Asian companies must gear up, consolidate, and merge to realize the capacity to compete in Asia, Western markets are free game. And technology—especially Internet and e-commerce technologies—will make it easier for Asian companies to move into Western markets. But a good idea still holds a premium, as Jollibee's Tan has demonstrated in the United States, and as several Asian technology are doing in Silicon Valley.

THE END OF THE ASIAN CONGLOMERATE

General Electric's CEO Jack Welch has shown that a large conglomerate can win in multiple market segments, but not always at the same time. Despite Welch's exemplary record, in recent years consumer appliance revenues have plummeted while other divisions excelled. And there are few GE-like conglomerates. In contrast, the wave of mergers and consolidations that mark the close of the twentieth century very clearly communicate the benefits of a focused, if global, reach in terms of core businesses and competencies.

Asia's conglomerates have been easy targets for global firms used to competing and to addressing the issue of increasing commoditization across product offerings and industries. In Asia, conglomerates grew up and diversified into an industry mix ranging from food processing to semiconductor assembly. During the miracle years, Asian apologists defended such willy-nilly, opportunity-driven diversification as the Asian way, replete with the inherent disadvantages that accrued to the Asian consumer: shoddy products, poor service, and high prices, for instance. Chipper Boulas, vice president at Booz Allen & Hamilton, cites a typical example: a Southeast Asian group with forty-nine companies, of which six accounted for 81 percent of the earnings made by its profitable companies. The group's five biggest loss-makers, meanwhile, dragged down those profits by 72 percent. "What were the other companies doing?" asks Boulas. A year before the financial crisis, when Harvard's Michael E. Porter bluntly suggested that Asian conglomerates were ill-suited for life in a competitive marketplace, he was roundly criticized by Asia's business elites and academics alike. A year after the crisis, Asia's most inexplicably diversified giants were beginning the process of dismantling their empires. But it was slow going. "More than 70 percent of business groups surveyed by Andersen Consulting in April [1998] said cost-cutting was their top priority, followed by postponing investments (42 percent) and adapting products (42 percent). Only 14 percent considered the gut-wrenching option of restructuring the group's business portfolio" (Tripathi, 1998, p. 50).

The reason that there are not many GEs may be that there are not many managers of Welch's caliber, and that of his predecessors, who have the talent to inspire and lead management across diverse industry segments. And Asian conglomerates were never a breeding ground for multifaceted competition-driven managers. Every Asian conglomerate is going through a series of transitions that will result, for the surviving entities, in companies almost unrecognizable from their form in the last half decade of the twentieth century. There are at least five reasons Asia's conglomerates couldn't last.

1. Lack of Focus and Discipline—Resources were used inefficiently

2. Liberalization—Competition puts pressure on margins and capacity to innovate

3. Globalization—International standards of quality and productivity were introduced

4. Professionalization of Management—The best and brightest weren't interested

5. International Consolidation—Major global players united to consolidate strengths and resources

Lack of Focus and Discipline

One of the greatest—and most obvious—fallacies of the Asian miracle was that every group could reap windfall profits from real estate development. Indeed, "Asians always rely on real estate appreciation and tangible goods for wealth, but I'm trying to change that model" (Kraar, 1998, p. 42), Stan Shih, chairman and founder of Acer, said in explaining why he was diversifying into software instead of real estate. Whether software will prove to be a good fit for Acer remains to be seen. Most hardware companies have found the extension a difficult one. But Shih is right when he criticizes conglomerates for getting into businesses they know nothing about.

The logic of the typical Asian conglomerate was found in opportunity. In a protected environment, opportunity-driven growth made sense. John Gokongwei, founder and chairman of JG Summit, has been one of Asia's most innovative taipans (major businessmen or industrialists) in identifying and financing opportunities, as Table 1.2 shows. To his credit, "Gokongwei kept property to 10 percent of his total holdings, and made only conservative real-estate investments," a strategy many other Asian taipans in 1998 wished they had followed. "He preferred to take advantage of government deregulation and piled money into developing businesses" (Tiglao, 1998, p. 46).

The propensity of conglomerates to chronically focus on asset building and market share expansion rather than profitability left them extremely vulnerable to financial travail as a result of the crisis, and market vulnerability as a result of liberalization and globalization. International banks providing cheap, dollar-denominated loans contributed significantly to the asset binge, and ultimately, the pressure to divest.

Food and agro-industrial products	Textiles and garments	Real estate and hotels	Banking and financial services	Power	Telecom	Cement	Petro-chemicals	Airlines	Other
Branded consumer foods	Cotton and polyester blended fabrics	Development of commercial centers, hotels and offices for sale, leasing, and ownership	Retail banking	Diesel, bunker, and coal-fired power generation	Local, domestic long distance, and international calling services	Manufacture, sale, and distribution of cement	Polypropylene	Domestic flight services	Electronic components
Agro-industrial products	Yarns	Hotel and service-apartment ownership and management	Investment banking				Polyethylene		Packaging products
Commodity food products	Garments	Residential property development and sales	Leasing				Other		Printing services
									Industrial brokering
									Industrial cleaning agents
									Securities investment

Table 1.2. JG Summit Holdings, Inc.

Liberalization

Liberalization across Asia demonstrated most dramatically just how unprepared most conglomerates were for competition, especially in areas outside their traditional strengths. Their shallow creative resources were able to generate few alternatives for reasonable competitive responses because for decades competition had taken a back seat to protecting low value-added manufacturing. As a result, consumer prices defied reason because inefficient manufacturers enjoyed a seller's market for their low-quality goods. Did they use the windfall profits to enhance their operations? History bellows a resounding no.

The Asian financial crisis quickly ratcheted up pressure to consolidate within industries. Many companies—including healthy ones—wisely looked for international strategic partners to help strengthen their position within key business sectors. Despite resistance to large-scale foreign equity and nationalistic calls to defend against encroachment by multinationals in some countries, the demands of Asian consumers—and their refusal to underwrite Asian conglomerates with their taxes—would ultimately force national consolidation across a wide spectrum of industries: food processing, semiconductors, telecommunications, automobile assembly, finance, and others.

Globalization

Globalization raised the efficiency and productivity bar. Getting over that bar required at least three things. First, the reengineering of business processes. Second, the acquisition of technology that would provide the information necessary to accurately measure efficiency and productivity and continually improve business processes. Third, manufacturing and service delivery processes that allowed the company to maintain quality despite efficiency and productivity pressures. The result? A new mindset incongruent with conglomerate safety strung across wide industry borders that protected group companies from the effects of competition instead of honing them in the marketplace.

Professionalization of Management

While some of the surviving portions of today's conglomerates will continue to be run by members of the founding families, in ten years that will be rare. In part, this will be because of dilution of share holdings and the shedding of unrelated businesses, but primarily as a result of competitive pressures and the increasing importance of serving the best interests of public stockholders.

Another reason is because the only way to recruit capable managers is to assure them an uninterrupted career path, free of "relative obstacles." Gold Peak's Victor Lo in Hong Kong is proud that he is the only member of his family involved in the company. And that's been instrumental to the tightly focused group's capacity for attracting management talent.

International Consolidation

Global consolidation in telecommunications, finance, transportation, and other industries to achieve worldwide economies of scale for these strategic sectors will derail conglomerate expansion into nontraditional businesses. Despite arguments citing national interest, national competitiveness concerns will continue to provide the opportunity for significant market intrusion by these massive global organizations into local Asian economies.

In summary, Asian conglomerates will not survive the effects of the crisis, liberalization, and globalization because their structures and cultures are ill-suited to the vast changes these forces are bringing about in Southeast Asian economies, and because they lack the resources—intellectual and financial—necessary to respond to them effectively. They are true corporate dinosaurs, whose downfall is being brought about not by the sudden impact of a meteor from outer space, but by the equally dramatic impact of never-before-seen economic and market forces.

THE TRANSFORMATION

While companies were falling like coconuts, as an international news weekly described one Asian economy in mid-1998 (Table 1.3), significant business model innovation—revolution, really—was taking place in Asia. For the most part, the revolution was being led by Asian baby boomers who were experiencing the first real crisis they had ever known, and relishing the challenge that set them apart from their elders. Nipping at their heels, an even more confident and pampered wave of "GenerAsians"—Asia's GenX—was watching developments closely. And despite the predictable mumbling about the euphemistic concept of colonialism, managers transplanted to Asia from the West were found not infrequently to be driving change in corporate structure and strategy. Western consultants enjoyed a field day trying to fix Asian corporations and banks.

Asia's new leadership was proving—again—that generalizing about Asia, a vast region containing 60 percent of the world's population, is a dangerous and misleading habit. At the peak of the Asian crisis and amidst the downfall of many of the former pillars of Asian commerce, Asian entrepreneurs, second- and third-generation managers in established family corporations, and professional executives were promoting profound changes in the way business is done in Asia that had little to do with fabled, esoteric Asian management styles. They were creating a new corporate character for their organizations and recreating the rules of competition.

MANAGEMENT AND CORPORATE CULTURE

Observers, analysts, and pundits rightly criticized Asian governments, ponderously uncompetitive conglomerates, and inefficient, poorly regulated banks for delaying structural reforms as the severity—and

	Currency	Stock Index	Market Fall	Unem- ployment	Prime Rate	Imports	Vacant Offices	PC Revenues
Indonesia	−83.2%	−35.0%	−88%	16.8%	65.0%	−33.4%	13.6%	−81.8%
Thailand	−40.2%	−48.0%	−66%	8.8%	15.5%	−39.5%	26.7%	−62.3%
Malaysia	−39.4%	−56.0%	−76%	5.0%	12.1%	−22.4%	10.6%	−55.2%
Philippines	−36.1%	−33.8%	−58%	13.3%	18.0%	−7.5%	3.5%	N/A
South Korea	−34.1%	58.7%	−71%	6.9%	11.5%	−36.1%	N/A	−46.3%
Singapore	−16.5%	−43.5%	−53%	2.2%	7.5%	−19.5%	8.7%	+19.5%
Hong Kong	Nil	−43.2%	−42%	4.2%	10.0%	−4.0%	7.5%	−3.1%

Source: Asiaweek, July 17, 1998, p. 41 and Bank for International Settlements; International Monetary Fund, World Bank, Jones Lang Wootton, and Dataquest.

Table 1.3.   The Reckoning One Year Into the Crisis.

prolonged duration—of Asia's financial crisis became increasingly apparent. The framers—and principal beneficiaries—of the Asian miracle fought an untenable battle to preserve a comfortable way of commercial life tied to privilege and payback.

But Asia's emerging leaders refused to be held back by their suddenly outdated predecessors. For this new generation, leadership has more to do with communication skills than connections. To them, success is a product of competitive advantage, not privilege. They understand well that every element of competitive advantage is under continuous siege, including the capacity to think faster than the competition. There are other differences.

Technology for this generation of leaders, for instance, is more than a productivity-enhancing capital expenditure. It is an investment in intelligence. The investment is expected to 1) provide an understanding of the company's real economies to attain global industry standards of efficiency and business process productivity, 2) identify best (most profitable) customers, 3) build new strategic models to capitalize on shifting profit zones, and 4) identify new business opportunities.

Next, effective people, not loyal bodies, are the critical resource. Getting the right people in the most important positions with the right tools and the mandate to do their jobs is requisite to survival. Third, market leadership is a product not of what resources are available, but of how they are used. Fourth, business decisions are not personal. There's a new, practical, detached coldness in decision-making, a price the fittest pay to survive: the loss of some of their humanity. Fifth, because corporations have no loyalty, neither do their executives. The highest bidder wins.

CORPORATE STRATEGY

The three forces of economic change in Asia—financial crisis, liberalization, and globalization—are not "events" in the sense that they have a beginning and an end. Rather, they are processes that instigate profound and continual change in market fundamentals (see Table 1.4). As those fundamentals have changed, business models—essentially business modalities established in response to

Process	Effect
The Asian Financial Crisis	Profound economic reform and corporate restructuring
Globalization	Internationalization of profitability, efficiency, productivity, and quality standards
Liberalization	Fierce competition leading to business model innovation

Table 1.4. Three Processes Driving Change in Asia.

opportunities presented by the circumstances of protectionism—have become irrelevant. As Adrian Slywotzky and David J. Morrison argue in their important book, *The Profit Zone: How Strategic Business Design Will Lead You to Tomorrow's Profits* (1997), vast change in the way Asian markets operate caused traditional sources of profit to dry up. Managers who decided to wait for profitability to return—like a seasonal well—gradually and belatedly realized that there would be no return to business as usual. But by the time the obvious was acknowledged, time had run out.

Many blamed banks for their failure, arguing that bankers were no longer lending. And indeed, many of Asia's banks no longer could lend. Others rode the interest wave, enjoying windfall profits at the expense of enterprise in the name of restoring stability to the financial sector. Others were afraid. But the most dramatic reason credit had become scarce for so many Asian companies was that their business models were clearly nonviable, and banks were beginning to realize this. Banks were also becoming concerned about the strength of the management teams of their clients. At Bangkok Bank, for instance, credit extended to the most profitable client segment—small- and medium-scale industries—one year after the advent of the crisis was roughly equivalent to pre-crisis levels. But the number of clients the bank was willing to lend to had decreased by about half.

For the first time, Asian bankers had to think seriously about whether there was a market for their clients' products, and whether their clients could offer their products competitively. Where rosy proforma financial projections provided by the client had formed the basis of credit worthiness in the past, bankers were now having to actually work to determine whether a proposal for financing reflected market realities and presented a competitive strategic framework for undertaking a project and developing the business.

But the real challenge was not in whether the banks would begin acting like banks, but in whether companies could respond to the need to think strategically, rather than opportunistically, about their businesses. To understand how dramatically this new reality dawned on Asian business, it is useful to define what we mean by the need for Asian business models to change to reflect new conditions. Perhaps GE provides the best example of a company that demonstrates the capacity—and the will—to continually shift its business model in response to shifting profit zones. Slywotzky and Morrison provide a more comprehensive summary of these shifts, but here's a concise version.

Jack Welch, known as a "fiery CEO," is probably best known for his statement that GE would become number one or two in every industry segment in which it operated. This was a call to quality. Welch rightly believed that he could out-position the competition by consistently delivering the best quality product available for a fair price. And it worked. Until the competition found that it could benchmark GE's quality, and match it. When that began to happen, GE was forced to lower its margins to maintain market leadership.

"By the mid-1980s, it was clear to Welch and other forward-looking managers that winning the market share game was not enough. The relationship between market share and profitability was eroding. In some industries, the downward price spiral was leading to the creation of enormous no-profit zones. In many cases, an inverse relationship between share and profit began to emerge. In industries as diverse as cars, coffee, and structural steel, the smallest players became the most profitable, and the largest players became the least profitable. High market share without high productivity was a losing hand" (Slywotzky and Morrison, 1997, p. 79). To boost productivity, Welch initiated the first process reengineering exercise on record, before Michael Hammer and Jim Champy rode the notion to fame. At GE, reengineering was called Work-Out. The program was designed to counter the productivity lowering effects of excessive bureaucracy. For example, when problems were encountered, employees were given the authority to stop work on the spot, solve the problems, and restart the process.

Work-Out provided GE with the means to restore profit margins while maintaining market share. Today, Welch remains obsessed with productivity gains, and the employment of new information technologies and e-commerce to further enhance productivity standards. In the early 1990s, Welch and his lieutenants faced a situation in which maintaining—let alone building—market share was offering the bleak prospect of lower and lower returns. In fact, the prospect of high market share becoming inversely proportional to profitability, as Slywotzky and Morrison suggest, was becoming obvious. Given these new conditions, GE took an entirely new approach to sustaining growth in revenues. One can imagine Welch and his lieutenants in brainstorming sessions becoming increasingly frustrated as they sought solutions to the threat of stagnant growth. In 1995, he launched a new initiative, Six Sigma, that has produced significant quality and productivity gains. In 1998, Welch expected the program to realize approximately US$750 million in net benefits (Byrne, 1998, p. 47). But in the same way quality wasn't enough to sustain profitability, neither was productivity. Welch soon found that his competitors could benchmark productivity, too, and pressure on margins returned.

At some point, Welch began to focus on the company's most profitable customers. Rather than allocate resources to building business with fringe customers—who may even be costing the company money—wouldn't it make sense to look at ways to increase the amount of business with customers who already value their relationship with GE? As a result, GE adopted a total customer solution approach to expanding business. That approach meant that GE would do more than provide a product. The company might supply another company's product to a customer, but it would finance the product, maintain the product, and provide an upgrade path. By expanding customer relationships laterally into related but new areas of service, GE expanded its "share of customer" in its most profitable segments.

Many Asian companies have worked hard over the past decade to boost the quality of their output, with good results. The moral in

GE's example for Asian companies comes in the next two steps: productivity and increasing share of profitable customers. But to address these issues, Asian companies need to first acknowledge that their old business models are outmoded, and that profit zones have shifted. As Slywotzky and Morrison also point out, there are many successful business models, but finding one that works is dependent on the company's willingness to look for one.

One of the most notable things about business model innovation in Asia is that instances of dramatic change can be found concurrently in a wide array of industries as a result of the comprehensive reach of the Asian financial crisis, and its severity. While there are some industries that invariably benefit from downturns—such as fast food, for instance, as executives choose to "eat down"—providing less impetus for change, even greater benefits can be realized by business model innovation during such times, as Café de Coral has demonstrated.

OPPORTUNITY

Let's consider market and customer-based opportunity for the New Asian Corporation. And let's demonstrate how even traditional industries like garment manufacturing offer sound profit opportunities to firms that have learned to think strategically and revise business models to fit new conditions. Garment manufacture takes place within the context of what consultant James Moore calls a business ecosystem, an evolving business model that is characterized by an extended value chain. At present, the extended value chain in the Asian garment industry is managed mostly by Taiwan and Hong Kong companies that undertake the high value-added components: design, logistics, packaging, and distribution. The manufacture of yarns, threads, fabrics, and garments is contracted to firms across the region that make up the low value-added component of the extended value chain.

Consider a Philippine garment manufacturer. The Taiwan manager of the extended value chain negotiates with the dependable Philippine manufacturer to produce a lot of garments for a European retailer. If the manufacturer has to source and probably import the quality materials required, it is unlikely that he will be able to meet the deadline. Besides, the manager of the extended value chain has a better network of suppliers that he knows and trusts.

So the manager buys the yarn from a supplier in Korea, has it dyed in Thailand, and ships to the Philippines along with fabric from Indonesia. After assembly, everything is professionally packaged—using materials designed by the value-chain manager—and shipped to the customer. But where is the customer benefit in this process? In three areas. First, the quality of custom design undertaken in Taiwan or Hong Kong. Second, the speed with which the order is completed and shipped. Third, the quality of the finished product, providing value for money. Where is the business model innovation that makes these companies more customer focused?

These Taiwan and Hong Kong managers have evolved from simple switchboard-type activity funneling orders from customers to manufacturers to managers of distinct processes involving everything from raw material purchase to marketing and promotion. Integrating these processes allows the different component organizations to specialize and achieve high standards of efficiency, quality, and productivity, increasing value to the customer and providing higher profitability for the company. At the same time, it allows the manager to stay lean. His value-added is intellectual input, which requires minimal capital expenditure.

THE NEW ASIAN CORPORATION

As already noted, Asia developed faster than any other region on earth, and has suffered through the worst economic downturn ever witnessed. There has never been an instance where a nation of nearly two hundred million people went from relative prosperity to the point where almost half the population could not afford to buy enough food to survive—in a matter of weeks, as we saw in Indonesia. Throughout Asia, and despite profound resistance that persisted well into the crisis, political, economic, and structural change has taken place with incredible rapidity.

These are defining developments not just for Asia, but the global economy. The Asia that builds on them—and the Asian corporations that learn from them—will be a formidable competitor. While many Asian companies continue to lack the technological or financial resources of some of their most important competitors, those shortcomings will be transitory. What is not transitory is the character and quality these companies require to survive and capitalize on profound change.

Allow us to reiterate that it would not be wise to take that experience lightly. Every economic downturn the United States has endured has made it a stronger economy. That will be true for Asia as well. Those who gloat over the demise of the Asian miracle and the fallacy of the notion of Asian values would better spend their time contemplating the competitive threat Asia and Asian companies will—and are—presenting to the future of their firms.

It's a new Asia.

CHAPTER TWO

The New Asia: What's Different and What's Not

—*∿*— "In the industrial age," *Forbes* magazine publisher Rich Karlgaard wrote in summarizing the discussions at a Forbes & GartnerGroup CIO Congress, "the inputs to wealth creation were land, labor, and capital." Two speakers at the Congress, economist Paul Romer and strategist Gary Hamel, Karlgaard explained, believe that the new inputs to wealth creation are:

- Hardware—the sum of all existing tangible assets such as land, minerals, food, factories, cars, and computers

- "Wetware"—human brain power, creativity

- Software—language, math, art, culture, recipes, code (Karlgaard, 1998).

Michael Porter, Harvard's competitiveness guru, says this another way: The key to wealth creation is no longer access to inputs (or resources), but how inputs are used. Both definitions highlight the importance of creativity in the use of inputs, or what Karlgaard calls "wetware." That makes Asia's sudden concern with creativity, not just hard work, understandable. Development in Asia has primarily been a function of input mobilization, rather than input optimization. As a result, educational infrastructure, or the innovation factory, was neglected in the rush to spread prosperity.

For the New Asia to prosper, both the government and the private sector must do three things. First, acknowledge that Asia's post-crisis strengths are fundamentally in contrast to its pre-crisis strengths. Second, accept the reality that those post-crisis strengths represent potential and must be developed. (Significantly, Asia's potential still lies in its people—not the fact that they are there, but the intellectual potential they represent.) Third, redirect resources to accomplish the task of developing new strengths.

For insight into how to do this, it is useful to review what is meant by the term "Asia," consider the new role of government in post-crisis Asia, and view how the private sector is adapting.

A GREAT IRONY

Perhaps the greatest irony of Asia is that it is looked upon as one huge, homogenous zone by just about everyone who doesn't live there. Some might argue that this is an effect of globalization; others, that it is the product of ignorance. While the economies of Asia are inextricably interdependent—and becoming more so—Asia's financial crisis illustrated the significant contrasts that exist between Asian economies, societies, and politics.

The most obvious crack in Asian unity showed up in the Indonesia riots just prior to the resignation of former president Suharto. Organized gangs attacked ethnic Chinese Indonesians, burning and ransacking their businesses, raping their women—frequently in front of their families—and taking their lives. Ethnic divisions are not the only ones obvious in Asia. There are important religious distinctions as well. As the final draft of this book was being prepared, Indonesian Muslims and the Christians were at each other's throats with consistently lethal results.

The Philippines is the only majority Christian country in the region, yet has a significant Muslim population, principally living on the southern island of Mindanao. Indonesia is the largest Muslim country in the world, yet the ethnic Chinese, the traditional targets of rioters' fury in times of economic difficulty, control the economy.

Even within Chinese societies, contrasts abound. Hong Kong, Taiwan, and Singapore are each distinct societies and business centers. Hong Kong is known for go-getter speculative investors and low value-added manufacturers, as well as for being a regional financial center. Taiwan is also full of entrepreneurs, but among them are those that have managed a significant and difficult transition from low value-added and original equipment manufacturer (OEM) contract manufacturing to original brand development, manufacture, and distribution of world-class products. Singapore is a tiny nation of private-sector bureaucrats, reflecting the interventionist policies of its well-meaning government.

The heavily American-influenced Filipinos are creative geniuses, excelling at theater and the arts as well as software development and big-company management. The Indonesians have frequently looked upon the Filipinos as their closest brothers in Asia not because of their Asianness—and certainly not because of their religion—but because they shared the unfortunate distinction of being the poorest nations in their part of the region. Meanwhile, the Filipinos and Malaysians have regularly insulted each other over the treatment of Filipino contract workers and rattled sabres over territorial jurisdictions.

Across Asia, resentment toward Japan remains surprisingly strong despite the important role Japanese investors played in support of the Asian miracle years. While Asia in a unified voice called for Japan to behave responsibly to help bring the region out of recession, many Asians chuckled that the Japanese economic invasion had ground to a prolonged and ignominious halt. Japan's financial debacle, however, should have demonstrated to the rest of Asia that basic economic fundamentals apply to high-flying Asian economies as much as they do to Western economies.

During the Asian miracle years, per capita GNP ranged from approximately US$400 in Indonesia to US$31,000 in Singapore. Hong Kong and Singapore were among the world's most competitive economies while Indonesia and the Philippines were among the most corrupt. Politically, the disorganized Philippine democracy was seen by leaders in the rest of Southeast Asia as an impediment to development although fisticuffs between Taiwan legislators failed to dent that economy's rapid growth. As Asia's financial crisis worsened, the dangers inherent in politically immature societies became evident in the overthrow of Indonesia's Suharto, destroying a damaging political dynasty but also erasing twenty years of dramatic economic development.

Other geographic regions suffer the same failure of local distinction that Asia does. But no other region is anywhere as large or populous. Practically the entire region, excluding Japan and South Korea, was an economic backwater for most of the twentieth century, and then grew faster than any other economy in history. The World Bank effectively rewrote its development handbook on the basis of the Asian miracle, praising prudent governments and highly productive, savings-minded Asians. By 1998, however, one year into the Asian financial crisis, 73 percent of respondents to the Asian Leadership Survey regularly conducted by *BusinessWeek* strongly agreed with the statement that "the crisis is the fault of Asian government policies."

Enlightened government was not the only World Bank success factor under scrutiny. Economists Jeffrey G. Williamson and David E. Bloom, both of the Harvard Institute of International Development, argued that the structure of Asian populations, not work ethic and high savings rates, were the principal catalysts for the Asian miracle years. "There are two problems with the conventional wisdom. At the beginning of the miracle years, Asian investment and savings rates were about the same as other developing countries.

"In other versions of the miracle story, government policy boosts savings and investment rates. But which government policy? South Korea's government-knows-best approach? Hong Kong's low-tax, laissez-faire philosophy? That's the second problem" (Goad, 1998, p. 1). Williamson and Bloom say that "savings and investment rose as mortality and fertility rates fell" (Goad, 1998, p. 1), with the effect that eventually the percentage of the productive population—working adults—was larger than the nonproductive segments. Unfortunately, and obviously, that can't go on forever. As more baby boomers retire, there will be fewer children entering the workforce. That means slower growth because, as we said earlier, development in Asia has been based on mobilization of inputs—particularly labor, as economist Paul Krugman argued in his 1994 *Foreign Affairs* article, "The Myth of Asia's Miracle."

Not all of Asia is set for slower growth, according to the Harvard economists, just most of it. The Philippines, for instance, is just entering the "bonus phase" of the demographic transition: a majority of productive workers in the workforce. But for most of Asia, growth will depend on what Rich Karlgaard, Paul Romer, and Gary Hamel call "software," or the capacity to replicate knowledge. Put another way, it is the capacity to boost Asian productivity and value-added.

How each country in Asia does that will depend on a number of things besides population, beginning with enlightened government.

STILL A DIVERSE MARKETPLACE

The Asian financial crisis heightened the discussion of social safety nets to protect the economically challenged majority. In reality, the pain was felt principally in the middle of the social strata in most of Southeast Asia, depending on how one defines middle class. In general terms it is safe to suggest that the desperately poor never benefitted much from the Asian miracle years, especially in Indonesia, the Philippines, and Thailand. The top-level population of Southeast Asia also was in many respects immune from the effects of the Asian crisis, at least compared to the middle class. While many founders of large Asian companies lost control or were destined to lose control as the financial crisis dragged on, lifestyles were not significantly diminished. This was not true for the burgeoning new middle class, which in Indonesia lost two-thirds of its wealth. Long-term small investors in Hong Kong lost veritable real estate and stock market portfolio fortunes.

Who is the middle class? As explained in *Asia's Best: The Myth & Reality of Asia's Most Successful Companies* (Hamlin, 1998), there's a complicated answer to that question. It begins with a report in the *Asian Wall Street Journal* that illustrated the contrasts in the structure of Southeast Asian economies. For example:

- In Singapore, the 33 percent of middle-class households with the highest incomes each earn at least US$3,200 a month. In Indonesia, the middle class only has to earn US$260 a month to make the top 33 percent.

- Reflecting differences in tastes and lifestyles, the middle class is twice as likely to live in air-conditioned homes in Hong Kong as in equally affluent Singapore, where the climate is hotter.

- Despite growing affluence, Asia remains a telecommunications backwater. In Thailand, middle-class households with cars outnumber those that have telephones (Wong, 1995).

That two hundred years of Western industrialization was accomplished in less than fifty years in Asia helps explain how such vast contrasts came about. Development has been fast but uneven within as well as without Asia's individual economies. As a result, contrasts in income are sharper and are potential sources of political instability, as demonstrated in Indonesia so dramatically in 1998. In the New Asia, the principal priority of governments should be dealing with those contrasts.

The task in the New Asia is how to manage these contrasts. Management guru Peter Drucker says there is a stark choice. One is to bring everyone down to the lowest level, or to raise everyone up to the highest. That's no choice at all (Video conference, Sept. 18, 1997).

TRANSITIONING GOVERNMENT

How does a country's transition from developing status to emerging status mirror the private sector transition from an entrepreneurship to a professionally managed firm? Ideally in three ways: the role of strategy is enhanced, systems and processes become critical to sustained viability, and people become the principal source of value-added, or competitiveness.

Let's define what is meant by emerging economy. *Emerging economy* is a convenient marketing term developed by global fund and portfolio managers to seduce investors to nonmainstream, or developing, markets. Developing economy, and certainly the term "under-developed," implies too much risk for jittery, inexperienced investors, often for good reason—because risk in these markets had to do with poor implementation of the rule of law, political instability and corrupt government, and inadequate private-sector management.

All those factors were still present before the crisis, as the Asian and South American markets painfully demonstrated. But the term *emerging economy* provided a good intellectual excuse to avoid reality and to take comfort in an artificial and exciting reality principally spun by American investment bankers and fund managers, but that also involved European and Japanese investors.

However, for purposes here, *developing country* refers to those countries that have embraced the basic reforms necessary to get an economy growing: acknowledging the importance of foreign direct investment, developing the export sector, and gradually lowering barriers to the free flow of goods and services. Emerging economies are those that are looking beyond these basic reforms to accelerate growth and distinguish themselves from the competition for investment and opportunity. The transition from developing to emerging country—like the transition from entrepreneurship—is not an easy one.

Strategy

Successful entrepreneurships frequently sacrifice profitability in favor of market share and brand awareness. Countries sacrifice value-added in order to create jobs. Both eventually find that they are generating greater revenues but with less and less impact on the bottom line: profits for entrepreneurships and budget surplus for countries.

For entrepreneurships, continuing business in the same, start-up fashion results in ever decreasing returns, stagnation, and bankruptcy. Therefore, strategy is required to first achieve profitability and then to sustain it. The first step in developing strategy is determining, given competition in both the private and public sector in the new global economy, which customers are preferred in terms of profitability. For entrepreneurships, this means determining how to increase the amount of business they do with these ideal customers.

For countries, the challenge is the same: What sort of investment is needed that will create the necessary kinds of jobs? How is the inflow increased from these investors? For both entrepreneurships and countries, the central issues are 1) developing an effective strategy that distinguishes the entrepreneurship or country from the competition, 2) effectively implementing the strategy, and 3) continually updating the strategy in response to evolving conditions in order to set the rules of competition.

Coming up with a unique strategy is difficult. Take, for example, the national development strategies of Hong Kong, Malaysia, and Singapore. All are inextricably tied to technology. They had better be, because their national development strategies are all the same. Yet none of these countries is particularly well-suited for development into a technology industry cluster. During a visit to Hong Kong in 1999, Microsoft chairman Bill Gates said, "There is enough demand here that Malaysia, Singapore, and Hong Kong could all be successful in (becoming) great software centers" ("How Mahathir Wrecked . . . ," 1999). "It's not a zero-sum game. It isn't like one city wins and other cities lose" (Lo, 1999).

For example, none of these countries has the educational infrastructure to support technology development. This is something they think they can remedy. None of them have the right people—knowledge workers—in the numbers they need. They think they can import them. None of them have a tradition of value-added innovation. They think they can learn.

Does that mean the strategy is flawed? Possibly. The one thing they have going for them is fear. Fear is an important component of success, and it played an important role in the development of each of these Asian countries and other successful economies. Hong Kong developed as a lonely capitalist outpost during the Cold War; Singapore was thrown out of the Malaysian Federation with virtually no resource other than true grit; and Malaysia was faced with the specter of a race war, featuring religious and ideological unrest as well. All of these countries were scared for their futures, as they are now.

Contrast this with the Philippines, where there was no sense of urgency in terms of what the future would hold as recovery began to take hold in 1999. On the contrary, there was an underwhelming sense of complacency. While the region's strongest economies were sweating about the future, the Philippines appeared content to blithely coast along in the illusory comfort that its economy was the least impacted by the recent crisis provoked by the Asian meltdown (as the International Monetary Fund was frequently fond of noting).

Even worse, there was no clearly articulated strategy for Philippine development. There was no goal nor vision of where the Philippines was headed. There was no indication that the administration of President Joseph Estrada had a firm idea of how it intended to capitalize on the country's strengths to accelerate development and prosperity. To be fair, the government did consistently recommit itself to the principles of free trade, and it wanted to do something about agriculture. But these were tactics, not strategy.

Systems and Processes

Systems and processes have to do with how efficiently and productively resources are used. For entrepreneurships, this means acquiring the technology and professional management necessary to achieve or exceed industry standards of efficiency and productivity—while maintaining quality—in order to stay in business. Industry standards of efficiency and productivity are not sources of profitability, but rather requisites of being in the game.

For emerging countries, systems and processes refer to bureaucracy and infrastructure. In the same way that entrepreneurships struggle to transition from informal and disorganized ways of conducting their business, emerging countries must struggle to professionalize the bureaucracy. In the way that entrepreneurships struggle with entrenched and uncompetitive cultures and habits to implement reengineered, technology-based business processes, emerging economies must overcome ingrained cultural hurdles and other obstacles toward more efficient and productive economic operations.

For the Philippines—even more so for Indonesia—compared to regional competition, the challenges were great. Could Philippine bureaucracy compete with that of Hong Kong, Malaysia, and Singapore? How about infrastructure? The answers seemed obviously negative. But then why is it that the Philippines was in fact effectively competing with these countries for investment, opportunity, and technology?

The answer lies in people.

People

The most difficult part of transitioning an entrepreneurship to a professionally managed firm is finding, recruiting, and retaining the best people. People are increasingly the "product" that firms sell, whether they are in manufacturing, retail, or services. People develop strategy, systems and processes, and products and services. Putting the best minds to work determines the quality in each of these areas.

For emerging countries, the task is to provide a talent pool of people with the right kind of training and effective intellectual tools. Few countries in Asia have done this well, except for Taiwan and, it seems, China. It should be noted that Singapore and Hong Kong have belatedly acknowledged this shortcoming and are working feverishly to address it. Education is the fastest growing industry in Malaysia by some reports. That's one reason they are sweating.

Other Asian countries should also be worried for two reasons. First, in the case of Indonesia, the Philippines, and Thailand, many of their best people are at work in other economies. While their dollar remittances are important, their long-term contribution to economic development would be far more profound if they were working in Asia. To get them back in Asia, governments must improve opportunities by developing effective national strategies and providing the systems and processes to make them work. Second, these countries and Malaysia have allowed their greatest competitive advantage— the productive workforce and the people's aptitude for training—to erode dangerously. Increasingly, as Asia turns to its talent pool, despite its huge population, it will find that the pool is inadequate because: 1) its development has been taken for granted, 2) national investment in education is significantly rerouted to the pockets of corrupt officials and their private-sector cohorts, and 3) the private sector itself fails to invest adequately in training and education, in part because until recently, government has not acknowledged education's strategic importance.

People are the source of competitiveness and they should be the priority consideration in the transition from developing to emerging economy. But to achieve their full potential, governments must also provide both the strategy that will focus national resources and increase returns as well as the systems and processes to ensure the nation continues to develop.

PRIVATIZATION

Effective government in the New Asia is small government. Asia is already home to some of the world's largest privatization programs, from power generation and water supply to construction and maintenance of transportation infrastructure. Given the scale of privatization, it's not surprising that many of these initiatives have had a bumpy time coming together. In part, that's been due to differences in valuation perspectives. In others, because competitors or consumers argued effectively that foreign ownership or management of privatized assets undermined national integrity. A Malaysian concern won the bidding, for instance, of the Manila Hotel but the Supreme Court overturned the results in the interest of something called Philippine national patrimony. Developer Gordon Woo's attempts to build infrastructure in Thailand resulted in massive losses when he failed to persuade feuding government agencies to agree with each other. Privatization of national airlines in Malaysia and the Philippines has been controversial and costly to the majority shareholders. Analysts argue that the management of the airlines are not up to the task of creating worldclass operations and have been slow to undertake market-dictated reforms.

Many less visible projects have faired little better. In Manila, for instance, consumers have eagerly anticipated a water utility turnover to two major consortia that will rehabilitate and manage the water system for one of the world's most populated cites. But in 1997, dramatic depreciation of the peso decimated funding plans, delaying for up to half a decade plans to expand the aging network. Nevertheless, the turnover resulted in massive savings for the government. When it turned over, the system was losing 60 to 65 percent of the water it pumped to leaks and fraud. In an *Asiaweek* essay, former President Fidel Ramos said, "No mechanism can allocate resources as efficiently as the market does. Nor is there any mechanism as effective in fostering investment discipline and in rewarding creativity, intelligence, and hard work," in explaining why privatization was a priority during his administration (Ramos, 1998).

Despite privatization's uneven history, Asian governments will increasingly rely on market forces to supply the demands of consumers and to achieve reasonable returns on resources.

LIBERALIZATION

When the financial crisis hit, economists and analysts warned Asian governments that there should be no backtracking on liberalization. While that was an important message for Asian officials and private-sector executives, it was not directed to the principal obstructionists: the United States and Japan. When Asia Pacific Economic Cooperation (APEC) forum ministers met to devise a liberalization timetable in mid-1998, "a United States negotiator noted that his team would need congressional authority to yield concessions" ("APEC Ministers . . . ," 1998), Japanese negotiators said "liberalization deadlines are at odds with APEC's tenet that member economies can implement policy changes on a voluntary basis." Meanwhile, the United States was blaming Japan for not pulling Asia out of the crisis by reflating its economy and increasing imports from the region.

The question of steady liberalization of key sectors is clearly not a problem limited to Asia. Liberalization must be led by the world's two most important economies. It is wholly illogical to expect developing economies in Asia to set the pace for liberalization. Nevertheless, that has in fact been the case, with the Philippines leading the change to free-market economies under the Ramos administration. The danger of the Asian crisis was that it would undermine the champions of liberalization, particularly as American and Japanese reluctance to meet deadlines and otherwise contribute to easing the crisis became more apparent. In 1998, both Asian and multinational executives felt that neither country was meaningfully addressing the Asian crisis nor the danger it presented to their own economies. Rather, liberalization was privately viewed as a license for Asia to export its way out of recession. Only when the effects of the crisis became clear in the earnings statements of Japanese and United States multinationals did the full urgency of concerted effort to resuscitate Asia begin to weigh on trade negotiators and senior government officials.

Within Asia, private-sector leaders lobbied heavily for continued protection. There was great concern that the region liberalize collectively to ensure that no country gained advantage over another. This was a ridiculous argument, as there was little chance of across-the-board industry parity in the region, given the sharp contrasts between Asian economies, although basic industries such as steel and petrochemicals fretted about dumping by other Asian competitors. Ultimately the issue for Asian business and policy makers was how long voters would remain patient while waiting for inefficient, long-protected domestic corporations to create jobs and provide value for money.

Fortunately for Asian consumers, by late 1998, the tide had turned in favor of accelerated liberalization of trade in the Asia-Pacific. The sole holdout was Malaysia. Unfortunately, Japan and the United States weren't helping. By mid-1999 APEC trade ministers gave up trying to reach a consensus, and they threw the matter to the World Trade Organization for resolution.

REGULATORY ENVIRONMENT

"The Asian crisis is about bad banking," Paul Krugman said in an attempt at explanation ("What Happened . . . ," 1998). Bad banking practices proliferated, by implication, because government failed to provide an adequate regulatory framework. There are at least two reasons why the regulatory framework did not keep pace with development. First, governments everywhere have traditionally let bull runs get out of hand largely out of the fear of accidentally killing a vibrant economy. MIT economist Rudi Dornbusch says the United States Federal Reserve, up until the nomination of chairman Alan Greenspan, routinely managed to clobber economies. Even if Greenspan has learned how not to do this, which increasingly seems to be the case, no one else has yet learned how to keep growth in check for much longer than a decade. So it is not unusual that Asian governments were afraid to touch the economy lest they break it. So it eventually broke itself.

Second, no developing economy in history had ever had unfettered access to cheap global funds, that, as author and consultant Kenichi Ohmae says, flow around the world beyond the reach of governments. One may ask, just how exactly does one go about regulating what management icon Peter Drucker calls virtual money in a free-market, global economy?

The Asian financial crisis at first appeared to make obvious the dangers of over-reliance on volatile virtual money. But it is unlikely that governments or the private sector would—or could—choose to do without it. Instead of moaning about the evacuation of volatile portfolio investments, Asia would have been better served if its governments had worked to restore confidence and get the investments back. Clearly, the problem was not that these funds were relied upon, but that governments and businesses thought it was a free ride. Although there was real need for government regulation in banking and equity markets, there was no way Asian governments could afford to try to control the flow of foreign capital in the digital economy.

The Asian financial crisis provoked reform, but it was in the manner that banks were regulated, corporations encouraged to compete, and failed enterprise was divided up. Any attempt to exert a meaningful measure of control on the flow of virtual money would force a proportional sacrifice in the prospects for recovery and growth, as Malaysia's currency controls will demonstrate over time. Nevertheless, business, government, and Western academics were still debating the need to restructure global financial architecture in 1999. There was only one thing clear, however, and that was that no one had an acceptable remedy.

POLITICAL LEADERSHIP IN ASIA

"Banthoon Lamsam is not a popular man these days. The chairman of the Thai Bankers' Association has been egging the government to close some of the country's sixteen commercial banks. 'Apparently here in this country, all financial institutions are to be funded by the (state-run) Financial Institutions Development Fund as a last resort. You can keep anything up—just pump air into it'" (Gearing, 1998, p. 47).

Banthoon believes that the marketplace should reward companies that make the investment required to be competitive. Companies that fail to make that investment to ensure competitiveness should be penalized by the market and allowed—or forced—to close shop. When government artificially protects poorly managed companies and banks from failure, it serves as a disincentive to good management. That's an argument Asian governments must take to heart.

Whether governments do or not, leaders like Banthoon say good things about the kind of corporate environment that will eventually dominate the region. From the looks of it, it is key private sector leaders, such as Banthoon, who are leading the region to international competitiveness. But they need their governments' support. That support took a backseat in the first year of Asia's financial crisis as governments rotated in and out of power or sunk into the depths of denial. And Asians were in no mood for faint-hearted leadership.

Developments in Hong Kong, Indonesia, Korea, the Philippines, and Thailand showed that the people of Asia have grown weary waiting for entrenched political regimes to bring about fundamental reform. These are defining acts for twenty-first century Asia, warning shots for an older generation of leaders that has found it profoundly difficult to pass on the mantle of leadership.

The message is clear: Get it right, or get out. The reasons are clearer still. As Urban C. Lehner, executive editor for Dow Jones Asia, said at a conference organized by the Asia Society, "[T]he capacity of Asia to make necessary changes is unproven. Reform has been slow and incomplete." That is, until the people get involved.

In Hong Kong, Korea, the Phillipines, and Thailand, non-mainstream leaders (or, legislators in Hong Kong's case) have been elected on the basis of their promise to fundamentally reform government, level playing fields, and generate opportunity. Indonesia promises not to be left far behind. It turns out that those who proudly boasted that Asian values accounted for the region's rapid growth knew very little about changing Asian values after all.

During the very early period of national development, it was fairly easy for government to rationalize playing favorites for business persons and family members who appeared to have the talent to get things done. But it is even easier to see now why that should never have been done. Very few of the tycoons supported by corrupt regimes ever developed the capacity to fend for themselves. They robbed legitimate and talented businesspeople from capitalizing on the opportunities they monopolized.

Ironically, there are Asian leaders who still refuse to heed the signs of changing times. In the same way that economic crises are cyclical (although the American economy has been trying hard to prove otherwise), so it seems that politicians in nondemocratic environments invariably refuse to let go, despite the certainty of their eventual downfall and disgrace.

It would seem that a truly enlightened leader—such as Malaysia's prime minister Mahathir Mohamad—would seize the moment before downfall is inevitable and, in the fashion of a true statesman, display the courage to acknowledge that his people no longer need him. Indeed, that his people will do better with a leader more in tune with the times and the population. Leadership is no longer about iron-fisted control; it is about capitalizing on the dreams of a nation that knows it can do better.

One thing is sure. Democratic reform is releasing the enormous energy and talent required to rebuild the Asian miracle. Leaders seeking the fast path to recovery will find it in their people.

A NEW MODEL FOR ECONOMIC DEVELOPMENT

BusinessWeek's Asian Leadership Survey (taken at their Annual Leadership Forum, 1998) provided some other interesting insights into the future of Asian economies. Eighty-one of the fifty-eight big-name CEO respondents believed that Asia's financial crisis presented "huge opportunities for Western firms." Fully 97 percent of the respondents acknowledged that "the crisis will force significant restructuring of the affected economies. However, only 67 percent believed that changes in Asia would reduce corruption, which 86 percent of respondents believed to be a major impediment to doing business in Asia.

Ninety-three percent of the managers who completed the survey believe that Southeast Asia will become more open to foreign investment, and 88 percent said that Asian companies "will move towards greater transparency in business transactions and financial reporting." Additional insights into the structure and priorities of Asian corporations will be discussed in Part II—The New Asian Corporation.

What is important here in these admittedly unscientific, but insightful, findings is that big-name private-sector executives appeared to see the future better than government leaders, regardless of the extent of their domestic financial crises or political system. Yet the private sector feels that for their vision to be realized, government must actively participate in reform by setting and enforcing new ground rules. In the New Asia, government will assume its most important role: that of leveling the playing field. That won't be enough, however; rule of law must closely follow, and that is where government credibility is at its weakest.

Fifty-three percent of the respondents to the survey said their investment plans had not been affected by the Asian financial crisis. This is opposed to 88 percent of respondents with headquarters in the United States who said in a January 1999 survey conducted by the Asia Society/ *The Asian Wall Street Journal* that they had either expanded or left unchanged investment in the region. Indeed, most respondents to the *BusinessWeek* survey felt that the region had become much more competitive. But these CEOs believed that companies in Asia should focus resources and strategy in core business areas. Information technology was seen as a key enabler, providing a critical contribution to competitiveness and productivity. While opportunities are abundant in Asia, they now have to be earned.

COMPETENCY ZONES

As Asia transitioned from the economic crisis and structural reform to recovery and enhanced competitiveness, increasing productivity and value-added became critical long-term determinants of regional economies' capacity to generate prosperity (see Table 2.1). The urgency with which business must address these issues is heightened

Country	1995	1996	1997	1998
Singapore	9.5	6.5	6.6	. . .
Indonesia	10.4	10.6	5.4	−3.0
Malaysia	13.8	11.2	10.5	5.0
Philippines	7.0	6.3	5.7	3.0
Thailand	10.5	7.0	−0.1	−0.3

Table 2.1.   Growth Rate of Value-Added in Industry.

Source: Asian Development Outlook 1998, Asian Development Bank.

by three factors: 1) the increasing size of the nonproductive population, 2) inadequate educational infrastructure, and 3) competition with developed economies for Asia's best minds.

Like Asian business, governments as a result will be forced to prioritize national resources to achieve development objectives. And in fact, Asian governments are trying to do this. The problem is that their priorities converge and focus principally on information technology, as we earlier noted. This is a problem for several reasons. First, there is little educational infrastructure to support a technology competence cluster or venture capital. Second, it's expensive and risky. Asia is trying to more than double the number of high-technology industrial clusters, all in the United States. Third, providing high value-added output is attained, continual heavy investment is required to sustain competitiveness and profit margins. The other end of this clash of national development priorities—and its impuetus—is that Asian countries find themselves competing ever more aggressively for contextually smaller pieces of a low value-added commodity pie when they find it impossible to transition to higher value-added industry.

Asian governments are going to have to be more creative in setting strategic development plans and learn to differentiate themselves from the competition. Strategy will begin with a new development model that reflects national strengths. As obvious as this seems, the notion of distinctive competence was lost in the euphoria of the Asian miracle. This was because most people looked upon the entire region, rather than Asian nations, as a miracle of uniform development for close to two decades. Analysts spent much time and energy trying to define a model that would explain the Asian miracle, not the miracles.

With the financial crisis, it became clear that there was no single Asian miracle. In many instances, economies had managed to develop more in spite of national development plans than because of them. Japan and Korea invoked overt government support of heavy industry, and yet their most enduring companies never fell under the government's watchful eye; for example, most of Japan's electronics firms succeeded by exception, not the Japanese model, according to Harvard's Michael Porter.

Taiwan relied on its entrepreneurial instincts, while Hong Kong got out of the way of business. Singapore and Malaysia tried to emulate the Japanese model of heavy government intervention and support, while Indonesia, Thailand and Malaysia, too, competed in an all-out race for job-generating foreign direct investment. Indonesia focused on a few favorites to corner industrialization and economic development investment, friends and relatives of former president Suharto. Malaysia was somewhat more expansive in its selection of favored industrialists. The Philippines, under the administration of Fidel V. Ramos, belatedly moved to stimulate competition and encourage domestic and international investment by dismantling monopolies, a plan which was beginning to pay off when the Asian financial crisis began in earnest.

As Slywotzky and Morrison demonstrated in their book *The Profit Zone* (1997), there is no one business model that works for everyone. In the same manner, there is no one development model that works for all emerging economies. In both instances, it is imperative that development models that fit particular circumstances be defined and implemented strategically.

In revising their development strategies to fit new realities, Asian governments should establish two basic ground rules. First, development models must compete with other models in the region for foreign investment, opportunity, and jobs. Second, the development models must reflect the particular strengths of each country. It may be appropriate to add a third ground rule, and that is to communicate with a sense of urgency. If there was one connecting element in Asia's successful development strategies during the miracle years, it was a sense of urgency.

For the New Asia, the likely manifestation of the urgent need to differentiate competing regional economies is the development of what are called competency zones, reflecting the strengths of each economy. It is important to note that while Asian economies compete with each other, they also invest in and trade with each other, although the crisis greatly dented the level of intra-Asian trade. But the level of intra-Asian investment and trade is a critical element of economic growth, as well as decreasing reliance on developed economies (Table 2.2). However, it is also indication that the regional economies should be complementary, not monolithic.

But competency zones are important for other reasons: They nurture mid-market enterprises and hasten market liberalization.

"We need to go back to fundamentals," Li & Fung chairman Victor Fung advised business and government leaders attending an Asia Society conference in Manila. "Asia has been driven by entrepreneurship—by SMEs," he argued, suggesting that the Asian asset bubble bursting and the increasingly troubled fortunes of big business didn't mean that the region's competitiveness had eroded.

Fung reminded listeners that Asia still had three fundamental components of competitiveness in its favor: a young, productive population, high savings rates providing domestic capital and liquidity, and a strong work ethic. The Philippine situation differed somewhat because it does not feature the high savings rates most other Asian countries do, as other speakers during the conference pointed out. However, foreign investors usually cite the productivity and educational attainment of the Philippine workforce as a principal investment incentive. This means that while the Philippines demonstrates the capacity to attract value-added foreign investment, doing so

Country	Developing Member Countries		Japan		USA		European Union	
	1985	1996	1985	1996	1985	1996	1985	1996
Singapore	36.7	48.4	9.4	8.2	21.2	18.4	10.1	13.4
Indonesia	17.2	31.5	46.2	28.8	21.7	16.5	6.0	18.3
Malaysia	38.1	45.9	24.6	13.4	12.8	18.2	13.6	14.8
Philippines	19.5	25.1	19.0	17.1	35.9	32.6	13.8	18.6
Thailand	27.1	34.0	13.4	16.8	19.7	18.0	17.8	15.7

Table 2.2.   Direction of Exports (Percent Share).

Source: Asian Development Outlook 1998, Asian Development Bank.

consistently is vitally important to recovery because there is little capacity for domestic capital formation.

Which makes Fung's point all the more important, but not just for the Philippines. Economic development is driven by small firms that supply multinationals and international markets, not the grandiose dreams of big business and conglomerates that rely principally on domestic consumption. "The basis of the Hong Kong economy is its 300,000 small companies. Forty percent of these companies are operating across borders in two or more locations. They are mini-multinationals."

Because these dynamic firms operate across borders, Fung says that liberalization is not a threat, but an opportunity; therefore "we should hasten the process of liberalization." Fung knows what he's talking about. His successful firm excels in managing what is popularly known as an extended value chain, a virtual organization encompassing raw material suppliers, manufacturers and assemblers, printers, and shippers, aside from its own value-added processes.

The success of his company is anchored on a network of relatively small firms that provide the input and services Li & Fung requires to profitably meet the demands of its European and North American customers. But the viability of that network depends on the free flow of goods and services between Asian countries.

Within Asia, mini-industrial clusters—competency zones— are already beginning to emerge. The principal features of these clusters are professionalism, quality, and innovation. While low cost remains a consideration in choosing Asian suppliers, it is not *the* consideration. The priorities are the capacity to meet commitments, produce according to international standards, and originality. Li & Fung also finds that the best yarn producer, the best textile manufacturer, and the best garment assembler are located in different Asian countries. Cost consideration then becomes not a matter of who can fulfill their part of the supply chain at the cheapest price, but how cheaply materials and finished product can be moved across borders.

In other words, liberalization contributes to the capacity of small companies to increase the value-added of their products and exports because the high tariffs that confined them to low-cost manufacturing are disappearing. As a result, they become integral components of an international value chain that consistently contributes in a meaningful way to local economies.

But if we look at who dominates the business agenda in politics and media, it is not these engines of growth, but big business. That doesn't necessarily imply that the agenda big business pushes is detrimental to the interests of mid-market (or small- and medium-scale) enterprises. In fact, in most cases they are in fairly close alignment. There are exceptions, of course. The obvious ones are local, uncompetitive manufacturers who have failed to create internationally competitive organizations and the large retailers who want to keep the market to themselves to the detriment of consumers as well as the economy.

The problem with big business domination of the business agenda, however, is that it creates the perception that the robustness of the economy is tied to a few large firms. This is true everywhere, so it is not a uniquely Asian circumstance. However, it takes our eyes off the fundamentals Fung believes really account for Asian prosperity, with the result being that both government and private-sector resources are funneled toward support of big business to the detriment of mid-market enterprises.

The fallacy of these circumstances was expressed to us by Banthoon (Interview with the author, June 3, 1998). Aside from recruiting fresh equity to rehabilitate his bank, Banthoon said that future profitability is closely tied to the mid-market sector. Even without the real estate asset bubble bursting, Banthoon says that big business, "with its grandiose dreams," has not been a profitable sector for the bank. Because all banks wanted to do business with the largest firms, of which there were relatively few, these firms were able to negotiate tough terms. On top of that, the Asian crisis actually made them a worse credit risk than well-managed, mid-market firms.

The lesson here is that recovery doesn't depend on how well big business does. Big business is a beneficiary of recovery. Recovery depends on mid-market enterprises, the true engines of growth.

ROUGH GOING

How are Asian governments contributing to the development of competency zones? So far, government initiatives to drive competency zones have been predictable and unimaginative—if grandiose. Malaysia's well-publicized effort to spawn a high-technology super corridor—larger than Singapore in area—is likely to attract less than a quarter of the more than US$4 billion in investment originally expected from high-technology behemoths like Microsoft, Sun Microsystems, and Oracle. More than anything else, Malaysia's folly has demonstrated that competency zones should reflect strengths, not wish lists. They should boost the economy's engines of growth, rather than serve as monuments to political achievement.

As noted previously, Malaysia does not have the population or the educational infrastructure to support the development of an indigenous, leading-edge technology center. Its driving force was not resources, but one resource—the prime minister, Mahathir Mohamad. The Asian financial crisis, the imposition of controversial currency controls, political instability, and Mahathir's own erratic behavior accelerated the super corridor's demise. But it is Hong Kong's proximity to Asia's largest talent pool of highly educated professionals that ultimately will relegate Mahathir's vision to a shadow of its intended grandeur. Hong Kong will spend close to US$2 billion to build an information technology (IT) zone in its effort to reengineer its economy and lessen its reliance on speculative real estate. However, even Hong Kong's success is less than assured. It produces one-third of the scientists and engineers it needs annually, yet limits immigration from the mainland, which produces 400,000 scientists and engineers every year. And, "with tens of thousands of mainland Chinese now working in Silicon Valley and other United States high-tech centers, the potential boost for China is huge" because many of these engineers are on their way home or have founded research ventures in China (Gilley, 1999). Shanghai will compete aggressively for the honor of being Asia's Silicon Valley, and it has the intellectual resources to do so.

Singapore also hopes to evolve into a high-tech mecca. Its vision of the future—called Singapore One—"envisions the networking of the entire island under an IT plan that has attracted fourteen multinational companies. The Singaporean government plans to spend nearly US$56.5 million for online education, entertainment, and information services, plus another US$1.03 billion for new computers in school labs and to wire up most of the island's offices, homes, and schools" (Gilley, 1999). Keep in mind that Singapore is a very small nation.

The Philippines provides some examples of how the development of competency zones and government incentives should proceed. The Philippines' chief benefit from the colonial era was its educational infrastructure, which after World War II was clearly and easily the best in Asia. But so was its economy. Both crumbled during the Ferdinand Marcos administration, and education deteriorated even more from lack of attention as well as exploitation. Still, the Philippines produces a huge number of engineers, teachers, and medical professionals. Its preoccupation with art and entertainment have also made it a creative and literary center. The problem for the Philippines is that there are not enough jobs for these highly educated, value-added, potential contributors to economic development. A look at foreign direct investment inflows quickly shows why.

The Philippines was less efficient in attracting foreign direct investment than its neighbors (see Table 2.3), and therefore has been unable to generate jobs for an under-mobilized work force with little to do.

Country	1993	1994	1995	1996
China	27,515	33,787	35,849	42,300
Hong Kong	1,667	2,000	2,100	2,500
Singapore	4,686	5,480	6,912	9,440
Indonesia	2,004	2,109	4,348	7,960
Malaysia	5,006	4,342	4,132	5,300
Philippines	1,238	1,591	1,478	1,408
Thailand	1,730	1,322	2,003	2,426

Table 2.3. Foreign Direct Investment (US$ million).

Source: Asian Development Outlook 1998, Asian Development Bank.

At the same time, it is evident where the Philippines should direct its resources and provide incentives to investors:

1. *Engineering-intensive export industries, including services, because of an abundance of low-cost engineers.* One Japanese construction company, for instance, has established a fully-owned engineering design affiliate in Manila staffed by nearly fifty full-time engineers designing projects primarily being undertaken in Japan.

2. *Publishing.* The Philippines is a rich source of writers and creatives.

3. *Entertainment, including production services and talent.* Major animation studios, including the Walt Disney Company, have set up shop. Industry figures are trying to make the Philippines an offshore Hollywood studio.

4. *Healthcare, including major surgical procedures.* American healthcare organizations recruit heavily in the Philippines.

5. *Software engineering.* Again, United States, Asia, and European firms recruit heavily in the Philippines where contractors supply major airlines, hotels, and other service industries with core business solutions.

While allocation of resources in the strategic development of competency zones is not as well-defined in all Asian countries, it remains clear that development strategy must be designed to capitalize on national strengths and conditions. Setting up what is in effect an artificial industry without the intellectual resources required for its support and development is an exercise in folly. Worse, it is an irresponsible waste of finances and time. Asia is impatient to develop, and Asians increasingly expect their government to make the right decisions, not the easy ones.

Consider the argument that Japan's best companies developed without much help from government, and that Japan's most notable industry failures featured very high levels of government intervention. We would argue that Japan's failure was its focus, the intent to build a textbook economy while the textbooks were being rewritten in the marketplace. First, the focus should have been capitalizing on resources, not creating them. It took the electronics companies to do this by capitalizing on their expertise in miniaturization. Second, it should have focused on the markets and the customers. For all its public expenditure, Japan was building monuments, not enterprises. Its private sector took that responsibility.

Instead of emulating Japan's development model as Korea and Malaysia have tried to do, they should be pouring resources into education in areas that will strengthen the distinctive competencies of their economies and people.

STRUCTURAL REFORMS

Structural reform will take a great deal of pressure off of Asian political leaders as government's principal task becomes levelling playing fields and enforcing the rule of law, rather than managing development. The responsibility for performance will lie with the private sector, not the government's luck at picking the champions of industry.

When we speak of structural reform, however, we speak principally of two distinct elements of economic infrastructure. One is the banking system, which is *not* the heart of all economies. It is the value creators or wealth generators that are at the center of economies— mid-market enterprise. That these entities are bankrolled—or at least were before the crisis—by financial institutions does not make banks the principal source of productive national wealth. It makes them gatekeepers.

A second element of economic infrastructure is the laws regulating trade. Trade regulation prevents or encourages the emergence of monopolies by stimulating or encouraging domestic and international competition. Because the trade policies of Western developed nations, the United States in particular, have been overtly supportive of free trade, Asian governments have generally been seen as inhibitors of free trade. Indeed, many have been. But as we have already seen, so has the United States, particularly in agricultural products, for the same reason that Asian governments have sought to protect certain sectors of their economies: again, the demands of politics. Those demands are generally rooted in sectors that hold economies back, not push them forward. Japan's stubborn resistance to opening up its woefully uncompetitive agricultural sector is an excellent example.

The need to remedy bad practices and policies doesn't mean change takes place when it should. In the United States, it took the savings and loan debacle to force regulatory change in an obviously volatile sector. Calamity, as Richard Farson, author of *Management of the Absurd* (1996), argues, really does seem to be the best catalyst of positive change. Yet in 1998, eight years after Japan's economic bubble burst, meaningful banking reform had yet to take place.

One year into the Asian financial crisis, regional governments were, for the most part, benignly encouraging banks to merge and consolidate. The government was propping up poor performers in the meantime, as Banthoon complained. Indonesia was still doing this in early 1999, although it finally closed thirty-eight private banks in March that year. Analysts believe the number should have been closer to fifty. Malaysia continued to insist that inefficient, government-connected conglomerates had to be helped in the national interest. It took Thailand until March 1999 to finally pass comprehensive bankruptcy legislation. In every instance, resistance was traced back to the interest of large industrialists and nationalists. And it held back recovery in Asia.

But while reform didn't proceed at the pace it should have, Thailand, South Korea, and the Philippines, in particular, showed that reform leaders—despite much opposition—would lead the region back from the abyss. Those nations and their corporations will be at a distinct advantage to other regional governments that sought to shelter inefficient conglomerates and poorly run banks from the effects of crisis, liberalization, and globalization.

CHINA AND THE YUAN

China looms large in the Asian economy as a competitor in export markets and foreign investment. Despite rocky episodes by foreign investors, recent tightening of intellectual property laws and enforcement, moves to get the army out of the private sector, an effective cleanup in customs, and increasing transparency and reform in the financial sector have suggested that China's leaders understand that sustained growth is closely tied to the observation of market dictates. For the rest of Asia, these reforms make China an even more serious competitive threat.

So it was not surprising that in early 1999, frazzled Asian investors reacted to what should have been light reading, sending regional stock markets into an emotion-driven tailspin. Writing in the government-sponsored *China Daily Business Weekly*, journalist Zhang Yan, quoting unnamed sources said, "As the financial markets responded positively after the Brazilian government let its currency float against the United States dollar, some analysts said the devaluation or floating of the yuan would definitely not be a bad thing" (Smith, 1999, p. 1).

Wrong.

Financial news services reported the comments on a Monday, suggesting they were a trial balloon for an impending devaluation. With the help of gleeful short sellers, jittery investors, still nervous about Asia's emerging markets in the wake of nearly nineteen months of financial crisis, blindly sent stocks and currencies across the region reeling. The Singapore and Philippines markets plummeted well over 5 percent. Jakarta dropped almost 5 percent, and Thailand was down close to 3.5 percent.

After the carnage, Zhang said, "I had no idea my article would cause such a reaction. I wouldn't worry about the yuan; the government is quite firm about not devaluing." Because everybody knows this, Chinese government officials didn't immediately respond to the panic, apparently assuming saner minds would prevail. Wrong again.

Premier Zhu Rongji finally spoke up in defense of the yuan, denying prospects for a devaluation in 1999, and probably preventing a sell-off in United States and European markets. As a result, United States markets rose strongly as prospects of instability in international markets (particularly in Asia and South America) appeared to recede.

The next day, most analysts safely and quickly suggested that there was little pressure to devalue the yuan. J&A Securities' research manager told the *South China Morning Post*, "There's speculation that they want to devalue the renminbi, but in terms of politics they are not going to do it now" (Internet edition, January 26, 1999). Yet other analysts kept speculation alive. CLSA Global Emerging Markets' chief economist predicted that China would devalue the yuan by 10 percent in the second half of the year. Eddie Wong, an ABN Amro economist, suggested that a devaluation would serve to enhance the competitiveness of Hong Kong's exports.

But there are a number of reasons why devaluating the yuan would work against China's long-term interests. First among these is that although currency devaluation may provide limited, short-term benefits, as Wong suggests, it decreases pressure on local companies to increase efficiency and productivity—to become better-run companies. As a result, the "private" sector's capacity for successful participation in the global economy deteriorates further. To survive as poorly run companies, executives insist that they need state protection in the form of high tariffs and other restrictions on non-Chinese players.

With billions of dollars worth of technically bankrupt state firms still on its hands, China is not in a position to coddle inefficient companies run by poor managers. To manage the financial and social fallout of large-scale state-sponsored corporate incompetence, it is crucial that government signal managers that they are expected to live in the real world and create value instead of using up scarce resources. Recent introduction of incentive compensation seems to be intended to do this.

Devaluation also removes the pressure on companies to become better value generators, perpetuating low value-added manufacturing. Likewise, it undermines the urgency of enhancing skills and technology because exports are driven by low labor costs rather than the value of labor and intellectual inputs. This means that prosperity spreads slowly, undermining confidence in government and its commitment to its people. There is not enough generation of wealth for the nation to prosper, so a very small percentage of people—industrial titans running globally uncompetitive firms—enjoy the benefits of development exclusively.

From an immediately practical perspective, devaluation would provoke chaos in China's banking and financial system just when serious reforms are beginning to take hold. The closing of state-owned Guangdong International Trust and Investment Company, or GITIC, provoked a spurt of reform that Asia's financial crisis failed to inspire. In an encouraging effort to demonstrate transparency and sound management, banks and investment houses have for the first time begun to announce earnings reports, even when the results are not entirely confidence-inspiring. Making negative but factual information available to investors is the preferred alternative to relying on investors who assume the worst.

Because of significant levels of foreign-currency-denominated debt and huge exposure to bankrupt state firms, a devaluation would decimate the banking sector and bring reform to an immediate and ugly halt. Much like the rest of Asia at the onset of the regional financial crisis, investors would abruptly run for safe havens and foreign corporations run for cover as the value of their capital investments sank.

Some observers believe that China has steadfastly resisted pressures to devalue out of a sense of fiscal responsibility to the rest of the region. There is certainly no argument that China's resolve has contributed in a very important way to stabilizing regional economies, providing good prospects for recovery in 1999 and growth in 2000. But any responsibility exhibited in terms of regional stability is a by-product of China's desperate need to preserve its own development. It does not want to see its wealth melt away overnight the way the rest of Asia's did at the onset of the crisis. Ultimately, that's the most important reason a devaluation will not take place.

Not that national prestige is an unimportant consideration. With the tenth anniversary of the Tiananmen atrocity in 1999—as well as the fiftieth anniversary of the state—China's generally thin-skinned government was anxious to present the public image of a nation that is competently managing its dramatic transformation into a market economy. And it wants to show that it can do this best in a non-democratic context, undistracted by the chaos associated with individual freedoms and rights.

Because devaluation is a sign of a weakening economy that cannot generate the wealth it needs to fund development, devaluation would be an admission of failure on the part of government at the worst possible moment politically, likely provoking profound change. Management icon Peter Drucker believes that China is simply too large and too diverse to survive as a single country anyway. Local governments have clearly enjoyed the degree of freedom economic development has provided by lessening dependence on central government. As a result, in the past six months, Beijing has moved to reassert its authority. But if central government undermines its moral authority to rule by an admission of flawed macroeconomic public policy, it is likely that state officials will quickly take advantage of that admission to argue that local government is efficient and attuned to local reality.

The final reason China won't devalue is that it would obliterate Hong Kong's property market, the principal source of the Special Autonomous Region's increasingly fragile wealth. China has had a hard time demonstrating that Hong Kong is doing as well under its rule as it did under the British. Part of the reason is that the British are no longer in power, and therefore no longer visible. It is easy for the United Kingdom to forget their own incongruities, especially since Chief Executive Tung Chee Hwa has so consistently demonstrated that his job is too big for him. Timing was also unfortunate, with the turnover taking place the same month Asia's miracle shattered.

The reality is that even without the problems of weak government and the regional malaise, Hong Kong is frightfully exposed. For the most part, the Special Autonomous Region's small manufacturing sector has steadfastly resisted pressure to transition to high value-added production, choosing instead to maintain reliance on cost competitiveness by shifting operations to Guangdong and other locations. Its services sector is under assault from both Shanghai and Singapore. And government has resorted to reinflating the property bubble under pressure from Hong Kong's property barons. The last thing Hong Kong needs is a devaluation in the yuan because it will serve to further undermine structural infirmities that the government doesn't know how to address.

Given all this, why all the fuss? In part, it could be that pressure for short-term respite appears increasingly attractive to a central government that, despite the lack of democratic reforms, must be much more responsive to public mood. Or, China may be tempted to put Japan on notice that failure to do its part to spur regional recovery won't be tolerated forever. But whatever the reasons for periodic panic, none of them make much sense. What does make sense is the rest of Asia's unease with China's voracious appetite for foreign investment and investors' giddy enthusiasm for this emerging mega-star economy.

THE EVOLUTION OF THE NEW ASIA

While the challenges before the New Asia are greater than ever, so are the potentials. Although growth is unlikely to mirror the heady rates of the past fifty years, the evolution of the New Asia over the next fifty will be at least as profound, particularly if it is successful in capitalizing on its greatest resource: the people.

The three forces of change in Asia are provoking a profound transition. The effect of the Asian financial crisis is the emergence of tough, battle-tested competitors that have adapted to survive and prosper. Liberalization is not only making Asian corporations more efficient and productive, it's making them, as well as the entire region, more cosmopolitan. The confluence of interest that is focused here is creating a new society that will set the standards of social and political tolerance in the next century.

Globalization encompasses lifestyle and values. Asia will have the most democratically elected governments serving the largest and most demanding group of consumers on earth.

But for all this to happen, Asia must release the creative capacity of what economist Paul Romer and strategist Gary Hamel say are the new input to wealth creation: hardware, wetware, and software. Asia has the input. The challenge is to accelerate the New Asia's capacity to turn that input into wetware.

PART TWO

The New Asian Corporation

CHAPTER THREE

Rising from the Ashes

In a 1997 column by Thomas L. Friedman in the *New York Times*, Teera Phutrakul, director of a Thai mutual fund, said of Thailand's crisis-related woes, "We all go through three stages. Stage one is denial. It's all a bad dream and will blow over. We paid a heavy price for that stage by trying to prop up our currency. Stage two is shoot the messenger. It's all the fault of [financial firm] Moody's rating agency for downgrading our credit. The third stage is admission and calling the IMF. Once you call the IMF [International Monetary Fund], the party's over."

Friedman wrote that "getting to stage three is not so easy. Malaysia's leader is still blaming Jews and currency traders for his woes. Not the Thais. They are now pointing a finger squarely at themselves. The motto here is 'Wea Culpa'" (Friedman, 1997).

Regardless of who was ultimately responsible for provoking the financial crisis, business and government alike eventually learned that the crisis wasn't going to be remedied unless it—and the reasons for it—were first acknowledged. Only then could it be effectively addressed. Truly successful Asian companies—as defined in *Asia's Best* (Hamlin, 1998)—were much more prepared to address the effects of the crisis than those who were simply along for the miracle ride. These are companies that practice management by international standard rather than esoteric (and convenient) myth.

There are several forms of denial that negatively affect the capacity of Asian corporations to compete with multinational corporations in Asian markets. One is the assumption that only Asians can understand Asians. The prevalence of that notion is remarkable, given the contrasts in Asia itself, and the difficulty defining a collective "Asian" in anything much more than geographic terms. Another form of denial is the argument that what works in Western markets probably won't work in Asian markets.

Let's take the "Asians only understand Asians" assumption first. At the risk of irritating one of Asia's important book retailers—generally something an author tries to avoid—the entry of United States superstore book retailer Borders into Singapore provides an excellent illustration of this point. Borders entered the Singapore market in October 1997, after the onset of the financial crisis in July. Despite the unfortunate timing, Borders' president of international stores, Vin Altruda, said in August 1998 that the Singapore superstore was "one of our better performing stores in terms of [sales] turnover" (Chen, 1998, p. 8).

Meanwhile, local bookstores had been feeling the heat of the crisis and increased competition with "double-digit" falls in sales since late 1997. Despite that setback, one of two major local retailers continued to insist that they "knew the mentality" of local buyers. "To Asians," the general manager of the chain said, "the Borders concept means 'I go and sit and read and then put it back and go home.'" This general manager saw no need to change the way his chain did business because "serious buyers should be 'freed from the hassles of pushing around nonserious buyers'" (Chen, 1998, p. 8).

It should be noted that the attitude toward Borders displayed by the general manager was in sharp contrast to the reaction of the other local chain of bookstores. Having already successfully experimented with a "mini-superstore" approach to selling books, including a small café and library-like decor, this retailer recognized the competitive threat, and is "not sitting still," according to a senior manager. The contrast in the approaches of these two representatives demonstrates one of our principal arguments, that the principles of excellent management are universal, and that in Asia, poor management is frequently explained away as being appropriate in the Asian context.

That brings us to the second assumption, that what works in Western markets won't work in Asia. It is hard to explain why this argument persists, given the inroads into Asia many industries have made over the past two decades. Fast food is an easy example. Virtually all of the major multinational chains have prospered, in part because the competition also initially saw American fast food as no threat in a region with a rich cuisine and demanding palates. But what of the popular notion that companies should think globally and act locally, in terms of modifying product to local preferences? That notion fits well with Borders' success in Singapore. "Borders has had to alter its book selection to fit the local audience. There is a bigger section of Asian literature in English. The nonfiction section has also been beefed up, as sales figures showed that Singaporeans were buying more books on mathematics, self-help psychology, and business than their counterparts in the United States" (Chen, 1998, p. 8).

And Borders sees the Singapore experience not just as evidence that the superstore concept works in Asia, but that it will work in other diverse markets as well. "Spurred by this success at the Singapore store, which Borders regarded as a test site for international expansion, the company is opening a superstore in London this month; another United Kingdom store in Brighton in September; one in Melbourne, Australia, in October; and another one in Glasgow, Scotland, in November. Borders' scouts are checking out still more international locations" (Chen, 1998, p. 8).

In an international conference convened in an attempt to explain the reasons for Asia's financial crisis, Toyoo Gyohten, president of the Institute for International Affairs, said that first, complacency arising from a general sense of arrogance resulted in the failure "to adjust to a completely changed environment." This was the "wetware" or emotional block to reform. Second, there was failure to correct structural and systemic deficiencies. Asia's software didn't have the capacity to handle globalized business. Third, at the "crux of market confidence, speculators—local and foreign—joined the attack." Consequently, the value of Asia's hardware plummeted.

Gyohten's assessment was a vast simplification of a catastrophic array of economic blunders. Accountability resides firmly with economic and political leaders. And clearly it should. The private sector throughout Asia has been an extension—certainly in big business terms—of government. The nature of that extension has varied, but rarely has it been at arm's length. Big business, for its part, demonstrated few signs of wanting to grow up until it had no choice.

Enterprises that didn't rely on government favors and learned to be competitive in global terms were frequently looked upon as rebels, faddists, or worse by both their peers and government. And it is these companies that most clearly demonstrate the qualities of the New Asian Corporation. These are companies that can compete and succeed by adhering to global standards of quality and productivity in liberalized, competitive markets and through difficult downturns in the economy. They take their hard knocks, yet they don't make excuses. They're too busy taking care of business.

Now, even top-name CEOs of Asian and multinational corporations acknowledge that big business has to change. Eighty-one percent of the respondents to *BusinessWeek*'s 1998 Asia Leadership Forum survey were either neutral or disagreed with the statement that "Family-controlled companies have a competitive advantage" in Asia. Just 3 percent strongly agreed. And only 5 percent disagreed with the statement, "Ownership and management should be separate." (See Table 3.1.)

The PriceWaterhouseCoopers survey conducted in the third quarter of 1998 "found broad agreement among CEOs in Asia for the proposition that 'Western companies have a lot to learn from the attitudes, practices, and philosophies of leading Asian companies,'" suggesting that learning should be a two-way exchange. What lessons should be learned was not provided. The survey report also noted, "There is one management area where Asians seem less sure of their

Question	Strongly Agree	Agree	Neutral	Disagree
Ownership and management should be separate.	29	29	34	5
Family-controlled companies have a competitive advantage.	3	14	47	34
The influence of families in many Asian companies will diminish over the next three to five years.	19	55	15	10
There will be more buy-outs of Asian companies by foreign investors.	33	66	3	2
Successful Asian companies will continue to depend on networking.	17	66	12	3
Asian companies should adopt a "Western" approach to business.	12	33	40	14
Asian companies will move towards greater transparency in business transactions and financial reporting.	24	64	9	2
Asian business should now focus on improving long-term financial performance than on long-term growth.	36	52	7	3
The economic crisis will require Asian companies to sharpen the focus of their business activities (i.e., reduce diversification).	45	45	5	3

Table 3.1. *BusinessWeek*'s Asia Leadership Forum Survey (Percent of 58 Respondents).

achievements: management training and education. Well over three-quarters of the CEOs completely or mostly agreed that the quality of local managers would improve if there were more indigenous graduate schools of business. The majority take the view that the best and brightest Asian students must be sent abroad for a world-class graduate business education" ("CEOs in Asia Upbeat . . . ," 1998).

Perhaps reflecting the anticipated trend toward increased foreign participation in Asian corporations and a likely preference for equity over debt development funding, 88 percent of the respondents agreed that "Asian companies will move towards greater transparency in business transactions and financial reporting."

If the sentiments demonstrated in these findings prove to be widespread, they foretell a vastly different Asian corporate sector from that which drove—and benefitted from—the Asian miracle years. Indeed, they suggest the emergence of the New Asian Corporation, an entity more global than Asian in business character. While there are many in government and the private sector who worry about a fading of the Asian character of business in Asia, the emergence of the New Asian Corporation represents much less the fading of an era than the transition to a new one. That era will be less traditionally Asian than the past, but it will reflect the new Asia in all its diversity and richness.

WHO'S RUNNING THE NEW ASIAN CORPORATION?

Who should be leading the New Asian Corporation? First, management whose vision is not limited by quaint cultural blinders. It is costly and time consuming to throw off old intellectual baggage. Second, management that is capable of responding very quickly and effectively to rapid change in the marketplace in innovative, creative ways. That is, managers who strive to set the rules of competition, not conform to them.

Café de Coral's Michael Chan again provides a good example. Like the fast food business throughout the region, Café de Coral was actually a beneficiary of the Asian financial crisis. As currencies plummeted and costs rose, formerly high-flying, power-lunch executives were forced to "eat down." As a result, nearly a year into the crisis, Chan was enjoying 20–30 percent increases in sales at his outlets.

It would be hard to fault Chan for sitting back and enjoying the windfall. Instead, Chan saw the crisis as an opportunity to increase profitability in a number of areas, and not just a time to enjoy increased sales. He viewed the crisis as a one-year window initially to lower costs in three important areas. First, he used the downturn as an opportunity to negotiate lower leases with landlords for sites the company didn't own. Of the group's 180 restaurants—including the Ah Yee Leng Tong and Spaghetti House outlets—twenty are company-owned. The company does not buy real estate other than for the purpose of building and running restaurants. Chan points out that just a 1 to 2 percent decrease in the cost of leases translates into HK$20–30 million in savings for the company. "That's important because of our narrow margins [in the fast food industry]," Chan told us.

Under Chan's leadership, Café de Coral was able to avoid many of the pitfalls other Hong Kong and multinational companies suffered during their 1990s' headlong dash into China. As many of the respondents to the Asia Leadership Forum survey said would happen, Chan began an early focus on profitability over market share. Still, the Chinese fast food chain enjoys nearly a 17-percent market share, down slightly from close to 19 percent in 1995.

How Western is Chan's approach to management? "Our company has a strong blend of Asian ethics and Western management style. Corporate culture is driven by a strong sense of harmony," he says. "Because of this, I spend long hours in meetings. I have to be very patient to listen to them, and reach a consensus." While Chan emphasizes harmony, he quickly notes that, "At the same time, we're blending in the profit motive."

Like Alphatec's Robert Mollerstuen, Bill Heinecke has made a commitment to building a business in Thailand. Now a Thai citizen, the son of American parents founded the Minor Group, "spanning food, hotel, and trading companies that control local Pizza Huts, Swensens, and a Ripley's Believe It or Not! Museum." Like Chan, Heinecke's fast food business was up—some 35 percent—in the first year of Asia's financial crisis. And also like Chan, Heinecke saw opportunity. He's using the cash generated from booming Pizza Hut sales and sales of "small stakes in a hotel chain to increase his holding in Bangkok's Regent Hotel. 'This is the time to buy really great assets,' he says" ("The Stars of Asia," 1998, p. 62).

Taiwan technology manufacturers have established an important position for themselves in the hardware components industry. Less well known is a company named Trend Micro, which has likewise established a name for itself in the software industry. Chairman and CEO Steve Chang, a former Hewlett-Packard executive in Taipei, started his own company in 1984, and it has evolved into one of the industry's top anti-virus manufacturers. "Big-selling products include PC-cillin, ScanMail, and ChipAway Virus. They give Trend hefty margins of 30 percent on its projected sales of US$100 million for 1998" ("The Stars of Asia 1998, p. 59). The company also does contract work for such icons of the industry as Netscape, Intel, and Sun Microsystems.

Chang didn't start out in anti-virus software. He began business customizing other companies' database products for the Taiwan market. "Software pirates kept ripping him off, so Chang developed a special set of codes to thwart them. He sold the rights to his idea for US$125,000 and realized that there was a growing market for computer security software" ("The Stars of Asia," 1998, p. 59). Soon, Chang saw the potential in developing software to combat software viruses, but needed software engineering talent that wasn't available yet in Taiwan. So he went to the talent. Now the company has facilities in Tokyo, Taipei, and the United States, but Chang himself is back in Taipei.

Glenn Tyler is the director of Poranunt Company on the outskirts of Bangkok. The company produces plastic paint pails. When the financial crisis hit sales, Tyler began to think of how he could lower production costs to increase margins and provide competitive pricing. In an article in the *Bangkok Post*, Tyler explained, "'A standard pail right now costs about 75 baht, 15 baht lower than a metal one. But it's still too expensive for the market. Our customers, because of the recession, needed something cheaper'" (Nivatpumin and Sivasomboom, 1998, p. 1).

So Tyler and his Thai engineers set about designing a new technology, called orbital turbulent injection, that provides faster resin flow at multiple points. Because the technology requires less pressure, Tyler's engineers were able to use a 400-ton injection molding machine instead of the 650-ton machine necessary with the older technology, lowering power costs. There was also an advanced technology benefit: a stronger product.

"The bottom line: a pail can be made for 55–60 baht that is stronger and lighter than a typical 70-baht product. Injection and production take twelve seconds, half the normal time. 'The Germans and the Japanese—they didn't believe that the technology could come from Thailand,'" Tyler said in the article. Neither did the Thais. When Tyler applied for a patent, he was told foreign technology couldn't be patented in Thailand. "This is technology developed in Thailand, by Thais, and I want to register it for my company," he argued. With patent in hand, Tyler has reached a licensing agreement with "German industry giant Mannesmann Demag to market the production process" (Nivatpumin and Sivasomboon, 1998, p. 1).

When Tony Tan celebrated the twentieth anniversary of Jollibee in 1998, he had grown to be one of Asia's most notable success stories. He had gone from owning almost nothing—he had contemplated getting out of the industry when McDonald's entered the market— to owning close to three hundred stores, twenty-eight located outside the Philippines in Asia, the Middle East, and the United States. Tan's success is based on global standards of service and localizing product, much in the same way Borders does.

"We do blend tests," says Raffy de la Rosa, Jollibee's vice president for finance, in other markets. As a result of those tests, the company customizes its product to appeal to local preferences. As a result, "In Indonesia and Malaysia we're doing quite well compared to the competition," de la Rosa says. "We also have to introduce local products, like *sambal*, hot sauce, and *nasi lemak*—a spicy rice and chicken dish" (Interview with the author, July 24, 1998).

But de la Rosa and Executive Vice President Ernesto Tanmantiong quickly admit that learning how to operate internationally has sometimes meant a bumpy learning curve. "We have two key learning experiences," they say. First was the degree and depth of management support provided to overseas' franchisees—60 percent of all stores are franchised. Requirements by franchisees for support turned out to be much greater than originally envisioned for a number of reasons, such as distance from the home office during market development periods following new store openings. "So we strengthened management," de la Rosa says.

The second challenge was simply avoiding the temptation to put up stores whenever—and wherever—sites became available. "Before, if we had a willing franchisee, we went into the market. We learned that we must be focused and can only do that if we focus our resources on specific markets. You can't just take sites. You must take prime sites to communicate the name and the product.

"We waited over a year for the Daly City location," de la Rosa says of the wildly popular entry into the United States market.

Like other dynamic Asian managers that see the financial crisis as a time of opportunity, de la Rosa and Tanmantiong have not enjoyed a trouble-free journey to industry leadership and significant international expansion. But they have made certain that they understand why they experience setbacks and what they would have to do to make sure those setbacks didn't occur again in the future.

Each of these glimpses at some of Asia's exciting young managers provides special insights into the New Asian Corporation and its leadership (Table 3.2). First is the emphasis on performance. Throughout Asia's history, people of contrasting ethnic heritages have been able to demonstrate that a savvy, determined manager can operate anywhere. That is true nowhere more than in Asia today—and likely tomorrow as well. The financial crisis quickly eroded the luxury of convenience and security in appointing leadership to Asian companies. What counts is the bottom line. Period.

Second, tremendous innovation is beginning to come out of Asia, proving the old truism that adversity is the mother of invention. This says a great deal about the confidence of managers in Asia. Despite the downturn, despite the challenges, the managers of truly excellent Asian companies realized from the beginning of the crisis there were opportunities to be capitalized on. The best managers set about doing so while many firms ran to government for help or a shoulder to cry on.

Corporate Strategy	Focus on key business processes and the development of new business models
Management and Corporate Culture	Premium on management expertise and strategic thinking
Opportunity	Market and customer centric

Table 3.2.   Characteristics of the New Asian Corporation.

Third is that these managers can survive and flourish anywhere—not because they are Asian or Western managers, but because they are smart, gutsy managers.

STRATEGY AND STRUCTURE

In a 1998 presentation at *BusinessWeek*'s Eighth Annual Asia Leadership Forum on "The New Asian Business Model," Dell executive Philip Kelly noted that despite being a year into the financial crisis, Asian sales of Dell's computers continued to expand. He attributed the continued growth despite the effects of the crisis to two attributes: customer loyalty and shareholder value.

"We have had to determine who our most profitable customers are and what markets are most profitable," he said. To do this, Dell has leveraged multinational relationships beyond national borders. But Kelly emphasized that, "Our customers need more help from us than ever before. We intend to be part of their solution." Doing that depended on attitudes within the organization, attitudes that were the result of a concerted effort by the company's leadership to sell vision and direction throughout the organization. Fast food entrepreneur Michael Chan agrees: "With 6,000 employees, I spend a lot of time managing by walking around, and a lot of time in meetings 'brainwashing,'" he says bluntly.

That sounds like a pretty soft approach to strategy and structure in the crux of a crisis. But it's worked. Scott Fraser, the executive director of Deloitte & Touche Consulting Group/Braxton Associates in Singapore, preaches a more structured approach incorporating the Braxton Business Model (Figure 3.1). That model provides a universe of eight interactive elements.

Fraser notes that all these elements work together, and when one changes, the others must. Like many of the managers we've discussed, Fraser argues that when the environment changed, it provoked a fundamental reassessment of goals, especially a shift from growth, or simply wanting to be big, to one of value formation through increased profitability. Asian firms are notorious for low return on investment

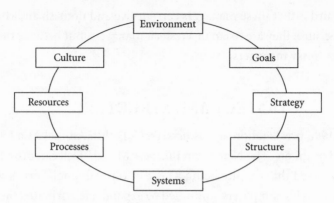

Figure 3.1.   The Braxton Business Model.
(Reprinted with permission.)

and productivity. As a result of the crisis, "Economic performance must be the measure of success" (Presentation at *BusinessWeek*'s 8th Annual Asia Leadership Forum), Fraser noted, not market share and certainly not market monopoly.

This shift has caused the "economic logic of over-diversified conglomerates to collapse," Fraser says. As the Asian Leadership Survey showed, managers in Asia by far acknowledge the need to focus resources and develop innovative business models that allow them to capitalize on new sources of opportunity and profit. This will require fundamental changes in structure, systems, and processes. This transition will be addressed further in Chapter Eight.

DEVOLUTION OF RESPONSIBILITY AND DECISION MAKING

The need for such profound shifts likewise demands a shift in business culture. Strong leadership is only one element in the development of a culture that lends itself to the creation of value through increased profitability and intense customer relationships. While conglomerates ruled it over the Asian miracle years, they were known, for the most part, for their autocratic, if benign, paternalism.

TA's Wong Hong Meng readily admits that his firm was no different. But Wong's boss and TA executive chairman Tony Tiah has been quick to hand over the reins to a new generation of younger managers that he believes are more suited to manage in newly turbulent and challenging times. Working through the transition is difficult. In speaking with Wong, he candidly admitted that he wasn't sure how smoothly the shift would take place, and not just because the older generation, including him, was trying to hold onto authority. "Sometimes," he said, "we feel that they are not aggressive enough because they are thinking of our feelings. And yet sometimes," he laughs with a sense of irony, "we do feel that they are too aggressive. So we are just getting used to this new system" (Interview with author, June 23, 1998).

Café de Coral's Chan feels that he still has to be involved in many details he'd rather not be involved in. However, he has worked diligently to develop managers who think for themselves. Part of his development strategy has been an aggressive profit-sharing scheme. "Every store is a profit center," he says, and "forty percent of each manager's salary is made up of incentives." The system—which includes full-time senior staff—has paid off in low turnover as well as sustained profitability (Interview with author, May 6, 1998).

Thai Farmers Bank's Banthoon Lamsam says the transition in Thai companies to a more Western approach to management represents a huge culture shock. "If the shock can be overcome," he says, "there will be a shift to higher performance." But despite the severity of the crisis and the urgency of reform, Banthoon says the transition won't go smoothly. "There is much resistance because people are embarrassed when they are measured precisely." Banthoon feels that it will be difficult to maintain the harmonious working relationships that were so critical in corporate Thailand during the boom years. "In the past, we induced harmony, but as competition increases, we have to get the best people in the most important positions of responsibility" (Interview with author, June 3, 1998).

Most observers of Thailand's banking sector during the financial crisis focused on speculation as to whether the sector would be able to adequately recapitalize and in what form banks would emerge from the crisis. Banthoon himself predicted that companies that had not made the investments in the technology and the people necessary to pull them out of the crisis would very likely be gone or unrecognizable in terms of their ownership structure in six months. A few weeks later, Thai Farmer's Bank reported a US$100 million second-quarter loss. "Its stock price plunged 65 percent, and analysts expect it will have to return to the market to raise yet more money," *BusinessWeek* reported ("Thailand: Banking Chaos," 1998), despite the bank's successful US$850-million equity place to foreign investors just months earlier.

The *BusinessWeek* article went on to say, "So it should come as no surprise that the talk these days in Bangkok is not whether a few of the smaller, weaker banks can survive. Instead, the question is whether any can be saved." Interviewed for the piece, Russell Kopp, a regional bank analyst at Dresdner Kleinwort Benson, said, "We are one step away from nationalizing the banking system." In a related interview, Thailand's Finance Minister Tarrin Nimmanahaeminda admitted, "The economy is in a shambles" ("Thailand: Banking Chaos," 1998).

Given those conditions, analysts' preoccupation with survival is understandable. While Banthoon clearly didn't relish a return to international equity markets under even worse conditions than those during the initial offering, he seemed to understand that attracting additional funds depended on Thai Farmer's Bank's capacity to be different, and not just second largest. Attracting funds a second time would be even more dependent on Banthoon's confidence in the structural reforms he was forcing. His capacity to break down resistance to reforms and instill a "performance mentality" was likely the most important factor in saving the institution. By late 1998, analysts were already suggesting that the Thai banking sector "may be the first in Asia to recover" ("Thai Banks May Be First . . . ," 1998).

As the experience of these companies suggest, survival and success in the New Asia depends on, in the context of the Asian miracle years, doing things and thinking differently. Conformance to accepted regional norms of business is a formula for failure. The New Asian Corporation is a company that distinguishes itself by being different, and frequently controversial. But not for the sake of just being different. These companies and their leadership are different because they are focusing on efficiency, productivity, and profitability in a new, outrageously competitive Asia.

GEN-X IN ASIA

In research involving the twenty technology companies with the highest five-year return on equity in the United States, Peter Cohan, bestselling author of *Net Profit,* found that the most important distinguishing characteristic of industry leaders is how aggressively they compete for the smartest people. And they pay incredible salaries both to attract and keep those people. Microsoft, for example, is said to have more than 3,000 millionaires among its present and former employees. Now that's what one could call a real stock option incentive plan.

A report by Nina Munk in *Fortune* magazine (1998) suggests Microsoft's incentives may be trend setting, but not unusual in the booming United States economy. Many experts have argued for several years now that competitive advantage is no longer resource or size dependent. Instead, the capital that matters are the people walking around the company drinking coffee and dreaming up new ideas.

Munk calls these people "gold collar" workers: the best and the brightest. And they create the best and the brightest companies in the world.

Now think about this. Virtually every one of the top technology companies in the world recruits heavily throughout Asia. The United States Congress enacted new legislation doubling the number of visas available to knowledge workers from other countries in response to heavy lobbying by technology companies. That shows not only how important it is to recruit gold-collar workers from wherever they may be found, it shows how important Asia's best and brightest are to the world's most important technology companies.

In *Asia's Best: The Myth & Reality of Asia's Most Successful Companies* (Hamlin, 1998), it is argued that one of the great ironies of emerging Asia is that developing economies are footing a big part of the educational tab for advanced economies. This is true both in terms of

private and public education, as well as the corporate education provided by Asian companies and multinationals operating in Asia to
supplement the region's inadequate educational infrastructure.

This is discussed in more detail in Chapter Nine, but for now what
this means is that while much of Asia is focusing on how to keep jobs
cheap, the world's best companies are aggressively recruiting the
region's most important source of competitive advantage: GenX gold-
collar workers. And they are going to keep doing this, too. Munk
shows why: "The unemployment rate for college graduates is 1.9% (in
the United States). If it were possible, the jobless rate for gold-collar
workers would probably be less than zero.

"In San Diego at this moment there are 3,000-odd open spots for
engineers and 2,000 positions for technical professionals. McKinsey
& Co., the big consulting firm, hires one in every ten Harvard and
Stanford MBA grads, but still its demand for talent outweighs supply:
'We've gotten to the point where we've tapped out,' says partner Lenny
Mendonca" (Munk, 1998, p. 62).

Declining student populations and continued growth in the United
States and European Union economies promises even greater competition for intellectual capital.

What does this mean for Asian companies that are competing with
hungry multinational firms for talent? First, it means some pretty stark
strategic decisions are necessary. Remember, Adrian Slywotzky and
David Morrison argue forcefully and effectively that the source of profits for firms is shifting as a result of the global forces that stimulate competition and enhance economic integration across political borders.

For example, when Coca-Cola's declining revenue growth opportunities suggested the industry had matured, Coca-Cola focused on
vending, which provided healthier margins than those available from
traditional retail sales. When vending growth began to slow, the company began buying back its bottler franchises, to again increase value-
added for the company.

When companies look at their industry and say they can't add value
because they can't afford people or technology, they are looking in the
wrong places. Future sources of revenue growth and profit will likely

come from completely different parts of the manufacturing or marketing chain. The capacity to identify those new sources is proportional to the company's capacity to innovate. And its capacity to innovate is dependent on the quality of its people.

The second implication is that companies will have to be willing to assume huge risks. For many, they must bet their futures, which makes TA's Wong Hong Meng's apprehension over the changing of the guard and Thai Farmers Banthoon's determination to do so understandable. Making the investments necessary to attract gold-collar workers will also be expensive. Turning over the future of the company will be gut wrenching, but as Munk says, the best and the brightest expect to have the remote control. They expect to be allowed to make things happen. And that's especially true in Asia, where the best and the brightest are at an even greater premium.

For those who think that Asian economies and companies can't afford this kind of massive shift in people valuation, we argue that the investment in keeping gold-collar workers is an investment Asian companies can ill afford not to make. That is, not if they expect to develop into high-value manufacturers and service providers. Asia's best managers agree. The competition for people is more than a competition for scarce intellectual resources—it is the race for the only resource that matters.

LIBERATION TECHNOLOGY

The book has thus far addressed the impact of the crisis, liberalization, and technology on the competitiveness of Asian companies; the critical importance of enhancing the efficiency with which resources are utilized; the productivity with which products and services are provided; and the identification of new sources of profit resulting in massive structural, system, and process reform. One year into the Asian crisis, it was clear that companies that had, as Banthoon suggested, made the investment in people and technology early were doing better than the competition. In May 1997, the results of a survey by British Telecom showed a higher acceptance of information as a strategic tool among Asian business directors than their counterparts in Europe and the United States. "Asia marked 91 percent, while Europe and the United States posted 76 percent and 74 percent, respectively. The global average was 82 percent" ("Survey Says Korean . . . ," 1998). Both the *BusinessWeek* Asian Leadership survey (see Table 3.3) and the PriceWaterhouseCoopers survey showed a high level of appreciation for the role of knowledge management in achieving competitive success.

Question	No Impact	Little Impact	Some Impact	Significant Impact
What impact do you think IT will have on your organization now?	3	12	24	60
What impact will it have in the next three to five years?	0	7	14	78

Question	Yes	No
Has your planned investment in IT for the next three to five years decreased because of the economic uncertainty?	21	78

Question	Not Important	Somewhat Important	Important	Very Important
How important are investments in IT to the achievement of your company's future goals and objectives?	3	19	26	48

Question	Essential	Occasionally Useful	Nice to Have	Can Do Without
As a tool for my business, the Internet is:	41	36	17	2

Table 3.3.   *BusinessWeek*'s Asia Leadership Forum Survey (Percent of Respondents).
Source: BusinessWeek 8th Annual Asia Leadership Forum Issues Survey, June 25, 1998.

After the paralyzing shock of the financial crisis began to recede, this awareness drove a panicked rush to make strategic technology investments. One major business systems vendor, previously considered too expensive for developing Philippine corporations, suddenly signed five major contracts in one week in July 1998. Consulting partners such as Andersen Consulting and Ernest & Young were likewise feeling the impact of formerly reluctant clients rushing to implementation.

Seventy-four percent of respondents to *BusinessWeek's* Asia Leadership Survey said investment in information technology (IT) was either important or very important for "the achievement of your company's future goals and objectives." Almost half said such investment was very important, and 60 percent said IT has significant impact on their organizations now, and 76 percent said IT would have significant impact in the next three to five years. Despite the effects of the crisis, 78 percent of the respondents said that they have not decreased their planned investment in IT. Demonstrating the increasing importance of the Internet to corporate Asia, 41 percent of respondents said that the Internet is an essential tool to their businesses. Another 36 percent said it was occasionally useful. Results of the PriceWaterhouseCoopers survey showed that "nearly three-quarters of CEOs believe that e-business will either 'completely reshape' or have a 'significant impact' on competition in their industries. More than half of the CEOs believe their industries will be challenged by nontraditional competitors using e-business as their main channel to customers. Fully a fifth see more than 20 percent of their [own] total revenues coming from e-business in five years" ("Inside the Mind of the CEO: A Survey of Asian Chief Executives," 1998).

Hard data backs up these perspectives. In an article in *Fortune* magazine, the International Data Corporation (IDC) reported, "there are already about eleven million Internet users in Asia. That's not all. IDC also forecasts that Internet commerce in Asia will explode from roughly US$500 million in annual revenues today to US$30 billion by the year 2001" (Chowdhury, 1998, p. 33). These results suggest that by the time the Asian crisis winds down, electronic commerce will play a fundamental role in the business models of most Asian companies.

If it is true (and it is) that quality and productivity are requisites of doing business and no longer a source of competitive advantage, then so is technology. In fact, acquiring state-of-the-art information technology is a requisite to being in business for the New Asian Corporation. While less than stellar technology was fine for corporations seeking to enhance efficiency and productivity in domestic markets with limited competition, the introduction of intensive global competition quickly changed that part of the success formula. But while acquiring that technology represents a financial challenge to many organizations—and another people challenge as they strive to retain their technology and knowledge workers—it also represents an important competitive threat to large domestic and multinational corporations. Asian corporations that make the investment enjoy the same opportunities to achieve enhanced efficiency, productivity, and business intelligence signaling shifts in the market that their larger and more resource-rich competitors enjoy. With most multinational firms already enjoying the technology, they represent a saturated market for systems developers and retailers. For that reason, enterprise system developers, such as SAP, Oracle, PeopleSoft, and Baan, have intensified their efforts to make their products available to smaller businesses.

Internet technology and e-commerce are important components of this development. E-commerce has two parts. The first is the introduction of electronic transactions in the supply chain, or business-to-business e-commerce and Internet commerce. When Asia's financial crisis began, retailers were busy developing the retail side of the chain in terms of the introduction of technology. The crisis made it clear that the backside of the chain was just as important to maximize returns on resources. In fact, business-to-business Internet commerce by some estimates is expected to grow to US$1.2 trillion by 2003. And Asian exporters will be an integral link in the global supply chain.

The second part of e-commerce, business-to-customer, is a much smaller segment, but addresses customer interface in a range of transactions spanning corporate communication to retail. Retail involves everything from creative and editorial services to the sale of manufactured products. Corporate communications provides the means for relatively small Asian corporations to bring their products and services to the attention of global markets at very little cost. In both cases, as respondents to the Asia Leadership Survey believe, the Internet is fast becoming an essential part of successful business activity in Asia.

A glimpse into how essential the Internet is and will be was offered by economists Philip B. Evans and Thomas S. Wurster when they proclaimed, "Every business is an information business." They argue that as dramatically as technology has affected operating processes over the past decade, "a more profound transformation of the business landscape lies ahead. Executives—and not just those in high-tech or information companies—will be forced to rethink the strategic fundamentals of their businesses. Over the next decade, the new economics of information will precipitate changes in the structure of entire industries and in the ways companies compete" (Evans and Wurster, 1997, pp. 71–72).

By mid-1999, China was thinking seriously about providing its 30 million cable subscribers with Internet services. Singapore had signed up 30,000 consumers for its high-speed multimedia network, Singapore One. And Japanese commuters had given up their comic books for cellular phones with Internet and e-mail capability.

Asia's financial crisis made the need to rethink strategic fundamentals a matter of survival, and the integration of information technology a fundamental enabler in that process. Thanks to Asia's easy adaptability—demonstrated by its willingness to adapt strategy and processes during the miracle years—Asia proved to be well-suited, despite early resistance, to major and continuing change. Indeed, no other region has changed as fast as Asia has in the twentieth century. Therefore, no one is as prepared to throw off the shackles of past success.

THREAT WARNING: GUYS, AND GALS, IN THE GARAGE

Technology and the competition for knowledge workers presents other threats to the New Asian Corporation and multinationals in Asia alike. And that is that GenX doesn't need the New Asian Corporation—or its competitors—as much as both need, desperately, GenX. Of all the frustrations managers in Asia will experience in the first two decades of the twenty-first century, this will be the worst.

First, there will be the enormous competition for the best and brightest people. That competition will not be limited to competition among companies, but will be further exacerbated by competition with the increasing attractiveness of entrepreneurship. Taiwan and Hong Kong are already great bastions of entrepreneurship. Thirteen months into the Asian financial crisis Hong Kong Chief Executive Tung Chee-hwa said he believed the Special Autonomous Region's entrepreneurs will be "the engine that pulls the territory out of its economic slump" (Entrepreneurs the Engine . . . ," 1998). As GenX's knowledge workers increasingly measure the attractiveness and remuneration benefits of working for major Asian and multinational companies with the challenges—and potentials—of setting out on their own, the companies will more and more frequently come up on the losing end of that decision.

Companies in Asia as well as other markets are having trouble enticing new recruits into the corporate lifestyle because the young people think to themselves, if one has to work this hard, why not do it for myself? For many GenXers, unmarried, highly educated, and concerned about the quality of life, security won't be entirely out of reach even if the experiment with entrepreneurship doesn't yield entirely happy results—there will be an insatiable appetite for capable people among corporate Asia.

While further limits on the brain pool has serious implications for Asian business, that may not be the most serious threat. It will probably be entrepreneurs in the tradition of Acer's founder Stan Shih, Trend Micro's Steve Chang, and Singapore's Sound Blaster king, Creative Technology co-founder Sim Wong Hoo. But the difference will be that they will take the entrepreneurial plunge before trying out the corporate alternative. Like some of the West's technology heros, these Asian business leaders have built major corporations up from shoestring operations in their garages. As the New Asian Corporation looks at the competitive landscape in the next century, it will see multiples of these kinds of leaders—looking for a place in history, and creating a life on their own—as well as a whole new group of dangerous competitors.

CHAPTER FOUR

Guanxi, Mergers and Acquisitions, and the New Asian Corporation

———~~~———

Andrew Fung set up ACL Consultants to provide business management training programs for the People's Republic of China government units. He established programs that included elaborate political and economic studies for senior officials, including city mayors, department heads, bureau chiefs of various ministries, and provincial governments. The programs were intended to empower government agencies, and to assist them in developing their capacity to service constituents in a fast-changing, sociopolitical environment. To the officials involved in Fung's programs, Fung was a teacher, a sharer of knowledge—a dispenser of power—through his methods of building capacity.

Fung benefitted greatly from his experience training government officials. First, of course, he made money. Second, and perhaps more important, he earned the goodwill of literally thousands of government officials that would be active at the local and national levels of government for most of his lifetime. That goodwill paid off in an important way when Fung went to work for Renful Asset

Protection, a corporate security firm founded by former Royal Hong Kong Police Force Superintendent Colin Hill. The company is part of the Renful Group of Paul Yip Kwok Wah, a prominent Hong Kong businessman.

Although Yip—once appointed Hong Kong Affairs advisor by the Chinese Government—has plenty of high-level connections (also known as the infamous and mysterious *guanxi*), it is Fung's reputation for getting things done that has been the biggest advantage to the company. After all, he helped build the capacity of local government units to assist them in fulfilling their responsibilities to society.

The fine distinction here is that Fung's network is doing its job, not distributing special favors. Given China's reputation for opaque deal making, that fine distinction can provide a mighty advantage for Renful's big-name clients: dependability. In the past, the quality of *guanxi* frequently depended on the size—and prestige—of the war chest, as TV producer Robert Chua found out when he went up against News Corporation's Rupert Murdoch for cable deals with Guangdong cable operators. Chua thought he was well-wired with relationships with the vice minister of China's Ministry of Film, Television and Radio, the head of China Central Television, and the chairman of the Chinese Television Artists Association. He wasn't. Murdoch and his mainland partners took all the deals. Chua got nothing.

Those familiar with the deal say it was Chua's concern with doing things the "Chinese way" that got him into trouble. His chief operating officer said, "The contract was thirty pages shorter than I would have written it. Every time there was a normal procedure to be done, Chua would say, 'It's not necessary, don't worry.' It drove me nuts. It drove the lawyers nuts. From day one there was a lack of compliance, but we didn't mention it because we were all supposed to be men of good will" (Berfield, 1998).

One of the principal benefits—yes, benefits—of Asia's financial crisis was the pressure it put on connection-dependent networks and the practice of handing out special favors to businessmen in good standing with the government. As we've seen already, the competitiveness of many of Asia's cumbersome conglomerates was limited to their capacity to curry favor at the highest level of Asian governments (see Table 4.1). The crisis exacted a high price in return.

"'The core competency of many Asian conglomerates lay in their ability to manage the bureaucratic process for approvals of projects,' notes C. K. Prahalad, professor of corporate strategy and international business at the University of Michigan. 'That competency is no longer valuable because the regulatory environment is changing. They will now have to develop skills in the few businesses they do understand, and discard the rest" (Tripathi, 1998, p. 50).

That doesn't mean that networking is dead in China, or Asia. Eighty-three percent of the respondents to *BusinessWeek*'s Asia Leadership Survey, for instance, agreed that "Successful Asian companies will continue to depend on networking." But the nature of that networking will be business-oriented, based on market reforms. "We must get reforms implemented quickly," Banthoon Lamsan says, "because the economy is so fragile." Asia's economies just can't stand much more opaque deal making and shoddy management by fat conglomerates.

Statement: "Connections are more important than strategy for a company to succeed in Asia" (percent agree).

Overall	66
South Korea	73
Japan	60
Taiwan	74
Philippines	56
Hong Kong	58
Thailand	69
Malaysia	79
Singapore	73
Indonesia	78
Australia	64
Asian Expatriates	62
Non-Asian Expatriates	53

Table 4.1.   Pre-Crisis Views on the Value of Connections.

Source: "Managing in Asia 5," *Far Eastern Economic Review,* 1997, p. 32.

Rob Goodfellow is a writer and researcher specializing in Indonesia. He feels that the dramatic shift to democratic freedoms have speeded the changeover from crony deal making to smart business decision making. He has related the positive experiences of business consultants and joint venture partners in Indonesia. One stands out, involving a consultant he calls Mary, who had set up a joint venture between a multinational firm and a major Indonesia company. According to Mary,

about ten years ago we did a merchandise audit and found that the consumables for our new company were four times greater than for a similar-sized company in Europe or the United States. The idea of doing an audit was first to introduce our partners to the idea of accountability, and second to give them a bit of a shock. We flew a team of accountants up and they went through everything. We attracted some critical attention immediately because all of the Indonesian directors had shares in the consumables network.

It was obviously in their best interests to be very good consumers.

They all got a percentage off the top. There was six percent each for the directors, four percent for the manager, and two percent for the foreman. It took a long time to sort it out, but ultimately we sent a very strong message across to our partners that this type of behavior was neither ethically tolerable nor, more important, in the best interests of sound, steady, profitable business. Now this company is riding out the Asian economic crisis and the message is getting through to the general business community here (Goodfellow, 1998, Internet edition).

SOUND, STEADY
PROFIT-ORIENTED PRIORITIES

Prapad Phodivorakhun, president of Mitsubishi affiliate Kang Yong Electric Company, provides good insight into the new business priority. "We see a challenge to our competitiveness ahead," he says, "as Thailand conforms to AFTA agreements to limit import duties to a maximum of five percent by the year 2003." Kang Yong is a manufacturer of consumer appliances that exports half of its production to Japan. Despite the Japanese recession and the impact of the Asian financial crisis, Kang Yong exports jumped 30 percent in 1998 from the previous year. Prapad is not taking his good fortune for granted.

He is concerned about competition in five areas. The first of those is low cost. Prapad understands that he is in the commodity business. To lower costs, Prapad has consistently upgraded the value-added of local content, especially in the design of products. His second concern is quality. Kang Yong's shop floor looks as if it were transplanted from Japan: clean, organized, efficient. Those qualities help ensure consistency of quality output. In one corner of the factory stands the remnants of quality controls victims: refrigerators with holes drilled into them, mangled fans, and other dismembered appliances.

Prapad's third concern is pricing. Kang Yong's parent provided critical assistance to finance operations during the Asian crisis by arranging for low-interest, yen-denominated loans with long payback periods from the company's bankers. The low interest was helpful, but in 1998, the deteriorating yen was a major challenge to both Kang Yong and its bankers. This is not to mention the effect of such deals on the Japanese banking system, the source of so many of Asia's ills. But for Kang Yong, it was still better than paying local interest rates.

Prapad's fourth concern was that Kang Yong continue to meet customer expectations, given rapid shifts in preferences. Prapad spent 100 million baht on training, hiring, equipment, and facility improvement, including sending new engineers to Japan for two years. More than thirty engineers have spent varying lengths of time training at Mitsubishi facilities there. Finally, Prapad was thinking about the future, namely the competitive threat that China presented to continued growth in exports. To meet that challenge, Prapad was preparing a second round of process reengineering to further trim costs and hike productivity. He has also managed to lower imported content to just 19 percent on average for the entire product line. Meanwhile, he's trying to convince those suppliers to set up shop in Thailand.

But Prapad was not planning to grow by merely cutting and trimming. When we talked, he was preparing plans to boost production of refrigerators from 250,000 to 500,000 by the year 2000. He had separate plans to boost production of electric fans. By 2000, he expected half of production to go to exports: "There are 550 million people in the ASEAN countries," he said. Because labor costs are lower in many of those countries, Prapad believes that Kang Yong's marketing program and product development efforts will be the two principal critical success factors. As noted before, productivity and quality do not provide that advantage, just the capacity to be in business.

BUSINESS NETWORKS

Neither connections nor networks are of much use to Prapad. Like both he and Rung, Alphatec's Richard Mollerstuen has counted on his reputation to perform to keep the company alive during a period of unthinkable turmoil internally. When Alphatec was established, Mollerstuen's model was based on a simple premise: professional reputation. Over the course of his career, Mollerstuen had established a reputation for delivering on his promises. That meant on-time delivery of quantity and quality. "There was nothing wrong with that model," he explained when asked what happened to Alphatec. What happened was that "DRAM—a type of memory chip—pricing and the local economy threw us for a loop. We [concurrently] went from funds always being available to nothing being available," he said.

Alphatec's founder, Charn Uswachoke, who worked for several multinational technology companies before establishing Alphatec, relied on family connections in Thailand to finance the acquisition of local production capacity owned by United States companies. Ultimately, Charn used some of the funding he obtained to finance other ventures, as well as to make questionable payments to outside directors. Connections helped give birth to Alphatec and very nearly brought it down.

That was bad enough, but to obtain much of the financing, Charn had been window dressing the company's income statements. Auditors in 1997 "found that Alphatec had created fake purchase orders to show profits that never existed. The company overstated its 1995 and 1996 profit by 1.8 billion baht each year, and 1997's first quarter earnings by 500 million baht. But Alphatec, in fact, had losses totaling 2.88 billion baht for those periods" ("Charn Resigns from Alphatec After Audit," 1997, p. 1).

This is the stuff that makes for the corporate communicator's worst nightmare. "In the first half of 1997," Mollerstuen says, "our debt level reached the point where we could no longer service it." This was clearly a critical juncture for Alphatec, and not just for the obvious reasons. If the company was to have any hope for survival, it needed to retain its skittish customer base. In the industry, stability—ironic given the volatility of the semiconductor businesses—is a critical success factor. Alphatec was exporting more than US$1 billion in output to major multinational technology companies who had to know that orders would be filled on time. That Mollerstuen and his staff had the credibility to convince these customers to take a billion-dollar bet—when the *Wall Street Journal* was regularly reporting the company's myriad problems—is truly remarkable.

"It was traumatic, at best," Mollerstuen recounted to us. "Overall, Alphatec has not lost its image [for quality and reliability]. Our customers have stuck with us. Our suppliers have stuck with us. To some extent, our suppliers have to work with us," Mollerstuen admits, "but to some extent, they just believe in us. Many are people that have worked with us for many years," he says. When Mollerstuen was last interviewed, he expected to realize profitability over the following six months, provided the company was recapitalized as planned (Interview with the author, June 1, 1998). Recapitalization—in the form of a capital infusion of US$40 million—did not occur until after the financial restructuring package was agreed to in February 1999. By June, Mollerstuen, now senior adviser, expected the company to reach 80 percent of capacity by the end of the year, and was investing US$14 million in new capacity. He also announced plans for a new factory.

Mollerstuen's network kept his company alive during an incredibly horrifying period. The company was hit by the revelations of massive fraud by its founder at the same time the Asia's financial crisis hit. To make things even worse, semiconductor prices nosedived. That Alphatec has survived—which most analysts didn't expect in late 1997—is a tribute to its incredible tenacity and determination.

Alphatec also represents Thailand's first experiment with a Western-style bankruptcy law that provides broader protection for creditors.

Because Charn had previously blocked efforts to recapitalize that would dilute his holdings, the company was unable to get back on its feet as early as expected without the benefit of the new provisions. But now, Alphatec has become a transparent blueprint for restructuring troubled Asian corporations.

While connections are out in the New Asia, networking is in. Most networking has to do with building and sustaining corporate image, to better enable the corporation to weather the inevitable storm. Fortunately for most, experiencing what Mollerstuen and his capable staff have gone through will likely remain a novelty. But all corporations will have to manage their images much more carefully to influence the business environment and generate new opportunities. This is discussed at great length in Chapter Five.

DEALS: MERGERS AND ACQUISITIONS

Connections have little to do with the New Asia's biggest deals: mergers and acquisitions. "A New York-based institutional investor, who recently turned down a private-placement offer from an Asian group, [noted]: 'We like businesses that are easy to grasp; their organization charts shouldn't look like the map of the London Underground'" (Tripathi, 1998, p. 49). Statements like this demonstrate the sadly deteriorated cachet of Asia's miracle years' conglomerates, not just in the consumer marketplace, but among international investors. But they also show that in tough times, quality of organization—or lack of it— is what counts. Perhaps that's why Sunthorn Arunanondchai, president of CP Land of Thailand's hugely diversified CP Group, told a gathering of business leaders in 1998, "We're taking out all noncore business, but unfortunately, we can't sell a business no one wants.

"But we have to keep on trying to sell anyway. Our group has 100,000 people, and we just can't maintain them in these conditions. We're talking with creditors to reschedule US$450 million." Despite these deplorable developments and the urgency of shedding noncore assets, Sunthorn said, incredibly, he still had to deal with "internal struggle due to resistance to selling."

Desire to hang on to family heirlooms wasn't the only impediment to outside investment in Asia's conglomerates. Malaysia's Prime Minister Mahathir publicly fretted that his country would be recolonized, and warned major business groups not to succumb to the temptation to, in effect, sell their souls to save their skins. Unfortunately for Mahathir and Malaysia's troubled business sector, the alternatives to seeking recapitalization through mergers with multinational corporations were few. Government plans to float bonds on the international market to provide funds to buy bad loans and rehabilitate the banking sector—freeing up funds for business expansion—were postponed when international credit rating agencies, which had all failed to anticipate Asia's financial crisis themselves, belatedly and probably uselessly downgraded the country's rating.

A United Nations survey in March 1998 showed that, "[A]ttracted by bargain prices and prospects for long-term economic growth, an overwhelming majority of nearly two hundred heads of multinationals surveyed said they were unshaken by the financial turmoil that has rocked the region since Thailand was forced to devalue its currency" (Lynch, 1998, Internet edition). By June, United States acquisitions of Asian businesses had reached US$8 billion, double that of 1997. "Wen-Tzen Lim, a mergers and acquisitions analyst at Securities Data, described the surge of investment by both United States and European investors as a 'historic moment' which he likens to the United Kingdom's 'big bang' when it opened its financial sector to foreign investors" (Walker, 1998, p. 5). While more than half of these acquisitions took place in Japan, acquisitions in Thailand were the third highest after South Korea. Acquisitions by European firms totaled another US$4 billion, and included deals in sectors from supermarkets to banks.

In June 1998, almost US$2 billion in new American-based investment funds had been set up to acquire distressed Asian assets. "They included several 'vulture funds,' so called for their hungry swoops on the distressed real estate that litters Asia's business landscape. Among them were a US$800 million fund launched by Houston-based developer Hines, which intended to invest more than 40 percent in Asia.

New York-based Greenwich Group International expected to raise US$2 billion to US$2.5 billion from American investors for Asian property purchases by the end of 1999" (Gilley, 1998, p. 43). Simon Murray, a long-time Hong Kong-based businessman, said, "This is the moment that many investors have been waiting for."

By the third quarter of 1998, a number of substantial mega-mergers were in the making or had been announced. Ford Motor Company was talking on and off to Kia Motors Corporation in South Korea. British Telecom announced its intent to buy 33 percent of Malaysian telecommunications group Binariang, following a competitor's filing for protection from creditors. Swiss cement giant Holderbank Financiere Glaris acquired 40 percent of a new company with the Philippines' Phinma Group. Soon, every major cement manufacturer would have a foreign partner. Two of Thailand's struggling banks had been acquired. There was significant pressure on smaller banks to merge throughout the region, and even larger banks were joining forces, such as the Development Bank of Singapore and the Post Office Savings Bank.

As the tide increased, Asian governments weren't alone in urging caution before rushing into the arms of foreign suitors. "You need to seek partners with the right strategic fit who can bring technology, brands or worldclass processors, not just money," AT Kearney Vice President and Managing Director Christopher J. Clarke warned. "Don't let your foreign bankers force you to divest your core businesses. If you owe the banks a lot of money, they are as desperate as you to find a solution, otherwise they have to write off their loans" (Pratap, 1998, p. 6), he said. That advice was right, if disingenuous, and problematic.

The most seriously distressed firms in Asia in 1998 were its wildly diversified conglomerates. Where the strategic fit lay was the priority question for buyers, and the difficulty in defining strategic fit—as well as internal and government resistance to foreign acquisitions—was holding the truly high-profile acquisitions back. This was a game the buyers could well afford to play. First, by waiting for diversified businesses to be spun off, investors were attempting to focus their infusions on core businesses or liberated subsidiaries that did in fact demonstrate strong strategic fit. In 1998, Jim Rohwer, best-selling author of *Asia Rising*, wrote, "Asian equity prices have moved mostly on the basis of financial news and have yet to fully absorb the bad news from the real economy: shrinking output, rising unemployment, and dwindling corporate earnings. Another sharp fall in company valuations is likely" (Rohwer, 1998, p. 82). Second, the longer they waited, the more desperate Asia's overweight conglomerates were becoming. In 1998, Asian governments were less capable of coming to their rescue. For investors, this was good business. But for the founders of the conglomerates and Asian governments, it was exploitation. Westerners were seen to be gloating over the misfire of the Asian miracle.

While big business and governments were complaining about an economic invasion from the West, Asia was stepping up its invasion of Western consumer markets. "Amid the turmoil" of the crisis, one report noted, "the United States consumer is emerging as a savior of sorts. Americans are the 'consumers of last resort in a world of excess saving,' says Rosanne M. Cahn, chief equity economist at Credit Suisse First Boston in New York" (Wysocki, 1998, p. 1). Southeast Asian nations were reporting record exports. By August 1998 Thailand had managed to build up foreign reserves to approximately US$11 billion, after blowing approximately US$35 billion on its ill-fated attempt to defend the baht just a year before. But that wasn't helping big business, which had traditionally exploited domestic economies. And for that reason, exports couldn't revive Asian economies on their own. But they were creating a new business elite that was enjoying windfall profits.

Meanwhile, big business—and its government benefactors— were looking at their own acquisition as the only reasonable means of survival. Mergers and acquisitions in Asia increased 21 percent in the first half of 1999 over the same period the year before, to US$33.9 billion.

GOOD REASONS AND BAD REASONS

A wave of global virtual corporate alliances and informal strategic partnerships in the early 1990s left most multinationals and their managers convinced that such soft alliances were messy and unproductive. What followed was outright mergers or acquisitions on a truly global scale. Multinationals were now staying focused globally on core businesses or very intensely related support industries. Entertainment, communications, banking, oil, and information technology all saw huge wedding parties, each subsequent joining seeming to outdo its predecessor in scale and reach. Not that these companies fared much better.

Mark L. Sirower, author of *The Synergy Trap: How Companies Lose the Acquisition Game* and a Wharton School visiting professor, has studied one hundred large mergers and acquisitions made between 1994 and 1997. "Roughly two-thirds of those deals met with negative market reactions," he notes, "and, for the most part, remained under-performers a year later." Sirower believes that mergers and acquisitions "are especially susceptible to three critical risk areas that can upset the best-laid plans." First of these areas, he says, is focus. "One of the most common mistakes in post-acquisition integration is to divert resources from some businesses to go after performance gains in others." The second area is competitor response. "Competitors will not sit still while an acquirer attempts to generate synergies at their expense," Sirower warns. The third area is strategy and organizational design. "Perhaps the most important challenge is to determine what is the new mission of the combined organization and how to organize to accomplish the new mission" (Sirower, 1998, p. 8).

Sirower notes that there are happy exceptions, but generally, achieving synergy from mergers and acquisitions even under the best conditions is tough. Sirower's argument, for that reason, is particularly important in the New Asia. Are mergers and acquisitions of distressed Asian firms wise? What are their prospects for generating synergy?

The bulk of mergers and acquisitions in post-crisis Asia are clearly opportunity-driven rather than strategy-driven, despite the talk about strategic fit, and these deals take place under far less than ideal circumstances. For example, Jim Rohwer notes that GE Capital "began seriously building up its Asian business in 1991 [and] until last year, the firm grew almost entirely by opening new businesses; now it is acquiring them (heavily in consumer finance, but also in insurance and equipment leasing as well as in a few 'nonstrategic' lines offering especially good value.)" (Rohwer, 1998, p. 85). In other words, these companies were just too cheap to pass up, sometimes despite the clear lack of strategic fit. It's a buy-and-sell game.

Rohwer notes two other reasons why mergers and acquisitions didn't take place at the rate originally expected, and why many were probably ill-advised anyway. Valuation, he says, given Asia's murky corporate cross holdings makes it difficult to know whether you are buying what you want and if you've actually bought it. Strategically, he says, "[M]any Western corporations are hesitant to jump into an Asian acquisition because they worry they won't be able to find enough local management to run their new operations. This is a problem that Dan Mudd, an ex-Marine who runs GE Capital Asia Pacific, struggles with daily" (Rohwer, 1998, p. 85).

It's fair to ask why Mudd would allow himself to be sidetracked by nonstrategic opportunities in the first place. His problem finding managers to oversee strategic investments makes the acquisitions even more curious. Perhaps the explanation lies in marching orders from CEO Jack Welch, who "made clear in the company's 1997 annual report that he sees the Asian crisis as an ideal opportunity for GE to grow its business in the region, comparable with the openings presented by the United States restructuring in the early 1980s, Europe's in the early 1990s, and Mexico's in post-1995" (Rohwer, 1998, p. 85).

If so, GE's growth objectives go well beyond the strategic game plan discussed in Chapter One. Opportunity to expand market share clearly remains a priority for this giant conglomerate, under pressure to sustain growth in its profitable concerns. Yet that's exactly the principal criticism of Asian conglomerates: the subordination of strategy to opportunity. Mudd's example shows that the company is making at least two mistakes: expanding outside its focus and doing so when it knows that human resources are in critical short supply.

Sirower says, "When asked to name just one big merger that has lived up to expectations, Leon Cooperman, the former cochairman of Goldman Sach's investment policy committee, answered, 'I'm sure that there are success stories out there, but at this moment I draw a blank'" (Sirower, 1997, p. 4). That's the last and probably the best reason mergers and acquisitions should be approached with a healthy dose of trepidation. The track record is still lousy. The first decade of the twenty-first century will reveal whether the 1990s mega-merger wave was in the best interest of shareholders, or just a giant opportunity grab that will not live up to rosy return on investment (ROI) projections. The same time frame will show whether the wave of Asian mergers that the financial crisis made inevitable will work better for consumers and shareholders alike than Asia's miracle years' conglomerates.

Sirower points out the biggest fallacy of merger mania. "For 1995, the total value of acquisition activity was over US$400 billion [in the United States]. By comparison, in the aggregate managers spent only US$500 billion, on average, over the past several years on new plant and equipment purchases and a mere US$130 billion on R&D" (Sirower, 1997, p. 5). There are obviously huge distinctions between the United States and Asian merger scenes, but the question is still valid: Shouldn't those funds being used for acquisition instead be invested in creating new businesses?

By logic, they should. By rights, they can't. Because of lingering restrictions on foreign investment and political sensitivity, all merger and acquisition activity is in effect an investment that likely could be improved upon. That is if funds were poured into creating new assets rather than acquiring old assets, whose value is extremely difficult to determine. This also means that ultimately, we don't know if new assets represent real opportunity. Outrageous, you may think. Well, what is outrageous is that acquisition premiums "can exceed 100 percent of the market value of target firms. Evidence for acquisitions between 1993 and 1995 shows that shareholders of acquiring firms lose an average of 10 percent of their investment on announcement. And over time, perhaps waiting for synergies, they lose even more" (Sirower, 1997, pp. 4–5).

If that's true with the United States' vibrant economy and stable political environment, imagine what the fright factor is for buying into pieces of timeworn, inefficient, and poorly managed Asian conglomerates and undercapitalized financial institutions.

A HAPPY EXCEPTION:
THE NEW ASIAN CORPORATION

There are exceptions in Asia—or by Asian companies—undertaking mergers and acquisitions. Look to Singapore's Excel Machine Tools. In 1995, at the height of the Asian miracle years, the Singapore government was obsessed with identifying strategy to sustain growth in the corporate sector and the economy. Along with Malaysia and to a lesser extent Thailand, the Singapore government exhorted its best firms to seek opportunities in other markets, both developed and undeveloped. Hungary and its robust economy was an attractive target. Singapore Telecoms made its largest foreign investment there, and Excel followed suit, purchasing the 103-year-old Hungarian operation of Csepel. There was a logic to the acquisition, aside from positioning in the developing East European market. Csepel produced a larger line of machine tools and provided technology that Excel did not have. Manufacturing processes were not impressive in terms of either efficiency or productivity, but the quality was top notch.

The question raised, of course, is whether Excel's resources would have been better applied developing the technology on its own. It turns out to be a very valid question because establishing synergy—and blending cultures—was every bit as difficult as one would imagine in such circumstances. The fact that Excel successfully integrated the companies, although an impressive if not remarkable achievement, doesn't affect the validity of that concern. Were resources applied in a way that would provide the greatest return on their investment? Probably not.

But the fact that Excel accomplished a very challenging merger of cultures and products that has worked well for the company argues that Western companies acquiring Asian firms with diverse cultures for whatever reason will benefit from examining the experiences of

Excel. The discussion should begin with a look at Excel's culture and value system. Executive Vice President Wee Yue Chew says the company's management philosophy is based on the following guiding principles:

- Human resource planning, management and development to meet tomorrow's challenges
- Proactive technological innovation to meet customers' needs
- Innovative management and operating systems to ensure efficiency
- Excel culture and value systems to foster team spirit and commitment
- Sharing productivity gains with employees to enhance their commitment to the company

The company places a great deal of importance on customer involvement and satisfaction. "We believe that it is no longer sufficient to have [only] customers," Wee explains. "It is necessary, for good business, to have customers who boost your product or services, stay with you, and bring in a friend for new business" (Interview with the author, June 25, 1998). To achieve that level of customer support, Wee cites three important pillars of customer interaction.

1. Frequent Interaction. "We believe in being market-oriented. Top management itself is in constant contact with customers, even to the extent of inviting them to Singapore and listening to their requirements and designing or making design changes to meet their needs. At a minimum, top management meets key dealers, customers, and suppliers every year to assess geographic market requirements. The product development team, based on this feedback, develops product engineering specifications. As a result we are able to introduce new designs and products on a yearly basis" (Interview with the author, June 25, 1998).

2. Responsiveness to Customer Concerns. "When a customer makes a complaint, no matter how minor, top management will get our sales/application engineers to respond without delay to demonstrate our concern to the customer and our responsiveness. When repeat orders are received from a customer, or if they recommend us to their friends—which is common—top management will host lunch or dinner together with their friends."

3. Customer Satisfaction Process. "We strive to satisfy and delight our customers. To strengthen this process, we have dedicated a department to keep track of our customer profiles, service schedules and records, and the nature of complaints. These records are analyzed for trends and forwarded to the Total Quality Innovative Committee. Top management uses these files to check [on customer satisfaction] and for customer visits. We believe that the salesman first sells the machine to the customer, but it is the after-sales service people who sell the second, third, or fourth machines to the customer. So we place great emphasis on after-sales service. This way, as our customers grow, we grow with them."

Shared culture and a strong value system drive these programs, according to Wee. "To be a world-class company, top management, over the years, has evolved and developed jointly with the staff a shared culture and values. These shared values are constantly reinforced, which is necessary to ensure continual support and commitment. The system is called Excel CAPs. CAPs stands for:

- COMMITMENT in his blood
- CHALLENGES in his soul
- CREATIVITY in his mind
- CONFIDENCE in his heart
- CONSISTENCY in his actions

- AMBASSADORS of Excel
- Positive work ATTITUDE at all times
- ABILITY to meet new challenges
- ADVANCEMENT with the company's goals
- ACHIEVEMENT oriented
- PROFITABILITY
- PRODUCTIVITY
- PROGRESS
- PROFESSIONALISM
- PRECISION

"Every Monday morning, top management does the Singapore Work-Out, sings the company song, and shares developments for the week such as customer visits to Excel, sales orders secured, or company trips. From Tuesday to Friday, every morning, individual department managers meet up with their subordinates to sing the company song, perform the Singapore Work-Out, and share developments on delivery or quality issues and obtain suggestions and feedback. Managers are responsible for constantly reinforcing our values."

Excel's long-term competitive advantage resides in its people, Wee says, and their continual development, and the company spends an average of 10 percent of payroll on development programs. Six monthly performance appraisals are carried out annually. Training is centered on four core areas: 1) basic skill training on the job; 2) trade skills and functional-based training; 3) career advancement training; and, 4) productivity and quality-related training.

In return for their commitment and continuous development in support of the company's objectives and goals, Excel has developed a reward system that links individual performance to company performance. Much of that performance has to do with how the company achieves its strategic plan, which is heavily reliant on the development of new, cutting-edge technologies, including laser and waterjet cutting technology.

"Every country has its own values and culture," Wee says. "In the same way, our company also has its own value system. When we hire, we look for people with the desired soft values." However, that wasn't possible with the acquisition of Csepel. Workers weren't hired, they were inherited. The contrasts in country cultures were huge. So were the company cultures. Although Excel has offices in the United States, Malaysia, and Thailand, Hungary presented a special set of challenges.

RECONCILING CULTURES

"The father and history of machine tools is found in Europe," Wee notes. Although Singapore has a well-deserved reputation for high technology, there was considerable pride among Csepel workers as the inventors of technology. Wee found that the company indeed had valuable technology, but very shallow managerial depth. The company did represent a good strategic fit in terms of its product line, which would serve to expand Excel's offerings to a heavier class of equipment. Nevertheless, there was considerable skepticism among Csepel workers for the prospects of the union.

Wee quickly realized that singing the company song was out. Under Hungary's former communist regime, "they had to do similar things," and they didn't want to be reminded of how life was then. From another perspective, Wee also didn't want to send the signal that things weren't going to change in the Excel era, including low productivity. But it was also clear that he would have to convince the former Csepel workers that Excel management wasn't going to sweep into the new acquisition and force near alien programs down their throats. In other words, Excel was sensitive to everyone's concerns.

"I started by talking to each manager and section head," Wee says, to see if they were open to change. He found that they were, but a great deal of hand-holding would be necessary. Wee spent two weeks every month in Hungary personally training and developing relationships. It was clear that Wee could buy technology, but not the motivation to make it turn a profit. But steady progress was made in changing the mindset of the Hungarian workers as a result of Wee's hands-on approach to managing change. "We turned the company around with productivity training and development," Wee beams. As a result of his efforts—and, of course, those of the workers—the Hungarian manufacturing operation has been extolled as a model company.

ACHIEVING SYNERGY

The unit has helped Excel develop its total company approach to growing revenues and profits. Whether Excel's acquisition of Csepel will prove to be one of those elusive success stories remains to be seen, however. Four years into the union, it is demonstrating a valuable synergy that has translated into increased profitability. It had also helped insulate Excel from the Asian financial crisis by making a resurgent European market a principal source of revenues. For Excel, timing was as important as the opportunity. So was luck.

As Excel's experience demonstrates, the prospect of achieving synergy is dependent not so much on technology, markets, and timing, although those are certainly critical considerations. It is people and the commitment to them that ultimately determine success or failure. Western firms may be acquiring value on the cheap in Asia, but whether that value is retained and built on will be determined by whether buyers demonstrate Excel's commitment to making acquisitions work.

CREATING OPPORTUNITIES

It has been made clear how Asian firms have relied on business acumen to survive dire circumstances and undertake a difficult merger. There are many notable examples of Asian companies—or companies run by Asian managers—that have capitalized on good business sense and foresight to build exciting new businesses. For instance, in Beijing, an enterprising entrepreneur proposed a unique—and attractive—financing scheme for the acquisition of new city buses. He would provide the buses at no cost, in return for exclusive rights to the advertising. This successful entrepreneur has now supplied buses to eighteen city governments, and his franchise continues to expand.

When Microsoft founder Bill Gates visited Manila, he presented a special award for creative application and business development to World Port, a company founded by Filipinos in Silicon Valley, now with offices in Manila. World Port develops Internet commerce and interactive data-driven Web sites. The company had participated in a competition intended to showcase Filipino talent. Its entry is called AuctionBoard, an innovative e-commerce site deployed in the United States that manages on-line auctions to sell a variety of products. There's been a lot of talk about the web providing the capability for consumers to source the best prices. World Port has developed a site that helps retailers find the most profitable customers. Albert Lopez, president and CEO of the company, says that over the eighteen months prior to Gates' visit, World Port's core business evolved away from simple "brochure" Web sites into high-end Web site consulting with satellite offices across the United States, Asia, and Europe. The company "is focusing its expansion into the markets where we have the greatest success: education and financial services," Lopez says.

World Port offers a comprehensive range of professional web consulting services including strategy consulting, analysis and design, applications development, legacy integration, system implementation, and audience/community development. "World Port clients," Lopez says, "often experience significant returns on investment—some in as few as six to eight weeks." World Port remains headquartered in Silicon Valley, comfortable in the world's most important technology hotbed. But it is an icon of Asian creativity and innovation. So is a similar company in Singapore called SilkRoute. "SilkRoute designs Web pages, produces on-line magazines, and conducts e-marketing for clients like Tiger Beer and Levi's. It wired up US$2.7 million in revenues in 1997. A subsidiary, Asian Manufacturing Online, develops business-to-business e-commerce solutions" ("Internet Thrills: . . . ," 1998).

Sunonwealth Electric Machine Industry Company manufactures miniaturized cooling fans for personal computers using a patented brushless technology developed in-house. The company says it was almost untouched by Asia's financial crisis and is building new facilities in Taiwan and China. It expected to double production at the height of the crisis. "But Hung isn't relaxing. 'A company like ours can have lots of capital, hard-working employees, and strong sales today,' says Hung, a high-school graduate whose down-home charm has won over many clients. 'But if you aren't looking at what you'll be doing three to five years in the future, you can find yourself suddenly out of business' " (Baum, 1998, p. 44).

Hung's company played an important role in solving a problem Intel was experiencing as its chips grew more powerful: overheating. "[Sunonwealth] says its mini-fans can be found in 70 percent of the notebook computers made in Taiwan. By advancing Sunon's technology with an in-house engineering team and lowering costs with automated production lines, [Hung] is now taking world market share from his leading Japanese competitor and enlarging his share at home" (Baum, 1998, p. 45).

Marjorie Yang—like Li & Fung's Victor Fung—has sustained growth in what many consider a sunset industry, garment manufacturing, by "providing everything from design work to production to packaging ideas, working with customers from beginning to end to give them exactly what they want. To survive in the global economy, more Asian companies must adopt Yang's blend of production and services" ("Making a Bundle . . . ," 1998, p. 53). In his research, Harvard's Michael Porter also demonstrates that traditional sunset industries can, in fact, be very profitable. He cites, for example, the Italian footware industry, a major export earner for that nation. Italian footware is profitable not because of the high quality or craftsmanship, but because of its wetware and software: innovative brainpower, culture, and tradition.

These are just a few examples of companies run by Asian managers that have succeeded by providing originality and value-added to their clients, not because they were offered or capitalized on connections to grow their organizations by freezing out the competition. Although cultural habits and traditions will hold sway in Asia for many years— honorifics aren't likely to go out the window, although prosperity will significantly impact lifestyle values—whether a business is successful in the New Asia depends on how well it is run, not how high-placed its connections are.

CHAPTER FIVE

Building Corporate Identity and Influence

—〜〜 "The queen of spin is losing a spin war," David Plotz wrote in the Internet magazine *Slate* of former *New Yorker* editor Tina Brown's final days at that literary institution. "Tina Brown," he said, "who essentially invented magazine 'buzz,' perfected buzz, made buzz high art (and made high art buzz)—is becoming buzz's victim." Brown's decline shows how precariously spinmeisters tiptoe from spin to spin.

There's only one thing worse than falling victim to spin, and that is failing to spin. Or to spin incompetently. Because "you live by buzz, you die by buzz," as Plotz quotes a former *New Yorker* editor "with malicious glee" (Plotz, 1998).

Although far from the "sassy, nasty, attention-getting" corridors of the *New Yorker* and its namesake city, the world's media capital, Asia is trying to spin, despite frequent sputters. Spin may not be a hard business issue like manufacturing productivity, strategic business modeling, and return on resources, but it is a critical opportunity generator. It is serious business for both public- and private-sector organizations.

SPINNING THE PUBLIC SECTOR

In response to persistent negative news reports on government's response at the height of the Asian crisis, Malaysia's National Economic Action Council (NEAC) formed a special communications team to take on a "proactive role, feeding media organizations, financial analysts, and economists with regular reports on how Malaysia's economic recovery plan is being implemented and the reasons for taking certain decisions" (Pereira, 1998).

"Part of the NEAC's task is to improve the perception of Malaysia," K. C. Leong, who headed up the team, explained. "If you allow only one side of the picture to be given, the perception created will not be accurate. We hope to be able to give our views to readers"(Pereira, 1998). However, Leong's idea of proactive spin was actually reactive—a transition to new communication realities of sorts. Instead of simply criticizing, or issuing not-so-veiled-threats of sanctions, Leong's team was writing to publications to at least try to correct perceived inaccuracies.

Leong cited a specific example. A critical report in the *Financial Times* about the government's decision to ease monetary policy— likely provoking increased currency speculation—was rebutted: "It is evident that Malaysia's recent move to lower interest rates is actually in line with the advice of . . . respected economists. I hope their views may also be taken into consideration in the name of objective journalism." The respected journalists NEAC referenced included Joseph Stiglitz, chief economist of the World Bank, who certainly had not recommended easing Malaysia's monetary policy, demonstrating a somewhat crude—and precarious—attempt at spin. But the real shortcoming of Leong's efforts was that they did nothing to shape public perception, which is easier to do than "correcting" public perception by writing letters to media.

Again in reaction to a series of sovereign downgrades by ratings agencies, Malaysia's government undertook a "trade mission to the United States to explain to investors there that the downgrading of the country's financial standing is not reflective of the country's industrial sector" (Jamaludin, 1998).

Indeed, "our industrial sector is very much different from the finance market," Malaysia's international trade and industry minister Rafidah Aziz explained. Although Prime Minister Mahathir had consistently warned of recolonization by Western corporations, Aziz said, "[I]t was important the Americans got the true picture of the country's industrial climate because it was one of Malaysia's trading partners. The mission would also inform investors [of] the measures being taken to overcome the economic slowdown and new policies pertaining to investment"(Jamaludin, 1998). The mission came none too soon; right after this announcement, international media stepped-up coverage of the political maneuvering Mahathir had undertaken to undermine a perceived political challenge by his then deputy, Anwar Ibrahim. Analysts' worries that politics was interfering with efforts to address economic issues were being heavily reported by international media, further undermining investor confidence.

It got worse when Mahathir abruptly fired his deputy and had him arrested, thrown in jail without bail, and beaten under the country's tough internal security act, an ironic holdover from colonial times, never before employed with quite the same arrogance and heavy-handedness. It was at that point that Mahathir destroyed his image as a leader and became a dictator instead.

It was downhill from there in the foreign media. Three especially harsh critics, the *Far Eastern Economic Review, Asiaweek,* and the *International Herald Tribune,* were eventually banned from government offices, which industry sources say actually had the effect of increasing domestic interest in the publications. The *Asian Wall Street Journal* was sued by Mahathir's son, Mirzan, after reporting that his career "was aided by other Malaysian companies and banks" ("PR Blitz," 1998). Malaysia's domestic media are controlled by close associates of the ruling United Malays National Organization (UMNO) party.

The strain of financial and political crisis had taken a toll. Not too much earlier, Karen Elliott House, president of Dow Jones International with responsibility for both the *Far Eastern Economic Review* and the *Asian Wall Street Journal* had told us about media freedom in Asia, an "honest newspaper can't make everyone happy all the time.

By being fair and accurate, at least you're right even if government gets angry about it. And you have to have reliable information to do business in a competitive world." She believes that most Asian leaders have come to understand the importance of timely and accurate information in a global economy. As a result, she suggested, Asian leaders are "learning to hold their tongues. There is more tolerance of accurate journalism" because "knowledge is power. Knowledge is profit" (Hamlin, "Marching Across Asia," 1998). This is why Mahathir was worried. Too much knowledge in the hands of his subjects could shift the balance of power.

About the same time that Malaysia was experimenting with spin, Thailand's government announced a public relations blitz "to build support and understanding for its financial reform package." The campaign was intended to brief the local public on the importance of taking tough measures to reform Thailand's troubled economy. "If I have to lose my job because my company went bankrupt for typical reasons," one bank employee was quoted, "I wouldn't feel anything. But now, I might lose my job because of the failed policies of our political leaders. I guarantee that in the next election, I won't vote for a person like this again"("PR Blitz," 1998). While Malaysia was concerned about salvaging relationships with investors and trading partners, Thailand's government was concerned with staying in power. For good reason, among the biggest victims of Asia's financial crisis are its governments—rather, the credibility of Asian governments to lead their people to prosperity and therefore their legitimacy.

That message—governments' inability to deal with the crisis—was becoming clear to Asian voters. Respondents to the *BusinessWeek* Asia Leadership Forum survey overwhelmingly agreed or strongly agreed that "the crisis is the fruit of Asian government policies." Only 21 percent of respondents disagreed. The results of another survey of four hundred senior executives in Asia reported by the political and Economic Risk Consultancy in its *Asian Intelligence* report "suggested a close link between the quality of a country's national institutions and its ability to steer a steady course through the current economic crisis" (*BusinessWeek*'s Asia Leadership Forum, 1998).

Unfortunately, of the countries surveyed—the original ASEAN members, plus Hong Kong, Japan, Taiwan, China, South Korea, and Vietnam—only Singapore and Hong Kong "were rated as having above-average institutions," according to the report. Even then, Hong Kong's slightly more-than-year-old government was sent a clear rebuke of its handling of the economy and its administration of the Special Autonomous Region in general in the first election exercise following the handover to China. A record turnout cancelled out that rebuke, despite an elaborate attempt to make voting a huge bureaucratic hurdle for citizens, who braved the terrible weather as well.

Massachusetts Institute of Technology professor Lestor Thurow said that the main question for Asia is not whether its countries were stupidly or badly run in explaining the crisis, but "which governments are going to be good at cleaning up the mess" (Fuller, 1998, p. 1). Those that weren't very good weren't going to be around for long.

When it became clear to Indonesians that former President Suharto's government was powerless in the face of the Asian financial crisis, it lost the last vestiges of credibility. If government could not bring back prosperity, then there was no longer any reason to endure the abuses and greed of Asia's arguably most corrupt government. Thailand's government had already been turned out once for similar reasons. As the new government struggled with reform issues, that same prospect threatened the government of Prime Minister Chuan Leekpai if the banking sector were not put back together in a manner satisfactory to constituents. With the Thai economy in shambles, as finance minister Tarrin Nimmanahaeminda admitted, time was running out for Chuan's government.

Despite institution of reforms intended to help recapitalize the banking sector, only Bangkok Bank and Thai Farmers Bank, the country's two largest, had been able to attract substantial international investor interest, although two smaller banks were acquired by foreign institutions. Together, Bangkok Bank and Thai Farmers Bank attracted a little less than US$2 billion, or about 10 percent of what some analysts believed would ultimately be necessary to revive the sector. Large losses posted in the second quarter and plummeting stock prices suggested that even Thailand's two largest banks might need to attract still more investors. But as Tarrin said at the time, "[t]hat window is closed" ("The Economy Is in a Shambles," 1998) as a result of further deterioration of the sector and the economy as a whole.

Banking reform centered over what to do with Siam Commercial Bank and Thai Military Bank. Siam's largest shareholder is the Thai Royal Family. Thai Military's is obvious. The perspective of those shareholders likely varies considerably from that of the average man or woman on the street, who reportedly feels that the government has no business bailing out wealthy investors. Unfortunately for Chuan and his ministers, those investors have enormous political pull. That's a dilemma Chuan didn't deserve, but had to deal with. His government was roundly praised by international observers for its focus on putting the country back on track. Chuan and troubled investors would have to make a carefully calculated decision over how much more pain the people of Thailand were willing to bear for the sake of people who were guilty of incredibly irresponsible banking.

The government's public relations blitz was designed to sell a program that was intended to "bail out Thailand's faltering banks at the lowest cost to the public," which involved selling bonds to distressed banks collateralized by bank securities. The government had "rejected proposals to take over the bad loans of the surviving banks by setting up a national asset-management company. Owners of banks that don't qualify for the rescue plan are expected to face writedown of their shareholder equity"(Sherer, 1998, p. 1), which meant that the government was trying to reach a compromise between rehabilitating deadbeat bankers and downtrodden consumers. Four banks and a number of finance companies were expected to be allowed to fail.

As a result of the announcement, the International Monetary Fund's (IMF) deputy chief of the Asia-Pacific region, Anoop Singh, said "Thailand is on the threshold of recovery" (IMF sees Thailand . . . ," 1996) giving the government's spin a boost. Singh tempered his enthusiasm, however, saying recovery would take years and depended in large part on the Japanese economy. But Thailand's government had not only undertaken a significant reform, it had clearly communicated its efforts, for the time being providing assurance that it was addressing the economy and concerns of voters.

The government learned its lesson well. In December 1998, it again took its message to the people when faced by legislative intransigence in its efforts to pass key reform measures. "Flanked by all his key ministers, Prime Minister Chuan Leekpai hosted a live public hearing to explain his government's determination to press with eleven parliamentary bills to modernize Thai business law despite opposition by some politicians" ("Thai Government . . . ," 1998).

What made this effort credible in Thailand—where it wouldn't be in Malaysia—is that Thailand's media is among the region's most loosely regulated. In Malaysia, government's dominance of media would have made such an event appear contrived, which indeed occurs regularly. Efforts to introduce talk shows on evening television in Malaysia have fallen short of candid exchanges, sometimes because comments are edited out before broadcast.

In the Philippines, during the first two months of his administration, President Joseph Ejercito Estrada was finding it increasingly difficult to create positive spin about his nation's recovery. In an apparent attempt to manage expectations in terms of government efforts to tackle the economic downturn, the populist president announced that the economy was bankrupt, provoking an outroar from big business seeking potential investors and struggling to manage trade relationships. After exhorting Filipinos to sacrifice everything to speed recovery, expensive and apparently unnecessary renovations of the presidential guesthouse and yacht provoked a similar outcry among other sectors, including the political opposition. His own media staff released a report showing the results of a survey in which 42 percent of respondents reacted negatively to a major policy speech called the State of the Nation Address, or SONA. (In the Philippines, almost everything has an acronym.)

Finally, Estrada announced that he was appointing a presidential spokesperson, apparently believing that incorporating more bodies— the Office of the Press Secretary is a large bureaucracy which includes two television stations—would solve his problem. Unfortunately for Estrada, the problem was not bodies, but competent bodies.

Asia's financial crisis accelerated the democratization of the region. What has popularly been called People Power has now been deemed responsible for the overthrow of governments in three countries: Indonesia, Philippines, and Thailand. In each case, financial crisis preceded the change in government (although the Philippines most debilitating crisis occurred thirteen years earlier than the rest of the region, almost exclusively as a result of massive and utter mismanagement of the economy). Change in government was followed by increased media freedom in all three instances.

In fact, there's an argument to be made that the Philippines' overthrow of Ferdinand Marcos was a warning bell for the region. It went unnoticed because in the blaze of growth the rest of the region was experiencing, it was easy to forget that the Philippines, the "sick man of Asia," was once Asia's leading economy. And, it was a long time coming. Marcos was able to cling to power years after the economy began to stumble. In 1998, the world saw that the cycle from downturn in the economy to virtual overthrow of the government had been greatly accelerated. Asians were expecting their governments to keep their part of the bargain—providing a strong economy—or they were history.

Even in China, the brutal Tiananmen Square repression was more a signal of the end of authoritarianism than of a return to the dark ages of free expression. While the People Power expression never seriously threatened the long-term stability of the government, it is difficult to imagine the same agressive response today not provoking a profound and long-lasting national crisis. Indeed, there is more evidence of free expression in China today than many long-time observers expected to see in their lifetimes. Prosperity, increasingly easy access to outside news—especially via the Internet—and a new-found tolerance by the country's leadership have changed what China's people expect of their government. They expect prosperity, or the opportunity to achieve it. Providing that opportunity to the people is government's reason for being.

There are still holdouts. In 1998, Malaysia's Mohamad Mahathir reacted to negative media reports by raging at *Time* magazine, "How dare you say these things!" (How Dare You, ..." 1998). When he felt that Anwar Ibrahim's friends in domestic media organizations linked to the ruling UMNO were undermining his authority, Mahathir had two pro-Anwar senior editors removed from their positions. Testing the limits of government patience was a dangerous game for other media, with government threatening to withdraw the publishing and distribution permits of errant newspapers. Singapore media were likewise tightly controlled, closely following government's lead in reporting the news. There was no significant competition to the market dominant Times Publishing Group. Government allows state-run Singapore TV to give "political parties free broadcasting time during elections only in proportion to their number of candidates." Since the ruling party has 81 of 83 seats in Parliament, guess whose message gets across? Singapore tried to go further in 1999, asking foreign TV stations "to restrict coverage of political parties that do not have a wide following" ("Singapore Seeks ...," 1999).

But clearly the era in which Asian governments could intimidate or bribe media into submission was drawing to a close. Even the most reluctant government could see that its power over free expression was waning, and that if it wanted to get its message out effectively, it was going to have to adapt to the new era. Not unexpectedly, the first attempts were crude and frequently bungled, but governments—and their opponents—were learning to spin for their lives.

That process was dramatically accelerated by the Internet. Because Singapore and Malaysia both aspire to become technology centers, there is little choice but to embrace the Internet and its culture of free speech and exchange. Once again, however, Malaysia undermined the effort to portray itself as a welcome destination for technology investment by forcing Internet cafés to register users and directing the police to track down users spreading rumors following the arrest of Anwar.

Perhaps the most powerful sign of Asian unity and individual expression was seen in August 1998, when eleven visitors from Thailand, Malaysia, Indonesia, and the Philippines converged on the nation of Myanmar to protest repression by the military junta. "The foray points to the rise of regional activity, as the nongovernmental organization, or NGO, movement takes off in Southeast Asia," read an article about the activists in the *Asian Wall Street Journal* (Wain, 1998, p. 8).

"NGO involvement is but one example of how ASEAN is being out-flanked as it tries to observe its core principle of noninterference in the affairs of member countries. Governments may not want to interfere, but organized private citizens do," author Barry Wain wrote. Clearly the period when people were accountable to their governments, rather than the other way around, was quickly ending. That became increasingly clear when Presidents Habibie and Estrada of Indonesia and the Philippines, respectively, openly broke with ASEAN's long-standing policy of refraining from comment on the internal affairs of member countries and criticized Mahathir for the treatment Anwar Ibrahim received in jail.

Whether or not they believed in what they were doing is perhaps for only the two presidents to know. But it was good spin: Asian leaders standing up for principle. And it further eroded Mahathir's credibility in the region.

SPINNING THE PRIVATE SECTOR

When Microsoft came under the scrutiny by the United States Justice Department and Congressional investigators in the late 1990s, it demonstrated just how dangerous it is to take corporate communications—including the capacity to effectively spin—seriously. With virtually no lobby capital to speak of on Capitol Hill, one of the world's most important companies and CEO Bill Gates, the wealthiest man in the United States, were left virtually "voiceless." This quickly proved to be a very serious predicament indeed. As one Microsoft employee, Jacob Weisberg, wrote, "A few months ago, everyone I met seemed to think that working for Microsoft was a pretty cool thing to do. Now, strangers treat us like we work for Philip Morris."

"Ironically," he moaned, "one of the charges leveled against Microsoft of late is that the company has sinned by *not* playing the Washington influence game forcefully enough. Only now, the analysis goes, is Bill G. realizing the mistake in neglecting to hire lobbyists, dole out huge campaign contributions, and so on. The theme of a recent front-page story in the *New York Times* was that the failure to flex political muscle demonstrates an arrogance and stubborness for which Microsoft is now paying the price" (Weisberg, 1998).

Weisberg went on to note that Microsoft has three lobbyists in Washington, D.C., compared to AT&T's fifty full-time representatives. AT&T gave US$1.25 million in political contributions in the "last election cycle" compared to Microsoft's US$43,500. Weisberg felt that was something to be proud of: "You haven't tried to corrupt the democratic process by handing out wads of cash" (Weisberg, 1998). Unfortunately, refusing to play the spin game made the company an easy target for seasoned operatives. As a result, Microsoft "increased its contributions to federal candidates more than fivefold"(Microsoft, Others . . . ," 1998). Given that a Democratic Justice Department was the manifestation of Microsoft's travails, it was not surprising that the targets of the company's new-found generosity were almost exclusively in the Republican fold. "In the 1991–92 election cycle, 79 percent of Microsoft's money went to Democrats; in the current cycle, 67 percent has gone to the GOP" (Microsoft, Others Make Political Contributions," 1998, Internet edition). Microsoft has always learned fast.

So will the New Asian Corporation, if it wants to exert some level of control over its destiny, to which Microsoft aspires. The difference between the crony capitalism of the Asian miracle years and the democratic capitalism of the New Asia is that political bribery will be legal—and transparent. It will be legal because politicians will actually have to run effective but expensive communications campaigns themselves in order to be elected. Democracy has many prices.

Underwriting political campaigns, however, is a small part of what we like to call corporate communications. We prefer the term *corporate communications* over public relations for two reasons. First, public relations is a narrow definition of corporate communicating. It is an important but relatively small part of the corporate communications function. Like government, corporate communications for the private sector has one core objective: building a strong identity in the marketplace. A strong identity helps the corporation exert influence on government, media, consumers, and other key constituents. These constituencies are called publics.

"Although public relations activities are relevant at all times, its overall contribution to success is even more vital during an economic downturn," according to Sam Black, former president of the International Public Relations Association. "Its contribution to the bottom line is relatively more important during a downturn than in more prosperous circumstances" (Shankar, 1998, Internet edition).

That was a fairly self-serving statement in 1998, at the height of the Asian financial crisis, but it was true Asia was changing, transforming institutions and markets into what we call the New Asian Corporations. That meant that old ways of dealing with government, the business community, and even customers was changing. That change meant that organizations needed a new way to exert influence, because the old ways weren't working anymore. And as Black said, corporate communications provides a cost-effective and efficient use of financial resources. Stated more bluntly: it's cheaper than advertising and, depending on circumstances, more effective as well.

Ultimately, corporate communications should reconcile distinctions between corporate identity and reputation. Corporate identity is an internal perception: what the company's internal stakeholders think of their organization. For example, a company in which obvious distinctions exists between what top management and employees think of the organization means that the organization is schizophrenic. Reputation is how external publics view the company. Problems arise when there are differences in how the company and the public view the organization. If a company does not understand how it is perceived, it may misread the extent of frustration or anger key constituencies feel toward the company. That's what happened to Microsoft. While it is one of America's most widely admired corporations, it was vulnerable among a key constituency: a Congress heavily lobbied by the company's most serious competitors.

WHAT MAKES REPUTATION?

If we compare *Fortune*'s lists of most admired corporations and the ten most profitable firms in the United States, it is pretty clear that size, profitability, and greatness, as perceived by interested observers, do not always correlate (see Table 5.1). Forty percent of America's ten most profitable firms are among *Fortune*'s ten most admired. All of the most admired corporations are very profitable, but Southwest Airlines is a much smaller company than the rest, albeit growing at a truly phenomenal—and unsustainable—rate. It would be safe to say that profitability contributes to good reputation. That may sound like a no-brainer, but how big a component of reputation is profitability? Also, no matter how much money a company makes, it can still find it difficult to make it into the most admired list (for instance, Philip Morris and IBM).

Sustained profitability generally depends upon good management. But look at General Motors. Although the world's largest company has improved many of its operations, "GM continues to underperform competitors in the United States. Its ability to execute even such basic functions as launching new vehicles on time remains a question. Europe, the shining light of GM's global empire earlier in this decade, is struggling" (Taylor, 1998). Leadership expert and author of *The*

Most Admired			Largest (Profit)		
Company	1997 Profit US$M	% Change	Company	1997 Profit US$M	% Change
General Electric	8,203.0	14.4	Exxon	8,460.0	12.6
Microsoft	3,454.0	57.4	General Electric	8,203.0	12.7
Coca-Cola	4,129.0	18.2	Intel	6,945.0	34.7
Intel	6,945.0	34.7	Ford Motor	6,920.0	55.6
Hewlett-Packard	3,119.0	2.6	General Motors	6,698.0	35.0
Southwest Airlines	317.8	244.0	Philip Morris	6,310.0	0.1
Berkshire Hathaway	1,901.6	(23.6)	IBM	6,093.0	12.2
Walt Disney	1,966.0	61.9	AT&T	4,638.0	(21.5)
Johnson & Johnson	3,303.0	14.4	Merck	4,614.1	18.9
Merck	4,614.1	18.9	Coca-Cola	4,129.0	18.2

Table 5.1. Fortune's Top Ten.

Source: "America's Most Admired Companies," *Fortune.* Mar. 2, 1998, p. 38 and Fortune 500 Index for 1998, April 27, 1998, Internet edition.

Leadership Engine, Noel Tichy says, "Over its lifespan, General Motors has destroyed US$17.8 billion in stockholder wealth, more than any other company" (Tichy, 1997).

Indeed, most analysts and brokers (there's an exception to every rule) would argue that other measures provide a better indicator of financial success than pure profit, such as annual growth in earnings per share.

In Table 5.2, we see that only one of *Fortune's* ten most admired corporations ranks in the top ten in terms of annual growth per share over a ten-year period. Only two are in the top twenty. None of the ten largest corporations in America find a place in the ten highest growth-per-share ranking. Table 5.3 looks at profit as a percentage of sales.

Although four of the ten most admired companies also rank in the top ten best performers in terms of profit as a percentage of sales, Hewlett-Packard ranks a low 164. The question is, is this a precursor or an ominous sign of soon-to-be-diminished reputation? Or, is the

Most Admired			Largest (Profit)		
Company	Annual Growth Earning/ Share 1987–97	Rank	Company	Annual Growth Earning/ Share 1987–97	Rank
General Electric	11.9	111	Exxon	7.0	185
Microsoft	43.3	7	General Electric	11.9	111
Coca-Cola	18.4	49	Intel	36.5	12
Intel	36.5	12	Ford Motor	2.2	251
Hewlett-Packard	16.8	64	General Motors	5.5	206
Southwest Airlines	31.1	15	Philip Morris	14.9	77
Berkshire Hathaway	22.4	32	IBM	3.3	233
Walt Disney	13.5	91	AT&T	4.2	221
Johnson & Johnson	14.8	78	Merck	17.6	56
Merck	17.6	56	Coca-Cola	18.4	49

Table 5.2.   Fortune's Top Ten.

Source: "America's Most Admired Companies, "*Fortune.* Mar. 2, 1998; p. 38 and Fortune 500 Index for 1998, April 27, 1998, Internet edition.

Most Admired			Largest (Profit)		
Company	Profit as a Percent of Sales	Rank	Company	Profit as a Percent of Sales	Rank
General Electric	9.0	111	Exxon	6.9	171
Microsoft	30.4	1	General Electric	9.0	111
Coca-Cola	21.9	3	Intel	27.7	2
Intel	27.7	2	Ford Motor	4.5	268
Hewlett-Packard	7.3	164	General Motors	3.8	305
Southwest Airlines	8.3	128	Philip Morris	11.2	65
Berkshire Hathaway	18.2	10	IBM	7.8	152
Walt Disney	8.7	119	AT&T	8.7	121
Johnson & Johnson	14.8	26	Merck	19.5	5
Merck	19.5	5	Coca-Cola	21.9	3

Table 5.3.   Fortune's Top Ten.
Source: "America's Most Admired Companies, "*Fortune.* Mar. 2, 1998, p. 38 and Fortune 500 Index for 1998, April 27, 1998, Internet edition.

company's PR so good that it has observers fooled? Are the products so well-appreciated—like Apple's computers—that it doesn't matter how well—or poorly—the company performs? Obviously not, or Apple, for example, would be keeping Hewlett-Packard company. (In 1999, Apple did make a dramatic recovery in both financial and perception terms.) As for the other two questions, it is impossible to sustain reputation long-term without substance to back it up. Therefore, in this case, low relative profitability—after a strong decade, growth in revenues is close to stagnating—is an indication of trouble ahead in terms of reputation, as well as financial outlook. Motorola, not on this list, is an example of a technology high-flyer that found it difficult to sustain innovation and market relevance.

Here's the insight: Being profitable doesn't guarantee the capacity to exert influence or to be well-received by the public. In fact, it can leave the company vulnerable. Again, witness Microsoft. However, corporate communications can't guarantee these things on a sustained basis without the substance of financial performance and astute leadership. Both variables are critical to the corporate brand.

The big public relations anomaly in all this is, for example, General Electric. The company's profit as a percentage of sales is not that much better than that of Exxon, and who doesn't know about Exxon's PR and management problems? GE has the lowest annual growth-per-share over a ten-year period among the ten most admired corporations. In its industry, it ranks number six. Yet no other company in the electronics and electrical equipment industry is among the most admired. Is GE's reputation, therefore, reliant to a significant degree on some great intangible?

Table 5.4 gives some similar examples from Asia. These Review 200 results appeared in January 1998, which means that the survey was taken during the first six months of the Asian financial crisis, well before the full impact was felt on corporate reputation. There are two striking factors in these lists. First, being profitable appears to be synonymous

	Review 200			Most Profitable (1997)	
Company	Profit (HK$M)	Increase	Company	Profit (HK$M)	Increase
Mass Transit	196.7	28.0	Sun Hung Kai	1,815.4	28.3
Cathay Pacific	488.3	27.9	Cheung Kong	1,570.6	10.1
Sun Hung Kai	1,815.4	28.3	Hong Kong Telecom	1,433.0	12.5
Cheung Kong	1,570.6	10.1	Henderson Land	1,232.8	15.0
Hang Seng Bank	1,088.1	6.3	Hang Seng Bank	1,088.1	6.3
Swire Pacific	981.3	18.6	Hutchison Whampoa	1,015.4	−10.1
Hong Kong Telecom	1,433.0	12.5	Swire Pacific	981.3	18.6
Hutchison Whampoa	1,015.4	−10.1	China Light & Power	620.0	10.2
China Light & Power	620	10.2	Jardine Matheson	536.1	−22.7
TVB	76.9	28.2	New World Development	533.0	21.9

Table 5.4.   Top Hong Kong Companies.

Source: *Far Eastern Economic Review*, Dec. 31–Jan. 7, 1998, pp. 16–17.

with being respected. Second, none of these companies are primarily manufacturers or creators of value. In fact, the companies are principally companies that create speculative value.

The Philippine model much more closely followed that of the United States (see Table 5.5). There was something more than money involved in reputation. Still, there were few creators of value, although the diversified Ayala group has manufacturing and food processing interests. San Miguel Corporation is a food and beverage producer, and Jollibee prepares food. But whether we are looking at most admired firms in the United States or different Asian countries, we see for the most part companies whose level of appreciation corresponds closely to excellent financial results. Still, it is true that there is no direct correlation: The top ten most profitable are not the same as the top ten most admired. To illustrate this point, it is useful to examine Intel's early days before its patents began to expire.

Although Intel has dominated the global semiconductor industry since the first IBM personal computer appeared, the company itself

Review 200			Most Profitable (1997)		
Company	Profit (P$M)	Increase	Company	Profit (P$M)	Increase
Ayala Corporation	243.6	2.5	PAGCOR	267.5	2.28
Jollibee Foods	16.84	72.27	Ayala Corporation	243.6	2.5
San Miguel Corporation	232.2	4.4	San Miguel Corporation	232.2	4.4
ABS-CBN	65.91	13.97	National Power	211.4	41.6
Shoemart	85.49	18	Metrobank	190.3	61.1
BPI	152.7	44.3	Manila Electric	193.2	14.8
Metrobank	190.3	61.1	Philippine National Bank	177.8	124.5
Pure Foods	3.9	78	Petron	161.7	5.4
Far East Bank	86.1	35.6	BPI	152.7	44.3
PCI Bank	110.9	23.6			
PLDT	291.7	18.8			

Table 5.5. Top Philippines Companies.

Source: Far Eastern Economic Review, Dec. 31–Jan. 7, 1998, pp. 16–17.

was significantly less well known for most of the PC's history than it is today. Rather than Intel processors with hyped-up names like Pentium, computer experts referred to "286s, 386s, and 486s," a series of new product models. Very few consumers were aware that a company named Intel produced these devices.

Two things changed. First, competition was introduced to the industry when Advanced Micro Devices and other companies began competing by manufacturing less expensive processors. For Intel, this is what Chairman Andrew S. Grove calls a "10X" change, or an inflection point (Grove, 1996). As a result of the sudden introduction of new rules of competition, Intel suddenly felt the need to establish a franchise for itself that radiated an image of quality—the best available. Second, ordinary consumers became an important market for the industry in its quest to sustain growth momentum.

From near anonymity, Intel successfully promoted a new brand image, which was intended to protect its franchise. The strategy was based on two fundamentals. The first was corporate branding. The ubiquitous "Intel Inside" became an assurance to consumers that they were purchasing a quality processor. Later, because of the popularity of nonbranded, assembled computers among consumers and small businesses, Intel established a network of what it called genuine Intel dealers. These were dealers that received training and special benefits in return for pushing Intel processors and not illegally altering processor speed or physical appearance (as some unscrupulous small-time dealers were known to do, especially in Asia). Developing a network of approved Intel dealers was supposed to help assure quality and product integrity for consumers. The second fundamental was product branding. Intel provided distinctive names for its products: Pentium, Pentium II, and Celeron, although that choice of terminology was sometimes the focus of considerable debate. The company even developed terminology for new technology introduced into the product line which sounded good but meant nothing. For example, MMX, which stood for a new set of instructions that made processors work faster, especially those used for multimedia applications and games.

By undertaking this strategy, Intel was seeking to instill in the collective market consciousness that all processors are not created equal.

Otherwise, they would have been in danger of "commoditization," or competition based solely on price, not quality or features. Although competition did introduce the element of price pressure, Intel has successfully sustained its capacity to obtain a premium for its products over the prices of competitors.

In the same way that corporate and product branding became a requisite for successful competition in a newly competitive industry and marketplace, so too will Asian companies have to think strategically about the value of a solid reputation as an element of competitive advantage. Naturally, solid products and services must back up the name, but as Intel clearly demonstrated, it is up to the corporation to convince the consumer why all processors, for instance, are not the same.

ADVERTISING VERSUS CORPORATE COMMUNICATIONS

Corporate communications determine the core messages that reside within all branding strategies. It is the keeper of the corporate brand. Advertising focuses on delivering product messages. Advertising executives will most likely howl wildly at that definition. But from this perspective, corporate communications is foremost a strategic function. Advertising acts on strategy to ensure continuity of message and relevance to the marketplace.

Reimaging at Petron, Cathay Pacific, and Hongkong Bank

The strategic role of communications is well-demonstrated by fuel company Petron Corporation, airline Cathay Pacific, and more recently Hongkong Bank. Both Petron and Cathay faced situations similar to that of Intel when its patents expired, or major inflection points that required extensive effort to build corporate identity or brand in increasingly competitive situations.

Petron is one privatization program that worked. Saudi-Aramco and the Philippine government each own 40 percent of the company, and the remaining 20 percent is owned by institutional and small investors. After Petron was privatized, the Philippine government deregulated the oil industry, allowing companies to adjust prices depending on market conditions, as well as allowing the entry of new players.

"Petron's corporate reimaging program is a strategy to boost the company's profile in a deregulated industry," according to Manager of Human Resources Antonio G. Pelayo. "The new Petron image is meant to convey our commitment to maintain market leadership and stay attuned to the changing needs of our customers.

"The new Petron image is epitomized by the new logo that we launched last year. At the service station level [our] new-generation outlets will bear the hallmarks of an industry leader—innovation, customer-friendly, and reliable," Pelayo explains (Interview with author, June 18, 1998).

In Cathay Pacific's case, changes in the operating environment were just as dramatic. As a part of Hong Kong's Swire Group, a respected British expatriate-run conglomerate, Cathay needed to transform its image from that of the flag carrier for the last obvious visage of the colonial era to an integral part of the service-oriented economy of Hong Kong. Cathay needed to become a Chinese company, not just in terms of its shareholdings—Swire sold much of the company to government corporations before the 1997 turnover at attractive values—but in the hearts and minds of all its publics.

As Stephen Pask, former managing director of East Asia of Landor Associates, the consulting firm that created Cathay Pacific's new image, tells it, the company required a bold image that defined its Asianness. They decided to use an ancient Asian art form, brush calligraphy, in their logo. A broad sweeping brushstroke provides the sense of flight, modernity, and Asianness that is both breathtaking and effective, transforming one of Asia's best-known and best-run "Western" airlines into an Asian corporation in the public's mind.

The Hongkong Bank likewise needed to establish a new identity with the handover of Hong Kong in 1997. Unlike Cathay, the bank needed to distinguish itself from those in Hong Kong and China, and therefore chose to rename itself HSBC. This was for two reasons. First, the bank had chosen to move its corporate headquarters from the former colony prior to the handover to Britain. It was no longer a Hong Kong-headquartered bank. The more practical reason was that there was an undocumented but palpable reluctance to do business with corporations registered in Hong Kong once sovereignty returned to China. This had to do with longstanding unease on the part of many of the region's governments and private sector executives, as well as current issues involving trade, borders, and investment.

HSBC began recreating itself as a multinational bank, and at quite a cost: US$50 million, not including advertising. That kind of investment clearly demonstrates the power of perception in corporate branding.

PRINCIPLES OF CORPORATE COMMUNICATIONS

Imaging, as each of these instances demonstrates, is a critical component in communicating the positive image of an organization. But it is only the first step. Corporate communications are built around six basic principles:

- *Publicity, Publicity, Publicity.* Joseph Pulitzer said it best: "Publicity is the greatest factor and force in our public life." For corporations in a competitive environment, the choice is to control the dialogue or to be controlled. This is the choice between managing perceptions and reacting to perceptions.

- *Control the Dialogue.* It is essential to manage and control public dialogue in order to set the agenda.

- *Everything Communicates.* Every action and every spoken or written word communicates a message. So does every unspoken word.

- *Target Constituencies.* Publics that must be persuaded to your view must be quickly and accurately identified in order to maximize returns on the communications budget and to achieve timely results.
- *Comprehensive and Long-Term.* There are no quick fixes when it comes to corporate reputation.
- *The Public Instantly Receives Information.* New technologies must be used to get the message out first and regularly.

Publicity, Publicity, Publicity

This principle, public relations, is important because it is credible in a way that advertising is not. Where advertising informs and announces, publicity demonstrates the message. But it is important to distinguish between publicity stunts and events that produce powerful publicity. While both capture attention, a stunt doesn't create a store of credibility; in fact, it frequently produces the opposite effect. This is also why it is important to communicate at the right times and with appropriate frequency.

Control the Dialogue

Controlling the dialogue, or spinning, frequently gets a bad reputation. Spin is messaging. Credible spin is long-term spin; that is, it's backed up with substance. Crisis spin also works, but not for long. This is where spin gets a bad name. Before the message deteriorates, it is changed. Rapid changes in message diverts attention—and news—from arguments that are difficult, or impossible to justify.

In both cases, spin works best when spin doctors are spinning up— or building—a message or reputation. Sustaining spin requires an interesting and relevant message, a venue, and a receptive media.

Government has traditionally been poor at generating spin in Asia. It frequently has been in a position to dictate coverage, so it doesn't have to spin and therefore doesn't learn how. We still see this in most of the region; however, Hong Kong, the Philippines, and Thailand, for the most part, enjoy a free press. Following the downfall of Indonesia's Suharto, the Indonesian press suddenly became independent.

The second reason is that unfortunately much of the Asian media has been—and is—for sale, again precluding the need to fashion spin, as it can be bought. It should be noted that media is not solely responsible for this deplorable level of unprofessional conduct. These are two-way transactions, and if the choice for a politician or a business is to pay for coverage or forego coverage, information fraud has been an easy sin to submit to. Fortunately, this is all changing.

A young generation of idealistic journalists is forcing change, at least in the countries that exercise freedom of speech. Another reason why the Asian media is changing is because there are some businesses—and their corporate communication counsels—who steadfastly refuse to pay off journalists. Unfortunately, these are not generally domestic firms or domestic corporate communications counsels. Here, professionalizing the industry is being driven by multinational corporations. A third reason behind the change is that international and regional media are setting a higher standard of professional conduct. That standard has been a very frustrating development for many businesses and politicians who feel their power to influence public opinion has been jeopardized. They're right, of course. However, the reaction has been notably immature—great bouts of ranting and raving about dumb or downright evil foreign journalists who don't understand Asia. As the influence of regional media has grown, governments and business have gradually settled down, and are beginning to learn how to interact. There's little choice.

As individuals, Asians have long been hungry for "unbiased" news. Malaysia and Singapore, for instance, still tightly control domestic media, and have tried from time to time to punish international media—the *International Herald Tribune,* the *Asian Wall Street Journal,* and the *Far Eastern Economic Review,* in particular—for publishing reports that made them uncomfortable. The *Review* and the *AWSJ* were both still gazetted—their circulation restricted—in 1998 in Singapore, but there were long waiting lists for both, which included numerous, high-ranking government officials. Meanwhile, Malaysia is the most important market for regional publications in terms of circulation, despite Mahathir's disdain for foreign media.

There is another aspect to the influence of the foreign media. Now that Asia is transitioning to take its rightful place as an important part of the global economy, unrestricted media and liberalization of the financial sector are critical precursors of advanced growth. Investors need information that is not "tainted" by government convenience.

All this strongly suggests that governments in Asia as well as indigenous Asian business must professionalize their media interaction.

Everything Communicates

The traditional view of corporate communications is focused on public relations. With media professionalizing, it is becoming increasingly important to find other effective ways of communicating with key publics, because professional media isn't interested in publishing corporate announcements as news. Again, the multinationals are setting the standards, particularly in the area of what has come to be called event promotion. Citibank, with the assistance of Burson Marstellar, ran an ambitious leadership program involving presentations to key clients by management gurus and former heads of state. The *International Herald Tribune,* The Economist Conferences, and *BusinessWeek* continue to run a variety of conferences and meetings that address contemporary business and public policy issues. These are branding opportunities that communicate an organization's influence in the region, and present the opportunity to interact with top business and government leaders. Large Asian corporations have also begun to participate in these meetings.

But there are also many micromeetings. For example, technology companies organize events that range from PC fairs to conferences on how technology can be used to address issues related to the changing competitive environment. Intel runs enormously successful PC fairs with its dealer networks that are attended by thousands of consumers who buy hundreds of nonbranded computers with Intel processors. SAP—the popular enterprise software company based in Germany—organizes meetings for top-level CEOs that show prospective clients how their solutions can dramatically enhance efficiency, productivity, and profitability in response to changing business conditions. Compaq, IBM, and Hewlett Packard organize similar meetings that are designed to appeal to the interests of key market niches, such as banking and finance.

The phrase *everything communicates* does not necessarily mean that one should be careful what he or she says (although that makes sense), but that there are many ways to get a message across to a key public. The only limitations are the levels of innovation and how return on investment is measured. Compared to traditional means of advertising, companies that focus on creative communications find that the allocation of financial resources is more efficient and the returns greater when initiatives are designed to focus on key market segments. This is a lesson Asian corporations will have to learn.

Target Constituencies

One of the principal benefits of a coordinated corporate communications program is its resource efficiency as corporate and marketing strategy focus on specific market niches. While other forms of advertising and communication—print and broadcast media, specifically— can be targeted to specific demographic profiles, the efficiency is nowhere near that of event management, for example. The principal point of targeting key constituencies is to conserve resources and efforts for allocation where they matter most.

In the same way that many companies, remarkably, do not have a good understanding of who their most important customers are, so, too do they lack a good feel for their most important constituents. The technology companies provide a good example. For years technology companies focused marketing and communication efforts on corporate systems experts rather than corporate decision makers, or the ones who sign the checks. The rationale was easy: Executives do not understand and do not like to talk about technology. The real reason was that it was easy to talk to systems experts because that is who the technology companies could relate to.

As the strategic role of technology has become more obvious, those senior decision makers who do not understand it have not-so-suddenly made their interest known. As a result, technology companies are jumping to figure out how to conduct this dialogue. An illustrative example involves the development of a fairly radical program intended to appeal to senior executives. The mandate was to design and implement the program. This caused incredible anguish in the organization, as successfully completing the project required that all of the existing rules for designing and running a meeting for this multinational client be broken. A great deal of time—and patience—was wasted in a verbal tug-of-war over why things had always been done a certain way by the personnel traditionally responsible for event management. When the meeting finally took place with the senior executives in attendance, it was clear that the company had successfully embarked on a whole new strategy, one where it could present its arguments directly to decision makers, reducing the time required to close contracts as well as improving the efficiency with which the company's message and arguments were delivered.

Comprehensive and Long-Term

In the same way that companies that invested in technology and people *before* the Asian financial crisis were better-positioned to deal with its effects, companies must invest in building corporate identity and the communications infrastructure necessary to respond effectively to a crisis long before the crisis hits. This infrastructure cannot be built after or during the initial impact of bad news or fortune.

Just as important, companies must begin developing an image that will provide the force necessary to influence events long before it must be called upon. It sounds like a cliché, but it is true that reputation doesn't appear overnight. It is also true that if a company has the wrong person in charge of its identity, then it may be creating more problems than it is solving.

Identity is a fundamental strategic concern. It requires development by a seasoned, experienced executive with a top management perspective of the total organization. It is ludicrous that very large companies will create corporate communications or public relations units staffed by young college graduates, yet we see this all the time. Just as ridiculous is putting journalists and lawyers in charge of corporate communications if they have no management experience. Lawyers are not trained to disperse information. For them, no news is good news. For the corporate communications executive, no news is a vacuum waiting to be filled with bad news. Journalists have the opposite problem: They want to tell everything, and look guilty when they can't. Some information is privileged and is appropriately withheld depending on circumstances. More than that, however, neither journalists nor lawyers have a management perspective—or for government, a leadership perspective. The corporate communications executive should be an individual who not only understands the business, but helps shape it.

The Public Instantly Receives Information

Like every other management function, the impact of information technology and globalization on corporate communications has been enormous. Powerful search tools like Lexis-Nexis and business and news sites such as those maintained by the *Wall Street Journal* and other publications have made it extremely easy to obtain information on companies all over the world.

It's important that the right information be there for researchers, writers, and analysts to find. And the right information for the company's perspective will almost always come from the company. This is another reason why corporate communications must be long-term and consistent. The other important factor in this discussion is how fast-breaking information is passed around the globe. There is very little time to determine a strategy after a crisis breaks or information relevant to the company's strategic plans becomes a news item. Here, technology works for the corporate communicator, helping to disseminate the corporate perspective quickly and accurately.

CONTROLLING DESTINY

Some corporations may be destined for greatness, but most will achieve their destiny in the New Asia only if they attain a level of control of the determining forces, including competitive developments in the industry, regulatory authorities, public sentiment, consumer sensitivities and desires, and the support of key stakeholders from employers to financial institutions. And then there is media.

Globalization of communications in the form of the Internet vastly reduced the capacity of governments and organizations to exert control on the flow of information—in the same way that it grabbed away governments' control over the flow of funds. It is senseless to try to reexert some measure of control. That's not going to happen as long as the business industry aspires to prosperous economies anchored on free and open markets.

It is therefore imperative that Asian governments and corporations learn how to effectively and consistently communicate under these new conditions. Control will not be administrative; it will come about by playing the game, and it will be called acquiring and exercising influence. But whether any organization is able to exercise influence long-term will depend on how well it lives up to the messages it communicates.

PART THREE

A Shift to Strategy

CHAPTER SIX

The Shift to Strategy: Betting the Company

W ashington SyCip, founder of the Arthur Andersen-
affiliated SGV Group and an Asian management icon, told a conference of managers in 1998 that, "I am not ready to accept that the year
of the tiger should follow an Australian saying, 'Rooster today, feather
duster tomorrow'" (SyCip, 1998). And he was right. Asia would be
back—but with a new rooster.

In the survey of Asian business executives taken by the *Far Eastern
Economic Review* just prior to the onset of the Asian financial crisis
(see p. 32), respondents overwhelming agreed that, "Connections are
more important than strategy for a company to succeed in Asia." This
was particularly true in Malaysia and Indonesia, with 79 percent
and 78 percent agreeing, respectively. But it was also true in Taiwan
with 74 percent in agreement, as well as Singapore and South Korea,
both with 73 percent in agreement. Interestingly, the Philippines
recorded the lowest level of agreement (56 percent), followed by Hong
Kong at 58 percent. Fifty-three percent of non-Asian expatriates
agreed ("Managing in Asia . . . ," 1997).

Harvard Business School's Michael Porter tells a story of a conversation with an Asian businessman that also took place well before the onset of the Asian financial crisis. Explaining why he was not concerned with strategy during the booming Asian miracle years, the businessman said in effect that he could do anything and make money—even by mistake—in that heady development environment. All it took was a few friends. "Porter came to Asia a few years early," Jose A. Concepcion III, president and chief executive officer of the RFM Group of Companies in the Philippines, said more recently (Interview with author, August 20, 1998).

Porter's tour through Asia and his prediction that the region's conglomerates would have to restructure and focus on customer-centric, strategy-driven growth sooner or later was met with strenuous objection to the arrogance of Western management gurus. By mid-1998, there were still howls bemoaning Western arrogance, but with a distinctly contrasting tone. Whereas pre-crisis criticism was of experts who preached the universality of Western management principles, in 1998 the Westerners were being warned not to rub it in.

Amidst the howling, Porter's message that opportunity-driven growth was fine for developing Asia—though not perhaps the over reliance on "connections," which led to incredibly poor lapses in judgement—was lost. Porter's message proved to be predictive. It was based on the assumption that changes in Asian economies and markets would require changes in the way companies operated. For Asian managers comfortable with the status quo, that message represented an obvious threat to their hold over industries and markets. Determined preoccupation with maintaining the status quo caused them to largely ignore the changes in the marketplace that were fundamentally changing the rules of business in Asia. The Asian financial crisis accelerated the pace of change.

- "Strategic planning? Who needs strategic planning? I built up my company from scratch to what it is today without strategic planning, so why do I need it?"

- "Market conditions are changing so fast, any strategic plan we develop will be obsolete in no time, so why bother?"

• "I guess strategic planning could be useful but we are so
busy running our business and trying to keep ahead of our
competitors that we do not have the time or resources to
undertake strategic planning" (Chan, 1997, Internet edition).

These comments, although they seem naïve, typify Asian pre-crisis
views. They illustrate why so many Asian corporations—aside from the
region's conglomerates—were so mentally, emotionally, and intellec-
tually unprepared to deal with the fiercely negative impact of the crisis.
But were Asian taipans exceptional in this respect? To try to answer that
question, think about what Jerry I. Porras and James C. Collins, authors
of *Built to Last: Successful Habits of Visionary Companies,* call the
myth of strategic planning among the United States firms they studied.

"Visionary companies make some of their best moves by experi-
mentation, trial and error, opportunism, and—quite literally—by
accident. What looks *in retrospect* like brilliant foresight and preplan-
ning was often the result of 'Let's just try a lot of stuff and keep what
works.' In this sense, visionary companies mimic the biological evolution of species. We found the concepts in Charles Darwin's *Origin
of Species* to be more helpful for replicating the success of certain
visionary companies than any textbook on corporate strategic planning," these two highly acclaimed authors note. They are not alone in
their viewpoint (Collins and Porras, 1994, p. 9).

James F. Moore says, "I observe companies that are drastically
affected by the changing ecology of business competition and that seek
ways to understand and shape the transformations engulfing them."
Moore believes that competitive strategy generally "ignores the context—the environment—within which the business lies, and it ignores
the need for coevolution with others in that environment, a process that
involves cooperation as well as conflict. Even excellent businesses can
be destroyed by the conditions around them" (Moore, 1996, p. 3). Like
Collins and Porras, Moore invokes the environmental metaphor to
explain that strategy evolves as a result of many factors, and cannot be
clinically devised. But it can be scientifically explained—in hindsight.

Gary Hamel and C. K. Prahalad argue that strategic foresight is a
quality shared by innovative companies like Honda, CNN, British

Airways, and others, but emphasize that rather than strategy reflecting some great or noble vision, it is more a dream of some perhaps improbable future, such as a PC on every desk seemed about a decade ago. And while strategic foresight in itself is important, Hamel and Prahalad suggest that, "The point here is that too often competitors are judged in terms of resources rather than resourcefulness. It was just such a misjudgment that led Manhattan's media mavens to label Ted Turner the 'mouth of the South, all show and no go,' at the very time the Atlanta-based firebrand was setting a torch to the cozy house of network news." However, like Collins, Porras, and Moore, these strategic experts do not believe that resourcefulness is the product of "an elegantly structured strategic architecture, but from a deeply felt sense of purpose, a broadly shaped dream, a truly seductive view of tomorrow's opportunity" (Hamel and Prahalad, 1994, p. 128).

For Adrian Slywotzky and David Morrison, strategy takes the harder form of straightforward business modeling based on critical building blocks that "make profitability happen" (Slywotzky and Morrison, 1997, p. vii). These building blocks keep strategic thinking focused on the customer, but not just any customer. The *most profitable* customers are the core that strategy—and the business model—is built around. There's very little dream involved in their model; instead, the quest for value for the customer and profitability for the corporation determine where and how a company evolves. But Slywotzky and Morrison illustrate their ideas through a set of visionary leaders that include Microsoft's Bill Gates, Intel's Andrew Grove, and GE's Jack Welch, suggesting that soft issues—leadership and charisma—play important roles in driving business model development. Meanwhile, Collins and Porras argue that great and charismatic leaders are not necessary to create—or evolve—a visionary company, nor are they necessary to create a good idea. All that is needed, ultimately, is the desire to create and develop a great company.

If the world's foremost authorities on strategy—irrespective of the terminology—have so much difficulty agreeing on what it is, how it is made, and what resources are required, how can we know that Asian corporations need strategy? Or what form their strategies should take?

Strategy is necessary for two fundamental reasons: to bring focus to top management's thinking and to foster creative thinking.

When management's thinking is focused, it is concentrated on the issues that most closely affect performance and development. It is able to resist the temptation of becoming distracted by attractive but unrelated profit opportunities. Resources are applied to strengthen and develop the company's core products and services. Everyone knows where the company is headed. Creative thinking works better because strategy prioritizes goals and objectives. When a company lacks strategic focus, its capacity to generate innovative, novel ideas is diluted because application to specific problems and challenges is inconsistent. Innovation requires incubation and testing of ideas. Shortened cycle times in all industries have increased the importance of focusing creative resources where they are needed most.

For the New Asian Corporation, then, what is strategy? To understand the answer to this question, it's necessary to return to the three forces introduced in Chapter One that are collectively redefining the way business is done in Asia, provoking profound and permanent economic restructuring. The first of those forces is the Asian financial crisis itself. Although the financial crisis quickly evolved into an enterprise crisis provoking recession in 1998 in many of Asia's economies, its origin, ultimately, was incredibly poor banking practices brought on by all the usual reasons, foremost among them inadequate, impotent regulatory frameworks. Some have argued that Asia's immature financial institutions and emerging economies were caught by the surprise effects of rapid information technology innovation and globalization. While technology and globalization help account for the severity of the crisis, they are not its cause. If they were the cause, the American savings and loans crisis in the 1980s and the bursting of the Japanese bubble economy in the 1990s would not have taken place. They happened because, like Asia, those environments demonstrated very poor regulatory infrastructure and incredible levels of irresponsible banking practices.

Lest it sound as if the crisis is being laid entirely at the feet of the banks and regulatory authorities, it is necessary to add that there was a clear and profound lack of corporate responsibility that aided and abetted—lobbied and egged on—the bankers while soothing any precipitous worries government authorities might have demonstrated from time to time. No one among the rainmakers—the miracle years' movers and shakers—is without blame. But as surveys already cited here have shown, government is ultimately responsible for keeping economic activity within rational boundaries, and therefore takes the brunt of the blame for letting things get out of hand.

What the crisis meant for Asian corporations was a heightened strategic sense of the importance of resources. Not so much in their availability but, as Porter, Hamel, and Prahalad argue, in the resourcefulness of their application. So strategy became a question of generating resourcefulness and innovation. Ultimately it was seen that generating resourcefulness is best accomplished in the context of focus on growth in profitability rather than growth merely in revenue and market share. The focus on profitability required that corporations ask themselves, "Given these new conditions, what will be our source of profitability?" Slywotzky and Morrison call these sources *profit zones*. The acknowledgement of the necessity to identify new profit zones is the first sign of the "evolution" of Asian corporate strategy.

Where crisis accelerated the restructuring of corporate Asia—in an appropriately messy, evolutionary manner—globalization accelerated the pace with which quality and productivity standards were uniformly applied across markets. The global marketplace was becoming—forever—a buyers' market. And technology is the principal catalyst of globalization and consumer empowerment.

For Asian corporations, globalization would require huge investments in productivity and quality-enhancing technology. It would also, along with the crisis, raise the premium on the value of the best people and improve the return on private-sector investment in education and training. Better people are not only the source of higher productivity and quality, but of resourcefulness. Pressure to meet minimum standards of productivity and quality will make Asia the fastest-digitizing region of the world in the next century.

Technology makes it possible to source—or just compare—goods and services from any corner of the globe at the speed electrons travel across networks. Increasing competition between Asia's exporters and, over the next twenty-five years, the increasing uniformity in quality and price that such competition provokes will profoundly alter the basic standards of doing business. Ultimately, the capacity of Asian corporations to attract a premium for their products and services will reside in how well they develop new business models that capitalize on new sources of profitability. This is the second sign of evolving Asian corporate strategy.

The third force that was buffeting corporate Asia was liberalization. If Asia's export-oriented economies expected to have access to the biggest economies in the world, then they were going to have to have access to Asia's. As we've argued, protecting Asian tycoons from foreign competition provided national economies very low returns in terms of uplifting common consumers by creating jobs and increasing the value-added of output. While access to Western markets was a powerful motivator for liberalization, the direct benefit of a more competitive corporate sector would ultimately result in improved Asian companies that are more profitable and create more—and better—jobs.

What liberalization meant for Asian conglomerates was that, first, many would not remain wholly—or even partly—Asian for long. Many would become quite something else, despite the intrinsic difficulty of merging cultures and operations, as discussed earlier. This would provoke a nagging firestorm of a senseless debate that was solely in the interests of the tycoons responsible for the flabby, uncompetitive character of the conglomerates and their political benefactors in the first place. Fortunately for Asian consumers, that was a debate the Asian tycoons were destined to lose. A second resulting effect of liberalization on conglomerates was that many be forced to ask themselves what business they were in, and focus exclusively on that business. Goodbye family heirlooms.

But the real beneficiary of liberalization would be the young Asian entrepreneur, who had the confidence—or the brashness not to care—to take on competition wherever they found it for the sake of developing an idea or a dream. From such a dream, a strategic plan would evolve to put a new business model into effect.

And this is the New Asian Corporation. Companies that develop original technologies, products, and services in response to vastly altered market realities, and as a result, define Asian corporate strategy (see Table 6.1).

THE QUALITIES OF THE NEW ASIAN CORPORATION

The most obvious characteristic of these companies will be their specialization on specific industries, product niches, and profitable customers. Frederick F. Reichheld, author of *The Loyalty Effect*, says in studies he directed, "We encountered evidence which supports the linkage between customer retention and profits. Seemingly insignificant changes in customer retention rates in several of our clients' businesses resulted in eye-popping improvements in profits. Then, we studied a wide array of industries, and found that a 5-percentage point shift in customer retention consistently resulted in 25–100 percent profit swings" (Reichheld, 1997).

Slywotzky, Porter, Hamel, Prahalad, and Fred Wiersema, author of *Customer Intimacy* (1996), all argue persuasively that unrestrained growth and dominant market share do not necessarily translate into profitability. Companies like Microsoft and Intel show that dominant market share can translate into unimaginable profits, but monopolies

Force	Effect
Profound economic reform and corporate restructuring	Shift in profit zones
Internationalization of profitability, efficiency, productivity, and quality standards	New business models
Fierce competition leading to business model innovation	Strategic plans

Table 6.1.   Three Signs of Evolving Asian Corporate Strategy.

are exceptions. Or are they? Another technology company, IBM, illustrates the experts' argument of how a near-monopoly can quickly erode. But what is true in all instances is that these companies are regularly challenged. Both Microsoft and Intel have experienced instances—such as Andrew Grove's famous inflection points, which outline the profound and irreversible shifts in the rules of industry competition—where the long-term viability of the company was at stake. Since the average Fortune 500 company has a life expectancy of around forty years, according to Reichheld ("The Forces of Loyalty versus Chaos," 1998) and others, these are healthy fears.

Both Intel and Microsoft are masters at resourceful use of intellectual resources. Extremely generous stock incentive plans help generate that energy. Despite that effort, they are regularly caught off guard. Microsoft was unnerved by Netscape's browser and Sun's Java programming language, and Intel didn't think development of processors for under US$1,000 was a serious competitive threat to their strategy of continual value enhancement. For both companies, niche players threatened the viability of the entire business model of two of the most successful companies in history.

That's the second good reason that Asian companies will focus on product and customer niches: leverage core competence. The first good reason, as discussed, is to focus on priority sources of profit.

Straying from a niche in the euphoria of success usually has unfortunate results. Singapore's Creative Technology is a good example of a company that's finding it hard to follow up on its first big success, Sound Blaster, a product that set global standards for multimedia PC technology. Although the company made a "remarkable turnaround" (Boey, 1998, Internet edition), by some reports in 1997, the turnaround was principally due to the cessation of new but unprofitable initiatives. Report cards were not yet in on whether two new products, digital video disks and the Sound Blaster Live!—representing an evolution of its principal sources of revenues—would be warmly received in the marketplace. Meanwhile, although the company expected to remain profitable in the face of the Asian crisis and slower growth in other markets, it downgraded revenues forecasts twice in 1998. Price

pressure was particularly intense on the company's low-end peripherals. And the company announced a US$8.3 million write-off that
surprised analysts (Ismail, 1998, p. 6).

Then, in early 1999, the company announced a bearish outlook due
to the Asian financial crisis and the effects of the Brazilian crisis. At the
same time, the company revealed plans to compete with companies like
Sony, Panasonic, and Philips in the "personal digital entertainment"
sector. Most analysts repeated warnings to leave the stock alone until it
became clear whether the company's latest product strategy would click.

Creative Technology may be trying a lot of stuff and seeing what
works, as Collins and Porras say of visionary companies. If so, it is still
very much in the "trying" stage. But indeed, all of Collins and Porras's
visionary companies, not surprisingly, experienced slumps from time
to time, usually when they got too close to comfortable. Microsoft's
Bill Gates notes, and he should know, that success can be dangerous:
"Every time we think, 'Hey, we've had a little bit of success,' we're
pretty careful not to dwell on it too much because the bar gets raised"
("The Bill & Warren Show," 1998, p. 41). James Riley, chief financial
officer of Cycle & Carriage, agrees. When his company won several
management excellence awards he spoke of his worry that his people
would become complacent.

Defining strategy makes at least one thing clear—strategy is messy.
It is chaotic. It is evolutionary. But it also has a number of clearly
definable characteristics. First, strategy equals focus on core competence. Second, it involves nichemanship, or concentration on profitable customer segments rather than raw market share. "Dominant
market share doesn't give pricing power," one analyst said of Creative
Technology, for instance (Borsuk, 1999, p. 13). Third, strategy provides for the resourceful application of resources, or innovative
approaches to technical, market, and financial challenges.

THE CASE OF RFM

Although a giant in domestic Philippine industry terms, it is also correct to refer to the RFM Group as a David who took on not one, but

two global Goliaths. Principally a food and beverage manufacturer, RFM has evolved from a milling and packaged food processing operation by dramatically setting the soft drinks and ice cream segments on their ears. In soft drinks, it shook up Pepsi and Coca-Cola— although those companies object to that evaluation. In ice cream, RFM took on the jewel of the Philippine corporate world and a respected international corporation, San Miguel Corporation. RFM is now the second-largest food and beverage conglomerate in the country, after San Miguel.

President and Chief Operating Officer Jose A. Concepcion III represents the third generation of a distinguished Chinese-Filipino family. (The company was actually founded by his maternal grandfather.) There is a well-known saying in Chinese folklore that the first generation sacrifices to make the family fortune, the second enjoys it, and the third generation loses it. So far, Concepcion is demonstrating that the old Chinese saying doesn't apply in his case. Profits increased an impressive 48 percent in 1998, the year Asia's financial crisis reached its dizzying peak. Concepcion forecasts annual growth in net sales of 15 percent through the year 2002.

As executive vice president in 1989, Concepcion pushed for the acquisition of a small local bottler, Cosmos, to move the company away from commodities and into value brands. Few analysts at the time could understand why Concepcion wanted to enter the cola wars with Coke and Pepsi. Cosmos had virtually no distribution network and catered to the extremely price-sensitive classes. Coke and Pepsi, as usual, were engaged in a bitter clash, ultimately leaving Pepsi struggling for profitability and survival. The franchise ownership for Pepsi finally changed hands in early 1997.

Cosmos was acquired three years into the administration of former president Corazon C. Aquino, following the overthrow of the dictator, Ferdinand Marcos. Filipinos were feeling liberated, good about themselves, and excited about the future, despite the difficulty government was experiencing with disgruntled, coup-happy, young military officers and with getting the government moving in general. Concepcion decided to market Cosmos as a distinctly Filipino beverage—given the prevalent undercurrent of nationalism—with all the glitz and quality of its powerful competitors. The company developed and launched a sleek advertising campaign celebrating the Filipino that made the market beam. For the first time, Cosmos was showing up prominently on the supermarket shelves.

And then a funny thing happened. RFM realized that there wasn't much money in supermarket sales, a fact Coke and Pepsi knew well. In fact, the most lucrative market for Cosmos would turn out to be its traditional market, where soft drinks were purchased at small neighborhood stores called *sari-sari* stores. Margins were better, and this was a pure cash business. No waiting for checks; no waiting for bank clearance. "*Sari-sari* is our most profitable distribution channel," Concepcion says, "and we're not as focused on supermarkets and restaurants" (Interview with author, Aug. 20, 1998).

Concepcion soon turned off the marketing glitz and focused efforts on increasing market share in traditional markets: extending distribution networks, developing relationships, and providing cost leadership. By 1998, Cosmos, by RFM's measurements, was the number two soft drink in the market, followed closely by Pepsi (which they hotly contest), and was contributing 54 percent of the group's profit. Like McDonald's chasing after Jollibee, Pepsi found it extremely unpleasant to be running after a local cola brand. Who says Asian brands can't compete?

But Concepcion wasn't through yet. After being named president and CEO in 1990, he purchased the Selecta brand of locally produced ice cream products. It is another superb—and extremely tasty—product that suffered from poor distribution and management as well as the sometimes heavy-handed pressure of San Miguel subsidiary Magnolia, which manufactured the market leader. Again, Concepcion's strategy was focused on quality as well as value for money. The product had always been distributed in tins rather than paper or plastic containers. Concepcion kept that piece of Selecta legend, but spruced up the can and the branding materials. Advertising focused on unique flavors and quality. To the market's surprise—and San Miguel's dismay—Selecta zoomed into first place. Giants fall hard—and not infrequently—in the Philippines.

A glance at RFM's corporate strategy shows essentially a well-focused food and beverage conglomerate that has expanded aggressively into segments closely related to its original food processing business (for more insight, see Figure 6.1). RFM, according to the company, pioneered the flour-milling industry in the Philippines and Asia. Concepcion intends to strengthen that focus through additional acquisitions. But what do a bank, a land development company, and a semiconductor assembler have to do with a food and beverage manufacturer?

Philippine Townships was formed when the industry switched over to contract chicken farming instead of managing their own farms. This freed up large tracks of land. There were then three choices: hold, sell, or develop. Probably as a result of the booming real estate market, the company opted to add value and then sell or lease segments of the developed land, principally as middle-income housing and industrial estates. One high-profile project—an upscale condominium-type building in Makati's privatized Fort Bonifacio—could have had serious implications for this division. Construction began just before the onset of the Asian financial crisis, but the company insists that

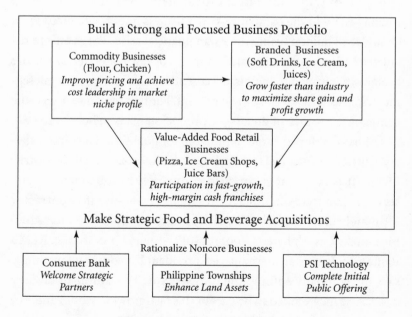

Figure 6.1. Corporate Strategy.

"predevaluation costs of constructing the building were secured . . .
securing, therefore, the margins originally planned by the developers"
(Interview with author, October 21, 1998).

The mystery of that explanation illustrates the significant depar-
ture of the company in constructing this site from its usual practice
of developing underutilized lands. It also demonstrates how easy it is
to succumb to the allure of real estate bubbles. But company policy
is not, according to Concepcion, to land bank for future development,
but to generate additional cash flows for the group through value
enhancement. The Fort Bonifacio experience shows how important it
is for RFM to stick to that strategy. As soon as it begins to view real
estate development as a core business, it will begin to take risks that
have potentially severe negative ramifications on the group. What is a
well thought-out strategy for generating additional cash flows without impinging on the financial resources of the company can quickly
evolve into a speculative gamble to reap windfall profits that ultimately
puts the sanctity of financial resources at risk.

Integrated circuits assembler PSI is another matter all together. This
company provided ₱943 million, in foreign exchange, in 1997 to the
Group. That translates into approximately US$4 million a month,
roughly equal to the company's core business imports, reduced from
about US$8 million before the Asian financial crisis. PSI in effect pro-
vided a hedge for the company's imports of raw materials for its core
business, allowing it to maintain a cost advantage in the soft drink segment, for instance, of close to 50 percent. For that reason in itself—the
company is a source of dollars—Concepcion plans to hold onto PSI.

PSI has developed a solid reputation for quality and on-time delivery. Customers include Hewlett-Packard, Motorola, and Texas Instru-
ments. It is far cheaper for such companies to subcontract these
services than to maintain factories themselves—but the contractor
ultimately takes the volatility risk so endemic to the semiconductor industry, as Alphatec's Robert Mollerstuen knows so well. RFM's
Ramon M. Lopez, an assistant vice president for corporate planning,
says the company entered the industry for: 1) a source of dollars;
2) because they wanted to be part of this fast-growing sector; and 3) a
return on investment.

Ultimately none of these are very good reasons for a strategic investment by a food and beverage manufacturer, and Concepcion seems to understand this. RFM has already reduced its holdings in PSI to 51 percent, down from 70 percent, and an initial public offering (IPO) is planned under which the company will relinquish majority control. However, the investment was hugely fortuitous in the context of Asia's financial crisis, despite the concurrent downturn in semiconductor prices, solely for its role as a source of foreign exchange. For that reason, it is unlikely that RFM will sell off its interest in the assembler at least until such time as Asian economies enjoy a sustained period of more or less predictable growth and stable exchange rates.

RFM also intends to dilute its interest in Consumer Bank, which plays an important role in providing financial resources in the supply chain, principally to suppliers. The bank finances suppliers and remittances are coursed through the thrift, which is a small institution with just sixteen branches. "Nevertheless," Lopez says, "we're still looking for other strategic partners to reduce holdings" (Interview with author, October 21, 1998). He notes that noncore businesses like PSI and Consumer Bank provide only 7 percent of total revenues for the Group.

Future strategic investments, Concepcion says, will be focused on food and beverage manufacture and will be intended to contribute to the goal of making the Group the clear industry leader. And he realizes that won't happen if RFM relies on internal financial resources. "Companies that are not up-linked will have a hard time raising capital," he says. "We will reduce our holdings to recruit foreign partners from among the world's best manufacturers in the industry. We will remain focused on the Philippines for the moment, but eventually intend to export to other regional markets." RFM already exports processed meats to both regional and Western markets.

"We will open up the company as long as it leads to greater shareholder value," Concepcion vows. "I'd rather have 10 percent of a large company than 100 percent of a small one" (Interview with author, Aug. 20, 1998).

In early 1999, RFM and Unilever formed a joint venture to capitalize on the Selecta success story and extend its franchise. At the time, Lopez said, "[W]e are completing negotiations with several multinational strategic partners who will provide needed capital and technology. Our strategy is to finish all possible joint venture and partnership talks in the subsidiary level to enhance the value of RFM and then proceed with the negotiations at the RFM Group level."

Strategic Lessons from RFM

In our quest to understand strategy, there are a number of qualities that RFM demonstrates that we should consider.

WILLINGNESS TO TAKE CALCULATED RISKS. The acquisitions of Cosmos and Selecta were both hotly debated. In both cases, RFM—up until then, a somewhat dowdy flour miller—was making a commitment to taking on long-standing industry leaders—in one case, a global leader; in the other, a regional conglomerate and one of Asia's most admired corporations, according to numerous regional surveys. Industry observers criticized the company for entering segments it knew little about in order to compete with multinational firms. The distribution networks of the acquisitions and RFM were said to be grossly inadequate. That brings us to the next quality.

RESOURCEFUL USE OF RESOURCES. RFM turned those shortcomings into an advantage, not always by design, but ultimately to its benefit. Competitively, it learned quickly that it made no sense to compete with Coke and supermarket and restaurant business where margins were nearly nonexistent. Instead, it capitalized on its 50-percent cost advantage at the *sari-sari* store level, and enjoyed the benefits of a purely cash business. Rather than use plastic and aluminum containers, RFM was steadfast in the use of imported bottles that helped finance production inputs because of the deposits collected up front of sale. RFM also read market sentiment and appealed to national pride: a Filipino company effectively competing with the big boys.

ACQUIRING, NOT DEVELOPING, OPPORTUNITY. When the company saw an opportunity involving limited competition it quickly capitalized by acquiring the capacity to compete, rather than developing that capacity. What analysts did not realize is that while RFM initially knew little about soft drink and ice cream manufacture, its executives knew a lot about marketing. This is discussed in detail in Chapter Eight.

FOCUS. Although the company has made some debatable forays into diversification, top management realized these do not represent the future for RFM. The volatility of semiconductor manufacture and real estate development has shown that these are two completely different industries, requiring different management skills, considerable risk on behalf of clients, and a different mindset. Selling to mass markets is worlds apart from selling to multinational technology companies and middle-class homeowners. Diversification has had its happy advantages, but Concepcion knows his company's greatest prospects are firmly rooted in food and beverage.

WILLINGNESS TO RECRUIT FOREIGN STRATEGIC PARTNERS. Rather than trying to preserve the family traditions, Concepcion acknowledges the future and the need to adapt to new conditions. For many companies this is not a choice of having 100 percent of a small company, but whether crisis, globalization, and liberalization will leave them with any company at all.

RECRUITING VERY SMART PEOPLE—AND LISTENING TO THEM. Although Concepcion's relatives—father, brothers, and cousins—continue to retain firm management control of the firm, Concepcion demands performance. He also makes it a point to recruit extremely intelligent executives that are willing to speak up to the boss. "People are our principal source of competitiveness," Lopez notes. "We have molded our managers to be a combination of professionals and entrepreneurs. They're hybrids."

THE CASE OF TRANS CAPITAL HOLDING

One of the interesting things about Asia is that for all the hype and talk, its technology sector is decidedly uninteresting. This is because it consists virtually entirely of multinational manufacturing facilities and contract assemblers, like RFM's PSI. Although margins are thin in this increasingly commodity-like industry, leading contract manufacturers have made fortunes on the basis of their capacity to provide quality, timely service and low labor costs. Contract manufacturers have replaced the garment sweatshops of an earlier era. That's not entirely fair, of course. Conditions are—of manufacturing necessity—much better for workers in semiconductor assembly facilities than they are for those unlucky souls who, for instance, work for contractors manufacturing Nike's athletic shoes (according to published reports.)

The facilities themselves and the equipment one finds inside them are much more expensive. But the reason they are in Asia is not that much different: low labor and low costs of doing business. Despite efforts to increase the value-added of electronic exports, that's been very hard to do for a number of reasons that have to do with everything from fears of opening up proprietary technology to lack of educational infrastructure. Educational infrastructure is the principal stumbling block, but Trans Capital Holding in Malaysia may be demonstrating that this view is more mindset than reality.

"As margins erode, you can't stay in subcomponents," says CEO Tan Say Choon. "We want an emphasis on R&D, but Malaysia isn't ready. The easiest way to get into R&D is to attach ourselves to Castlewood" (Hiebert, 1998, p. 56). Castlewood is a company established by hard drive pioneer Syed Iftikar, who had helped to found Seagate Technology and Syquest Technology. The company has developed 2.2-gigabyte Orb disks—similar to the popular Zip and Jazz disks produced by Ionics Corporation—that could revolutionize high-capacity, carry-it-with-you storage peripherals. When Iftikar offered to build the drives under contract with Tan, Tan quickly accepted—and took a 5-percent interest in the company that he hopes to expand to 10 percent. He's in good company—investors include Japanese manufacturers Sanyo and Aiwa. Iftikar liked Trans Capital because of its management and engineering depth and experience, as well as the Penang infrastructure, where many high-tech companies have operations.

Tan expects the alliance to "boost Trans Capital's revenue to 1 billion ringgit (US$237 million) by 2000, up from 220 million ringgit in 1997" (Hiebert, 1998, p. 56). That won't help Tan solve the problem of the lack of value-added technicians and engineers and research facilities, however. (Intellectual and educational infrastructure will be explored further in Chapter Nine.) But Tan has shown, like RFM, that value-added strategy doesn't have to be reliant on in-house technology and brains. It can be bought. That's a solid strategy, according to Peter S. Cohan, author of *Net Profit* and *The Technology Leaders*, who says both Microsoft and Cisco have relied heavily on the purchase of technology to grow capability and markets.

THE CASE OF GOLD PEAK INDUSTRIES

Although an incredibly entrepreneurial manufacturing culture is evident in Hong Kong, value-added industry development has been elusive. Although Gold Peak's core business can be said to be commodities-based—the manufacture and distribution of batteries, electrical installation products, automotive electronics, cable products, loudspeakers, and high precision parts and components— President Victor Lo Chung Wing has transformed a family-owned corporation into a modern, professional Asian multinational with three major listed subsidiaries in Singapore since its own listing in 1984. "It is evolving from an operating manufacturer into an industrial investments holding company with a diversified portfolio of high-quality industrial investments. Gold Peak currently employs more than 12,000 people in manufacturing, research and development, marketing, and distribution in over ten countries around the world, with total assets exceeding HK$5 billion and an annual turnover exceeding HK$3.5 billion" ("Managing Asia," 1998). As a result, Lo says he spends only about 25 percent of his time in the office, due to travel demands.

That means that like RFM's Concepcion, Lo has had to attract professional managers to whom he can quickly delegate significant levels of authority, in contrast to the usual Asian family-run firm in which a patriarch holds sway over the organization. "Human resources are the most important resource of the company," Lo says. "I delegate very rapidly and a long way" ("Managing Asia," 1998). Unlike Concepcion, Lo is the only member of the family to remain with the company, and he frequently says that his position is available. Lo says that although some family members remain shareholders of the company, in order to convince smart, professional managers to join the firm it was necessary to demonstrate that there would be no bumping up against family members and glass ceilings during the struggle up the corporate ladder. "In the early days, I spent a lot of time recruiting managers," Lo recalls. "I had to convince them of the commitment to transform into a professional company" ("Managing Asia," 1998).

A strong leadership profile was also important to attract the strategic partners Lo knew would be necessary to finance the development of the company, again a reality that RFM's Concepcion and Trans Capital's Tan have acknowledged is necessary. Like both of those companies, Lo has regularly used strategic investments to acquire technology to expand his production base into related—"not too diversified"—fields. The company remains solely a manufacturer of electronic equipment and batteries.

Significantly, Lo has also been able to parlay strategic investment into an admirable R&D capability, something other Asian companies must also learn to do if they want to build their capacity to use resources efficiently.

From these examples that span three distinct industries, it is evident that persistence in focus, acquisition of technology, professional management, willingness to recruit strategic partners, and a quest for increased value-added and resourcefulness in the use and application of resources are vital factors in developing strategy.

WHAT ALL THIS MEANS

Slywotzky and Morrison argue that companies must ask themselves a number of fundamental questions. One certainly stands out: "What is your principal source of profit?" (Slywotzky and Morrison, 1997). As companies in Asia have thought about this question, it became clear that any shift in profit zone was unrelated to diversification. Instead, as seen in these instances, significant focus was a tightly held principle of development even before the onset of the Asian financial crisis. Other Asian companies have experimented with diversification and realized that was not where increasingly scarce resources—principally equity and brains—should be allocated. When Gold Peak's Lo was asked whether he was getting involved in the buying binge of cheap Asian assets, he replied that many of those assets were indeed cheap, but in such terrible condition that in terms of opportunity cost, acquisition just did not make sense. There were so many other ways to capitalize on resources.

The strategic partnerships discussed are not taking place between distressed firms, but between strong companies with excellent management that have their eyes on the future and are managing for it. This is an important perspective for anyone who wants to do business in Asia: The best opportunities will be found in Asia's best companies. Investment in Asia is better directed toward a highly productive asset than one that has to be restored to life at great costs, to finances, time, and human resources.

Finally, strategy is an integral, critical component of doing business in Asia. Opportunity-driven growth has given way to strategy-driven growth. Long-term viability will be driven by the capacity of companies to devise and implement strategies that incorporate new business models focused on specific sources of profit. By doing this, they will become adept at changing the rules of competition in their industries, as RFM and the other companies examined here have done. If they are lucky, they won't forget that they have to keep doing this over and over.

CHAPTER SEVEN

The First Source of Competitiveness: Productivity and Innovation

———〰— 66 W e do not benchmark with other hospitals in the Philippines," says Jose F. G. Ledsema, the president and CEO of St. Luke's Hospital in Manila. "Rather, we benchmark against the best hotels, the best hospitals, and other best companies around the world" (Hamlin, "The New Competitiveness," 1998). His approach to setting productivity standards and establishing and sustaining a culture of innovation is a critical competitive competence in an increasingly competitive marketplace. Benchmarking the best organizations anywhere is setting new standards of productivity and innovation in the Philippines—and the rest of Asia—for his industry.

THE NEW PRODUCTIVITY

MIT's Paul Krugman popularized the issue of what economists call total factor productivity with his famous 1994 *Foreign Affairs* article, "The Myth of Asia's Miracle," but his was not the first voice to raise the issue of low Asian productivity, as he points out in that article. However, he was the first one to be listened to carefully, probably because his article—unlike others before it—came to the attention of an influential audience. Krugman's stature, and the reputation of *Foreign Affairs*, surfaced the argument in a dramatic way that Asia was going to have to work smarter. Even for Krugman, however, getting respect for the argument was difficult. Attracting detractors was much easier.

Put simply, his argument was that Asia's growth was almost entirely attributable to mobilization of resources, principally people and foreign investment, and not from value-added in the form of productivity, technology, or quality enhancements. As disingenuous as his argument sounds now, it provoked a storm of controversy among insecure Asian government executives and corporate chieftains ensconced in inefficient, protected companies. Singapore's senior minister Lee Kuan Yew—particularly incensed over Krugman's comparison of the Singaporean economy with that of the old Soviet Union under Joseph Stalin—took to regularly thrashing Krugman and his argument. Criticism, as usual, was principally spin-based, not factual: Krugman didn't understand Asia, Asian values accounted for Asia's success, his data was wrong. All of this, of course, made Krugman an extraordinarily famous media star—especially in Asia; he was the economist who stood up to Lee. Consequently, Lee began to read and talk quite a lot about productivity and innovation.

And Lee wasn't the only one. Other analysts joined the bandwagon, warning that "many Asian countries have depended on a plentiful supply of relatively inexpensive labor for their development, but they have neglected productivity considerations" ("Asia Must Address . . . ," 1998). In truth, Singapore and Taiwan have consistently allocated substantial resources to research and development, and investment in R&D in Japan is substantially higher than that in the United States. But this is incremental R&D that enhances existing technology, much of which is imported. Taiwan, Singapore, and Malaysia have invested with considerable success in basic research, but it has not produced a "big bang" product.

Because increased productivity, Krugman notes, is "primarily due to increases in knowledge," by 1998, most of Asia found itself not only in severe crisis, but without the resources it desperately required to boost productivity in difficult times. Thereby it was unable to improve the competitiveness and value-added of fat Asian conglomerates and other uncompetitive companies who were beneficiaries of protected marketplaces. Asia found itself with very few alternatives to increase its "knowledge," let alone manage it.

Krugman illustrated in alarming prose how serious this situation was. "Singapore's growth has been based largely on one-time changes in behavior that cannot be repeated," he wrote. "Over the past generation the percentage of people employed has almost doubled; it cannot double again. A half-educated workforce has been replaced by one in which the bulk of workers has high school diplomas; it is unlikely that a generation from now most Singaporeans will have Ph.Ds. And an investment share of 40 percent is amazingly high by any standard; a share of 70 percent would be ridiculous.

"But it is only when one actually does the quantitative accounting that the astonishing result emerges: All of Singapore's growth can be explained by increases in measure inputs. There is no sign at all of increased efficiency." As a result, Singapore, he predicted, "is unlikely to achieve future growth rates comparable to those of the past" (Krugman, "The Myth . . . ," 1994).

And with very low unemployment and high levels of foreign investment, what would be the source of Singapore's growth? This is where the contribution of Krugman's Ph.Ds and knowledge workers in general would come into play. Singapore—and Malaysia and Hong Kong, in particular—must learn to "think" more, in the manner of Sony's engineers working away at creating original products like VCRs, Walkmans, and digital cameras.

Ironically, the panic that characterized efforts to understand and resolve Asia's financial crisis eclipsed Krugman's productivity argument. While it is understandable that priority was given to stabilizing Southeast Asian currencies, ultimately it became evident that even that problem required movement in the direction of financial systems reform and corporate restructuring. And productivity issues would be central to efforts to restructure private-sector organizations. The

Standard Chartered Bank released a report in August 1998 that argued for "more thought to enhancing productivity in order to further enhance competitiveness" in Hong Kong. "The report said talk about Hong Kong's lack of competitiveness because of high costs and a strong currency is 'misplaced.' Drastic depreciation of the Southeast Asian currencies has not enhanced the competitiveness of the countries concerned, but destroyed financial stability and wiped out companies and banks" ("Bank Calls Productivity . . . ," 1998).

This is an argument Michael Porter is fond of making. Porter views currency devaluation, for instance, as a component of worsening poverty that, along with downward pressure on wages, prices, and profits, contributes to loss of foreign investor confidence as well as the immediate relative higher cost of imports. Worse, developments make productivity enhancements even more difficult to undertake, contributing to lagging productivity and increasing downward pressure on wages, prices, and profits. Increasing the value of currency, in contrast, puts pressure on corporations to boost productivity.

The struggle of Japanese corporations with a strengthening yen in the 1970s and 1980s clearly shows that Porter is correct. Automobile and electronics manufacturers invested heavily in productivity-enhancing technology and systems to dramatically lower costs of productions. From this challenge emerged such landmarks of modern management as just-in-time manufacturing and inventory control. Japanese factories were rapidly automated to further lower costs, and subcontractors were pressured to introduce their own cost-saving, technology-based productivity programs.

In the case of the Asian financial crisis, the pressure to boost productivity was uniform across the region's most troubled economies, principally because the entire region suffered currency meltdowns in tandem. But the pressure was greatest on Singapore, where devaluation was much less severe than in the rest of Southeast Asia, and especially in Hong Kong and China, where currency values were maintained artificially. High taxes on outward-bound remittances kept a lot of investment in Singapore, a fact infrequently discussed in the debates over currency controls. China relied on currency controls, and

Hong Kong—with the moral support of China—stuck resolutely to its United States dollar peg, while conveniently forgetting other principles of free market dynamics in its effort to punish currency speculators.

None of these countries, however, found weaning domestic corporations from straightforward input mobilization to productivity-led growth an easy task, in the same manner corporations found the switch to strategy-led growth a complicated matter. For corporations, the notion that market leadership didn't necessarily translate into profitability was a huge conceptual leap. For governments trying to stabilize and reposition their economies for growth, the idea that simply putting more people to work would no longer translate into impressive growth in GDP was, likewise, a major obstacle to reform.

For example, Hong Kong Chief Executive Tung Che-hwa promised early in his administration "to change the economy into one more dependent on high value-added real enterprises, such as software development companies, biotech firms, and commercial research labs, and less on stock and real estate speculation," according to the authors of an Asia Society report, *Hong Kong: The Challenges of Change*. The report said the chief executive "by temperament abhors a speculative economy in which people get rich quickly through luck and market acumen, not hard work and real innovation" (Lian, 1998).

Although it can be argued that market acumen represents value-added, transforming a speculative economy—particularly one in as unique circumstances as Hong Kong—into a true high value-added economy also requires very bold brushstrokes. When Tung used those brushstrokes—by announcing a plan to accelerate construction of government-subsidized housing, thus driving down real estate costs overall—the Hong Kong taipans who were used to growing enormously rich through real estate speculation howled. And as a result, the stock market plummeted. Despite the increasingly stark realization that Hong Kong's artificially high real estate values—the British colonial government had limited land auctions, keeping demand high—could not be sustained, the taipans had too much at risk to go quietly along with Tung's plans. In the meantime, there was little indication that they were restructuring their businesses into more sustainable, value-added orientations. It was the small and more entrepreneurial firms that would fill the productivity and innovation gap. So, the major obstacle to reform was not just conceptual, but political and perceptual as well.

The Case of Café de Coral

Meanwhile, Café de Coral's Chan was adding value to his business by cutting processing costs. In conversation with Chan, he explained he was centralizing food processing for the restaurants, a process that was expected to take up to twenty-four months. When completed, Chan expects to realize savings of about 2 percent over the next two to three years. Automating food processing will realize increased efficiency by limiting waste, and will enhance productivity by reducing the number of people in stores.

At the head office, Chan has also shepherded the chains through a reengineering process that shaved approximately 1.5 percent from costs over three years. He expected to realize a similar decline in costs as the company entered the next phase of this exercise. "Reengineering at the head office caused a 'cultural revolution,'" Chan said. "Everyone had gotten used to doing things a certain way. By removing redundancies and enhancing productivity of staff, we achieved significant savings." The program cost Chan US$10 million, but provided an excellent, and necessary, return (Interview with author, May 6, 1998).

The Case of Shangri-La

In Singapore, the struggle was less against entrenched taipans than it was against the government labor union. This tiny nation's union movement is, like most everything else, government-managed. As a result, the National Trade Unions Congress (NTUC) is itself an impressive business conglomerate, operating a frightening array of businesses ranging from supermarkets to taxi services. Why a union is in business is an interesting question, but that would distract from the principal argument.

The tight labor situation in Singapore resulted in two developments, both of which would become major issues for government as a
result of the Asian financial crisis. First, a seniority system developed
that not only provided security of tenure, but allowed low-level, low
value-added workers to receive compensation commensurate with
more critical positions purely on the basis of longevity of service. Second, large numbers of low- and high-value workers were recruited,
ranging from domestic workers to software engineers.

As Shangri-La's hotelier John Segreti said, tight labor conditions
resulted in absurd organizational and productivity anomalies, such as
a janitor with twenty-five years' history with the firm pulling down
pay equal to college-educated front-desk personnel. But it was worse
than that. Mid-level executives who had been holding the same position for a decade or more were being compensated at levels that did
not reflect their contribution to the organization, nor to profitability.
Just longevity.

That was bad enough. Because employees and executives like these
knew that there was virtually nothing that could be done to reprimand
them or to provoke improved performance, the quality of service—
Shangri-La's pride—began to deteriorate rapidly during the final years
of the Asian miracle. As the crisis set in and tourism began to falter,
the low productivity and out-of-sync cost of these employees became
apparent. "In Singapore, the longer you're around, the more you
make," Segreti says, "but lower productivity means more benefits expense" for the hotel. It also resulted in some "pretty crazy titles" as the
company struggled to differentiate roles of new and long-term
employees doing the same jobs.

But the problem is, what do you do? Although some multinational technology firms had fired large numbers of workers, particularly disk drive manufacturers, in the days leading up to the
crisis, no respected Asian company—especially a fixture of Asian success such as the Shangri-La—had ever retrenched significant numbers of employees for any reason. And like most other Asian
conglomerates, the Shangri-La was "a very patriarchal company,"
according to Segreti. However, when the choices came down to

profitability or continuing losses, it was clear that changes would have to take place.

Segreti had his mandate, but it was not one he relished. He first had to ask himself, "Who can I trust to help me with this?" And as he looked around at his executive committee, it was clear that the entrenched interests it represented would quickly undermine the reforms he had in mind. For close to a quarter of a century, many of these employees had watched general managers come and go. For them it was fine if the general manager wanted to act like he was in charge, so long as he didn't really try to take charge.

That situation was allowed to go on for so long, Segreti says, because "if you've never known bad times, you're not used to reacting. Labor was never an issue. If you had a problem, you threw labor at it. But over the years, of course, the cost of labor skyrocketed." Segreti knew enough about Asia and people management not to force necessary change upon the organization, but to empower his executive ranks.

"I don't compromise. But I put things in the local context. I got a local group of executives to implement the charges by empowering them to accomplish goals." For Segreti, that group was a reconstituted executive committee (Hamlin, 1999).

Once assured of the support he would need to implement drastic reform in the way the hotel was operated, Segreti then set out to make Singapore history by retrenching 188 employees at a cost of S$7 million. That move made Segreti the subject of relentless media attacks over several months. Media in Singapore is closely aligned with government, and the unions and the government are one and the same. The attacks, therefore, didn't come as a surprise.

Segreti was able to stand fast during the most difficult period of the retrenchment because his bosses were among the first Chinese families to embrace a much more corporate outlook toward business as a result of the crisis. This is clear in the people they hire and, as Segreti demonstrated, they are not afraid to embrace new ideas. As a result of that commitment to a new style of corporate management, Segreti has been able to make significant investments in productivity-enhancing technology, as well as redesigning systems and procedures.

He has established a tradition of pay for performance in Asia's most important and impressive hotel chain, in place of the old system of rewarding loyalty. After all, what's loyalty worth when the benefits only work one way?

The second issue Singapore and its companies would have to address was the need for imported labor. On the lower end of the scale, Singapore imports most of its menial labor. Singaporeans generally refuse to do many of these tasks, driving up the cost of labor for unskilled and low value-added employees. As the Asian financial crisis began to impact the Singapore economy, it became difficult to justify these costs. On the higher end of the scale, knowledge workers were more important than ever, but there was an increasingly short supply, as Singapore competed for talent with other regional and Western economies. Of all of the region's productivity problems, this would be the most serious and long-term.

The Case of Overseas Chinese Banking Corporation

Overseas Chinese Banking Corporation was experiencing a similar problem: Security had bred mediocrity rather than excellence. The company was finding that good people were too impatient to wait around for key positions in a seniority-based corporate structure. As a result, the bank instituted a performance-based appraisal system featuring key performance indicators that are measured regularly. The system also provides for variable bonuses, variable incentives, and share option schemes based on performance. OCBC is clearly serious about performance and productivity.

They are so serious that in 1995—one of the bank's best financial years—top management called in international consultants McKenzie & Company to look at returns, customers, and products with a view to boosting returns on investment and profitability. That analysis didn't lead to retrenchments, but it did result in redeployment with more people on the front lines where they count, according to sources knowledgeable of Singapore's secretive banking industry.

Like many organizations during the Asian miracle years, OCBC grew a bureaucracy in the back rooms that, instead of supporting the front line, was holding it back. The bank decided it needed fewer people supervising the people who were making money, and more doing just that on the front line.

The front line itself was evaluated. Analysts believed they had found the front line's network to be too big. As a result, the bank reduced the number of branches it operated from fifty-eight to forty-eight, and more were scheduled to go in 1998 before a top management change in September. Pervious to the McKenzie study, OCBC had allowed financial subsidiaries to operate independently. Following the study, the subsidiaries were made into branches. When that happened, it seemed clear that a number of redundant branches were feeding off each other.

But the bank's real problem wasn't redundancy, but a lack of competition between branches, resulting in low productivity and profitability. Removing branches wasn't revitalizing the bank; it was strengthening the culture of security and mediocrity it had hoped to dismantle. With profitability increasingly under assault as a result of the effects of the Asian financial crisis, it was clear that cutting itself to growth wasn't a viable strategy. OCBC needed to grow.

To make it grow, the family-owned bank broke from tradition and recruited an outsider, Alex Au Siu-Kee, to become its new chairman and chief executive. Formerly vice chairman and chief executive of Hong Kong's Hang Seng Bank, Au is considered by many to be the father of Asian retail banking. That's quite a distinction in a region where banks have traditionally relied on commercial banking and investment in government securities for profits.

Au also had experience with stodgy old banks. He transformed Hang Seng from an institution that prided itself on its low-profile conservatism into a retail powerhouse boasting 8,000 employees and 147 branches. But Au also built on fundamental strengths: high liquidity, strong capital base, and lean cost structure. Profit growth came from expanding, not shrinking, its network and by focusing on profitable customers and expanding the business that Hang Seng did with them.

Like he did at Hang Seng Bank, Au was also looking for ways to boost productivity and profits at Hang Seng, including exploring new delivery channels such as Internet banking. Although OCBC has more people on the front line than ever, it also has more branches with no people whatsoever. Fourteen branches are now completely electronic, yet full service, providing not just deposits and withdrawals, but passbook updating and other previously labor-intensive services. The bank's marketing line for these services: "Anytime, anywhere, anyhow."

Through the Internet, customers can already check balances and transfer funds, and the bank is working on key e-commerce initiatives that will include more productivity-boosting services.

However, OCBC continues to struggle with the effects of the Asian financial crisis. In 1998, profits plummeted 27 percent as a result of provisions made for expected loan losses, and "covering its exposure to Indonesia, Korea, Malaysia, the Philippines, and Thailand. The provisions rose 65 percent from the previous year" ("Oversea-Chinese Banking's . . . ," 1999). But significantly, operating profit rose 7.2 percent.

The Case of SM Supermarket

Despite the effects of the Asian financial crisis, Roberto D. San Juan of SM Supermarket—a subsidiary of giant mall developer and retailer Shoemart—says sales at SM Supermarket were up 20 percent in 1998. If new stores were added, growth rockets to 60 percent. But the long-term impact story at SM Supermarket is how technology is revolutionizing manufacturer/supplier-retailer relationships, boosting productivity, and lowering costs for both sides.

For many of the reasons Segreti said seniority-based appraisal didn't work well in Asia, most reengineering efforts fell short as well. First of all, people were used to throwing people at problems, and mediocrity was so prevalent that a lot of bodies were thrown at the problems to make sure they were adequately addressed. Gross inefficiency reigned as a result, and nowhere was that inefficiency more prevalent than in manufacturer-retailer relationships.

This was a problem for both sides, says San Juan, but it was especially serious for manufacturers. Because of delays in receiving feedback on retail sales, stock outages and overstock situations were prevalent in the industry. Without more timely information, it was virtually impossible to closely mirror supply to demand. As a result, supply lagged behind demand, with the result that sales were lost. As interest evaporated, when supplies arrived, they didn't move.

Procter & Gamble and Wal-Mart pioneered electronic commerce and close cooperation between manufacturer and retailer to avoid such circumstances, as well as to lower transaction costs and accelerate response times. While casual observers wouldn't be surprised to see similar relationships at work in Hong Kong or Singapore, they probably would be surprised to see how rapidly e-commerce is evolving in Asia's emerging economies. In SM Supermarket's case, more than 150 suppliers are already connected electronically.

Real-time feedback to manufacturers allows for better planning of production cycles. For the manufacturers, it allows more precise allocation of resources depending on market conditions and response to new product offerings. For retailers, quality of service and products is enhanced by the assurance of regular supply of popular items that are well within recommended shelf-life parameters.

Electronic transactions take a number of forms. In SM's case, actual electronic purchase orders are issued to manufacturers or their distributors. Confirmation of receipt is automatically generated by the manufacturer and an order number assigned. Any changes that take place in the order by SM are automatically updated, improving the percentage of orders delivered correctly, even with last-minute changes. Notice of dispatch is sent to SM electronically, and SM later acknowledges delivery electronically. In some cases, invoicing is also accomplished electronically, as is notification of remittance to the supplier's bank.

Such changes provoke enormous cultural upheaval within organizations. Enterprise resource planning (ERP) solutions like these frequently require that whole businesses rework their operations processes. For one reason, real-time data entry is making many support positions redundant. For another, today's ERP solutions make it impossible for some business functions to take place until their logical precursors have occurred and have been entered in to the system. That doesn't mean that they shouldn't take place, of course. On the contrary, there's obviously little choice. But that doesn't make them easier.

THE MAIN POINTS

There are two dramatic changes that are being driven in Asian corporations by the need to enhance productivity. The first is the transition from pay-for-loyalty to pay-for-performance. The second is the introduction of very advanced technology. These changes are taking place rapidly because of the crisis, globalization, and liberalization. And they are provoking enormous cultural revolutions within corporations and economies.

There is considerable resistance to changes like these, both within governments as well as corporations. Government opposition to economic reform and corporate restructuring in Indonesia ultimately became a major contributing factor to bringing about the sudden removal of former President Suharto in Indonesia. Disagreement over reforms in Malaysia resulted in a deep chasm between Prime Minister Mahathir Mohamed and former Deputy Prime Minister Anwar Ibrahim. The threat from Anwar was so great, in Mahathir's view, that Mahathir resorted to the sort of crude disinformation campaign to discredit his former deputy possible only in circumstances where media and the freedom of expression is tightly controlled. As a result, conditions under which productivity and competitiveness remain low were perpetuated.

But as Indonesia had already found, there would be no turning back the clock of reform and free market liberalization, although Mahathir had dramatically slowed the process, with severe consequences. In early 1999, despite government attempts to spin the economy, "industrial production remained in decline, loan growth had yet to pick up, nonperforming loans were growing, and the important property sector was still suffering from a huge oversupply" ("Analysis: . . . ," 1999).

Although the changes taking place in Asian economies and companies elsewhere were wrenching, they were also essential to safeguard the prosperity of future generations. For many, it was too bad that times had to change, but that wouldn't hold reform back long. As one report argued, "If Asian companies are to emerge from the region's current slump leaner and more competitive than before, they will have to get the most of their workers" ("Pay and Productivity: . . . ," 1998).

THE NEW INNOVATION

Prior to the onset of the financial crisis, not many managers in Asian corporations felt their firms were very innovative compared to multinational corporations. The most innovative Asian corporations, at least in the eyes of their beholders, were found in Australia and the Philippines, according to the *Far Eastern Economic Review*'s "Managing in Asia" survey (see Table 7.1). Thirty-one percent of respondents agreed with the statement, "Local companies are more innovative than multinational companies," for Australian corporations. The number for the Philippines was 26 percent. Indonesia followed closely with 25 percent. Only 14 percent of the respondents felt

Country	Percent Response
Overall	19
South Korea	19
Japan	16
Taiwan	19
Philippines	26
Hong Kong	19
Thailand	15
Malaysia	16
Singapore	14
Indonesia	25
Australia	31
Asian Expatriots	20
Non-Asian Expatriots	14

Table 7.1. "Local Companies Are More Innovative Than Multinational Companies."

Source: Far Eastern Economic Review, Managing in Asia Survey, 1998.

that Singapore companies were more innovative than multinational corporations.

Clearly, there are some problems with these numbers, especially considering the response from Japan (16 percent). But for years, Japanese have been told that they are not really very innovative, but very good at adapting and optimizing technologies and products for particular circumstances. And what of the considerable number of respondents that felt two of Asia's most slowly developing economies, Indonesia and the Philippines, are actually more innovative than multinational firms?

There are companies in both countries that demonstrate an impressive level of innovation. In the Philippines, Jose Ledesma's St. Luke's Hospital is one of them. The surprising innovations he has incorporated will be discussed further on. It comes as no surprise that two of the Philippines' most enterprising entrepreneurs, fast-food chain Chow King's Robert Kuan and Jollibee's Tony Tan Caktiong, sit on Ledesma's board, or that Kuan is the chairman. To take the relationships further, Tan is Kuan's partner in Chow King. These entrepreneurs have a knack for identifying what consumer desires are not being met, and then filling the vacuum. They're helping Ledesma do the same thing in his industry, healthcare. It's interesting that fast-food principles of innovation can find application in a hospital!

Indonesia, for all its repression of entrepreneurial creativity and its funneling of opportunities to Suharto's friends and family, is not without its creative oases, but they are admittedly a bit hard to find. One is Bluebird Taxi. This company has revolutionized service quality in its industry by its innovative approach to building relationships with both clients and five-star hotels, where it stations much of its fleet. Despite repression during the Suharto administration, the Indonesian media has also proven to be a stubborn beacon of creative resilience, both editorially and graphically. A company with the memorable name of Great Giant Pineapple Company has capitalized on the entrepreneurial fervor of its founders to capture a large slice of the multinational-dominated pineapple business, a solid source of foreign exchange during Indonesia's tough times.

But one should not lose sight of the fact that most managers of Asian corporations just don't consider their companies very innovative compared to their multinational competition. When considering that productivity enhancements frequently represent the flip side of innovation, this resource shortfall becomes even more serious. In *Asia's Best* (1998), significant levels of innovation among Asia's best-managed firms were observed. But innovation principally took the form of marketing, promotions, and, in a few cases, development strategy. One company that has excelled in both cases is the Philippines' Smart Communications.

When Smart entered the Philippines' recently liberalized telecommunications marketplace, it did so with its eye not on the 300,000 or so wealthy individuals that could afford to own cellular phones, but the millions of Filipinos considered too poor to think of paying airtime charges, let alone actually purchasing a cellular phone. So rather than provide a pricey service targeted at the same customers every other provider was going after, Smart decided it must provide an extremely cost-effective service that would appeal to laborers, salespeople, and rank-and-file employees. To keep costs down, the company relied on analog technology rather than the sexy digital cellular alternative other new market entrants were introducing. Then, Smart initiated a volume-based pricing strategy that would set the market on its ear, and they promoted the service aggressively. As a result, Smart zoomed to market leadership within three years.

That was a smart strategy. Success stories like this help make up for the fact that Asia has very little potential for developing innovative, value-added products in either the manufacturing or service sectors. To understand why, it is necessary to go back to Paul Krugman's argument centered on total factor productivity. Krugman argues that Japan—whose development experience has little in common with the rest of Asia—"is staging an unmistakable technological catch-up" (Krugman, 1994, Internet edition) with the United States, but that the pace of that catch-up is slowing for the same reason that Southeast Asia was unable to sustain its rapid growth: Productivity and efficiency enhancements are lagging behind the more creative United States economy.

So the obvious question is, "How do we create an innovative environment?" In a subsequent chapter, it is theorized that educational infrastructure has a lot to do with the capacity to innovate. Value-added innovative industrial clusters in the United States are generally located in areas where education infrastructure complements private-sector research initiatives. But there is more to creating innovative culture than educational infrastructure. If Asia is to wait on infrastructure development for the innovation it needs to spur industrial growth, the outlook for fully resuscitating Asia becomes bleak indeed.

Asia must devise a means to breed innovation into its organizations if they are to prosper in the face of crisis, liberalization, and globalization. Luckily, innovative organizations are not waiting around for their governments' support.

The Case of St. Luke's Hospital

A hospital is not exactly the site one would expect in a discussion of Asian creativity and innovation. That just proves how fallible it is to rely on stereotypic first impressions. Jose Ledesma's hospital is one of the most innovative organizations to establish itself in twenty-five years of observing Asian enterprise. Because the educational hotbed of innovation isn't available in the Philippines, Ledesma takes his quest for innovation to the centers of innovation in the United States.

Ledesma is a regular visitor to key American medical facilities and equipment manufacturers. During his tenure at the hospital, he has institutionalized the consistent acquisition of state-of-the-art medical technology. As a result, Ledesma says that "people are amazed to learn what's available in the Philippines." What's so innovative about regularly importing technology? The technology is still developed elsewhere. While the technology is important for Ledesma, it is not for its sake alone that he is such a busy acquirer. "It makes it easier to recruit young Filipino physicians when they know they will come home and have the same technology" (Hamlin, "The New Competitiveness," 1998).

For Ledesma, innovation and productivity lies not in the technology itself, but in the people who use and develop it. While many Asian companies struggle to retain their best executives and knowledge workers in the face of relentless recruitment efforts from Western and multinational companies, Ledesma is taking the battle for brains into their own backyard. Ledesma finds that maintaining state-of-the-art technology has other intellectual input advantages as well. "It makes real exchange of experts possible," he notes.

In the same way that Filipino physicians don't want to practice in an environment devoid of state-of-the-art equipment, it is impossible to invite leading physicians from other institutions to visit the hospital and demonstrate their experiences with technology if that technology is not present. So Ledesma also sends physicians for training in the United States. Many Asian institutions are reluctant to send physicians for training because of the temptation to remain longer than planned to expand studies and even to take new employment opportunities. Ledesma believes that the knowledge that state-of-the-art equipment is back home relieves some of that temptation. So far, he's never lost a physician to the temptations of life and study in the United States.

Benchmarking the technology of American hospitals is not limited to equipment for Ledesma. "Most people say that St. Luke's is the cleanest hospital in town; yet, we are definitely far from satisfied and say that we are still dirty because we benchmark against the best hotels in terms of cleanliness. Our billing system has greatly improved, yet we are far from satisfied because we benchmark against American Express in terms of their billing system and especially in terms of their always protecting the customer from unwarranted charges. This is one of our major strengths," Ledesma says of the hospitals benchmarking tradition, "always knowing that the best can be made better, and exerting every effort, every human and financial resource, to make ourselves better" (Interview with author, September 17, 1998).

It has already been noted how Ledesma leverages his benchmarking exercises to recruit and train physicians and to facilitate international exchange. He uses this practice in other innovative ways as well. For example, "we looked at room amenities at hotels, and found that the best hotels offered television with cable facilities, refrigerators, fax machines, computers with Internet connections, business centers, etc. We determined that we can do better than hotels. Color television sets, refrigerators, and telephones have always been standard amenities for our private rooms. Now, our suites have computers with *free and unlimited* Internet access and individual e-mail addresses, fax machines, VCR players, microwave ovens, in-room billing review, and even menu selection for those with normal diets. Our business center offers secretarial and messengerial services not only for patients but also for doctors. A concierge is also available for all patients."

Does that sound like any hospital you've ever visited?

Ledesma relates a story about an experience he had recently in a five-star hotel in the United States. He went to the concierge to request that a typewriter be brought to his room, which was not equipped with a computer or fax machine. The concierge told him bluntly that the hotel did not make typewriters available to guests and advised him to visit a nearby copy center. When Ledesma returned to the Philippines he told his assistant to make sure that never, ever happened in the hospital. If the "guest" wanted a typewriter, even if one had to be taken temporarily from the administration offices, the guest was to get one.

To most of us, St. Luke's undoubtedly looks quite a lot more attractive than most hospitals. Ledesma knows that amenities alone stand no chance of distinguishing his hospital from the competition in the realm of life-and-death technology, but they do show just how seriously the hospital takes the "guest," and not only his or her medical needs. Many specialists believe that emotional health and mental happiness are frequently major contributors to good physical health. While amenities may not create happiness, the comfort they provide certainly makes a contribution.

Most notable is how Ledesma has leveraged investment in state-of-the-art technology to lure some of his country's best medical minds back home to work and train other physicians. While each of Ledesma's innovations can be emulated, including this one, it will take his resolve to do so. More importantly, in the meantime, Ledesma will be way on his way to his next innovation.

The Case of Henderson Land

While Hong Kong's chief executive was pledging to maintain the American dollar peg for the Hong Kong dollar in mid-1998, real estate values showed no sign of recovery. Already down 40 percent, some analysts argued that values were going to decrease even further. When Hong Kong became the Special Autonomous Region, it merged irrevocably—and to its detriment economically, at least for a time—with China. That change in status meant that Hong Kong changed overnight from a colonial outpost, the world's most competitive economy, and a window to China—a status for which there was no pretentious contender—to that of a Chinese city competing with every other Chinese city. There's an easier way to say this: There's nothing special about Hong Kong anymore, except its past.

Plummeting property values created huge headaches for developers, as well as the purchasers of developed properties. For developers, there were at least two problems: convincing potential home-owners that prices had hit rock bottom and helping purchasers who had signed up to buy properties at pre-crisis prices obtain loans to cover the obligation. "Banks base mortgages on current market value, not the purchase price" (Wong, 1998, p. 3). Afraid of being caught in the same asset deterioration trip, Henderson Land, a major Hong Kong developer, needed an innovative plan that would convince buyers to act right away.

That plan evolved into a financing package offering price guarantees. "The guarantees amount to a bet by Henderson that Hong Kong's sliding property prices will rebound. Under the program, if the market price for the new homes is below the current purchase price in two years, Henderson will cut the amount due to be repaid on its loans to buyers by as much as 22 percent of the total sales price" (Wong, 1998, p. 3).

Henderson first offered the guarantee to new purchasers at 10 percent of the total value of the home, but quickly lowered the price to 8 percent when competing developers offered other incentive plans. While it is a gamble—some analysts expect prices to fall significantly over the two-year period before the new homes will be revalued—

Henderson's plan is intended to generate badly needed revenues now. If the gamble fails, Henderson will likely have given up its entire profit and more on the developments. But in the meantime, Henderson stays in business, generating fresh revenue streams for future business.

The Case of TAL Apparel

Long considered a low-tech, low value-added industry, as we saw with Li & Fung, top garment manufacturers in Hong Kong are taking garment manufacturing high-tech. They are making big profits as a result of original R&D and taking on more of the supply chain, from design to retail. "They provide a model for Asia's other aging industries, be it toys or footwear" (Granitsas, 1998, p. 52), supporting economist Michael Porter's thesis that traditional industry can be high value-added industry, too.

Hong Kong's garment industry has quietly become a major export: US$22 billion worth in 1997, "a seventh of the world trade in apparel." Much of the work of actually manufacturing garments takes place outside of Hong Kong, up to 80 percent by some estimates. "But the nucleus, and the profits, remain firmly in Hong Kong." TAL Apparel was founded in 1947 and "employs 17,000 garment workers in factories in Hong Kong, Thailand, Malaysia, Taiwan, and China" (Granitsas, 1998, p. 53).

What is particularly remarkable about TAL, however, is its reputation. "TAL is best known for its investments in R&D, and its manufacturing muscle. It makes and sends more than 23 million men's dress shirts to the United States each year from its factories in Asia—that's the equivalent of one in every eight shirts sold in the United States annually. And in recent years, TAL has spent US$2–3 million annually on R&D" (Granitsas, 1998, p. 53).

The investment has paid off. The company has received two patents on new wrinkle-free clothing technology, according to managing director Harry Lee, "and we have six more pending" (Granitsas, 1998, p. 52).

INNOVATION IN ASIA

Examples like these show that innovation is alive in Asia. Although it is principally tied to soft areas, such as promotional strategy and the like, the innovative application of technologies is slowly beginning to have some of the impact Asian companies require to boost productivity and efficiency. News of new surgical procedures developed by St. Luke's bright young physicians in the next few years won't be much of a surprise. Hong Kong's garment manufacturers are already applying new technology to new products and managing a dynamic extended-value chain. Although original research budgets remain very small (compared to the percentage of revenues invested by leading multinational corporations), Asian companies are establishing an important tradition reliant on original technology.

Nevertheless, if Asia is to sustain resurgent growth once recovery takes hold, it will have to rise to the challenge of productivity enhancement increasingly based on indigenous innovation. So far, only Japanese and Taiwanese companies have demonstrated the commitment and resolve necessary to accomplish that goal. For now, Japan has reached an impasse and hasn't figured out how to leap the next development hurdle toward installing fundamental, original technology across industries. Taiwan still shows promise.

Emulating the creative chaos of the world's hot beds of innovation is a huge challenge for Asian governments and corporations. Contributing to and benefitting from that process is a requisite goal. As Asia transitions into what was supposed to be the Asia-Pacific Century, more companies must acknowledge the importance of investing first to realize those dividends.

CHAPTER EIGHT

The Second Source of Competitiveness: Market Intimacy

C ustomer intimacy guru Fred Wiersema advises companies to "stop thinking in worn categories" in order to visualize who their customers are. "People—changeable and volatile—not stable categories, buy products and services." Wiersema believes that demographic categorization of market segments and customers "blinds us to the heart of the question, which is: 'What makes these customers potentially good people to connect with?'" (Wiersema, 1996, p. 127.)

Wiersema and other management experts, such as Slywotzky and Morrison, suggest that a better understanding of why customers are good people with whom to connect takes on new significant strategic importance in highly competitive markets. Slywotzky and Morrison argue that this is because competitiveness has become a much more complicated issue than it was in the past. For example, competition based on quality, or "industry leadership," as Wiersema and consultant Michael Treacy, co-author of *The Discipline of Market Leaders*, say, is difficult to sustain, in part thanks to increasingly affordable hard and soft technology. As GE's Jack Welch learned, it was not enough to be number one or number two in each industry segment in which it operated. Motorola, for example, demonstrated that it could compete on the basis of quality with Japanese manufacturers such as NEC and Mitsubishi. Nokia and Ericsson in turn showed that they too could humble Motorola. The result of this dynamic is that the mobile phone and pager industry must continually demonstrate incremental product enhancement to sustain industry leadership. But the rewards are also becoming consistently thinner and thinner.

Neither is productivity, nor cost leadership, easily sustainable. Wiersema calls this "best price." The Internet has made best price competitiveness an incredibly elusive goal, providing customers huge arrays of choices in books, cars, computers, flowers—virtually anything. Whole industries are suddenly commoditized. Ayala Corporation's Rufino Luis Manotok, head of strategic planning, said in response to a survey given by the author, "The fast evolution and convergence of information and communications technologies is empowering corporate and household customers, giving them not just more information and choices, but also allowing them to compare products and prices faster and cheaper—or at nearly zero cost! More and more, as customers become more educated and aware of the choices before them, we have to improve our ability to respond to their needs better and faster." Again, efficiency, quality, and productivity have emerged as basic requisites of being in business, rather than sources of competitive advantage.

Companies competing on these bases assumed that broad demographic categories of potential customers would want the best quality or the best price in specific, desirable product categories. As competition increased and returns on market share expansion contracted, it became clear that broad demographic categorization provided virtually no indication of what particular customers—especially the most profitable customers—really wanted, because that information didn't describe the customers or their circumstances. Neither did it provide insight into what related areas of customer needs corporations could potentially meet. In order to increase the amount of business companies did with their customers, they needed to know them better. They had to become customer intimate. When they did, they would be in a better position to provide what Wiersema calls a best total solution (see Table 8.1).

As discussed earlier, Singapore's Excel Machine Tools' business model has evolved to reflect its increasing orientation to best total solution in order to improve its interface with customers. This was the natural result of the company's business model evolution. The model originally initiated closer working relationships to compensate for "holes" in its product line. Instead of waiting for orders, the company began to participate in designing factory floors and work lines, including recommending equipment manufactured by its competitors that would work best for the client. The strong client relationships that developed continued to pay off for the company as it expanded its own product offerings as the result of a major strategic acquisition.

As Wiersema warns, Excel's focus on best total solution does not mean that quality and productivity are not important. On the contrary, they are fundamentals that make Excel a major player in its industry, while its best total solution makes the company an industry leader. To sustain industry leadership, Excel works hard at introducing new technologies (such as laser and hydro cutting technologies) and boosting productivity. Remember, Excel's executive vice president Wee Yue Chew hires three people for every four that he needs. But Excel works even harder at understanding its customers, and at understanding what it can do to help make its *customers'* businesses successful.

Best Quality	Best Cost	Best Total Solution
Product leadership	Operations efficiency	Market intimacy
Constant incremental enhancement	Constant incremental improvement	Constant expansion of related services
High levels of innovation and creativity	High productivity	High levels of relationship building

Table 8.1.   Value Disciplines.

ASIAN EXAMPLES OF QUALITY, COST, AND TOTAL SOLUTION LEADERSHIP

One doesn't have to look very far to find other examples of quality, cost, and total solution leadership in Asian firms. Let's take another look at some of the firms that have been examined in this study. Table 8.2 shows which "discipline," as Wiersema and Treacy call it, is the priority for these firms. The table also shows how the other disciplines play important roles in these organizations.

In some instances, what might be called discipline focus is in transition. For example, in recent years, Ayala Land has diversified into low-cost housing from its traditional residential, office, and retail development projects, which were marketed on the basis of quality at top-of-the-market prices. Increasing prosperity in other market segments, as well as near saturation and significant competition in the top end, has made this "new" segment attractive to the company.

The transition from high-end to low-cost housing poses several problems for Ayala. The first of these is the process of developing a new business model. Head of strategic planning Rufino Manotok says, "What keeps us on our toes is the continuing change in competitive dynamics as business models are upturned by economic realities and new technologies. The continuing challenge to us is maintaining market and industry leadership amid a more competitive environment and, from time to time, difficult economic conditions" (Response to author survey, 1998). In 1998, Ayala purchased low-cost housing developer C&P Homes. The initially well-received deal turned sour when difficult economic conditions pummeled both stocks. The new partnership would have significantly enhanced Ayala's position in the low-cost segment. After agreeing to purchase 38.4 percent of C&P at ₱2.25 a share early in the year, the shares were trading at ₱0.50 in September, when Ayala announced that the companies had agreed to suspend talks amid rumors of surprises during due diligence. Publicly, Ayala said it was impossible to justify acquisition of the stock at the pre-agreed price in view of its decrease in value over the subsequent few months.

Company	Best Quality	Best Cost	Best Total Solution
ABS-CBN Broadcasting	**Programming**	Efficient	Varied offerings
Alphatec Semiconductor manufacture and testing	Reliability	**Competitive**	One-stop shopping
Ayala Land Property development	**Premier developments**	Low-cost housing	Integrated development
Cycle & *Carriage* Auto retail and service	**Mercedes, Mitsubishi, Proton**	Hedge certificates of entitlement	Product range
Bangkok Insurance Insurance	**Comprehensive**	Competitive	Varied product offerings
Café de Coral Fast food	Innovative menu	**Affordable meals**	Menu rotation New chains
Excel Machine Tools Precision machining tools manufacture	Precision	Competitive	**Array of related services**
Jollibee Fast food	**Filipino food**	Affordable	Family orientation
Kang Yong Electrical appliances	World-class	Competitive	Product line
Petron Petroleum refining, wholesale and retail	**Service**	Competitive	Total care
Purefoods Food processing, distribution and retail	Ingredients	**Competitive**	Array of products
RFM Food processing, distribution and retail	Packaging and promotion	**Competitive**	Array of products

(*continued*)

Table 8.2.   Asian Leadership Examples.

Company	Best Quality	Best Cost	Best Total Solution
Shangri-La Hotel Accommodations	*World-class*	Competitive in segment	Business and leisure facilities
Sime UEP Properties Property development	**Innovative**	Low-cost housing	Integrated development
Singapore Airlines Transporation	Young fleet	Competitive	**Nurtures relationships with best customers**
Smart Communications Telecommu-nications	Network reach	**Aggressive**	Cellular, land, and paging services
St. Luke's Hospital Medical services	**Best equipment and top physicians**	Socialized pricing	Array of services
Thai Farmers Bank Banking services	Service	IT banking	**Varied product offerings**

Table 8.2. (*Continued*).

Note: Bold indicates area of emphasis by Asian firms.

The plan had been to capture "a window into the low-cost housing market, where demand for housing is high. 'They [would have] gotten a low-income (housing) business in the shortest possible way,' says Iva Gutierrez, an analyst at DBP-Daiwa Securities Philippines. She explains that if Ayala Land had begun from scratch, it would have taken the company a long time to penetrate the low-income segment" (Reyes, 1998, p. 13). One analyst said the acquisition would have increased Ayala's 1998 profit from their previous forecast of ₱5.57 billion to ₱6.03 billion.

The second challenge for Ayala will be operations. Michael Porter argues that it is very difficult for one company to lead in highly contrasting market niches, even in the same industry. To illustrate his argument, he cites the failure of major "full-service" airlines to compete with the United States's Southwest Airlines. Southwest Airlines is probably the most successful short-haul, no-frills airline in the history of passenger service. It is so successful, Porter says, because operations are finely attuned to fulfilling the airline's mission of providing low-cost, dependable service (see Table 8.3).

In fact, large United States airlines such as United, Northwest, and American found it so difficult to reconcile systems that small feeder airlines were established as independent subsidiaries, autonomous divisions, or alliances with completely separate organizations. None, however, have worked particularly well. They persist because of their role in "feeding" passengers into the majors' profitable full-service system, however. This continues to distinguish these small networks, which exist to support larger systems, from Southwest Airlines, which neither requires support nor supports larger, full-system airlines.

Southwest Airlines	Typical Full-Service Airlines
Point-to-point (no hubs), short-haul service between medium-sized cities and airports	Hub and spoke system centered around major national and international routes and airports
Very low prices	Complex fare structure ranging from high-priced, "regular" tickets geared to business travelers to non-refundable "economy" promotional fares for advanced ticketing
Automated ticketing; limited use of travel agents	Ticketing through large sales staff and extensive use of travel agents Sophisticated computer reservation systems linking multiple airlines throughout the network
Limited passenger services	Full passenger services including multiple seating classes and assigned seats, beverage and meal service, movies and in-flight entertainment, baggage handling and transfers, and connections
Standardized fleet	Mixed fleet to accommodate varied flight lengths and route demands

Table 8.3.   Southwest Airlines Comparison.
Source: Porter, Michael E. "What Is Strategy?" from On Competition. Boston: Harvard Business School Press, 1998, p. 48.

Porter notes that these uneasy relationships also exist in other industries, such as furniture, where Ikea has perfected a similar low-cost business model that is wholly distinct from more typical furniture manufacturers.

For Ayala, the question is whether it is possible to reconcile low-cost housing operations with middle and high-end developments. There are clear operational implications—such as procurement, quality and productivity standards—but more than contrasting operational priorities must be reconciled: corporate culture and values, training and personnel skill sets, and marketing thrust, to name a few.

Then there is market perception itself. Specifically, will Ayala's foray into low-cost housing affect the market and perceived value of the company's premier developments? Or conversely, will the company's reputation for high quality at premium prices put its low-cost housing projects out of reach in the consumer's view? These are tough issues that many large, global firms are also struggling with. For example, luxury German automobile manufacturers like Mercedes-Benz have or plan to introduce low-end compact models. Large hotel chains, such as Marriott, have tried to diversify across market segments to serve both luxury and economy segments.

The rationale for such strategies is clear. As Ayala found out from observing the competition, margins may be lower in the low-end side of the market, but the market is very large. But can a company like Ayala, for the three reasons already discussed, effectively compete in a dramatically contrasting industry segment? Ayala is determined to find out, and the logic for doing so is hard to resist. If it is successful, Ayala Land will have transformed itself from a company focusing principally on quality leadership to one that emphasizes best total solution.

In fact, Ayala Corporation already provides total solutions in its existing segments by providing insurance and financing to purchasers through other group companies, commercial developments near residential subdivisions, and utility services. But even in the provision of those services, substantial contrasts will be experienced when these support services are retailored to the low-cost housing segment. Loans and insurance policies will individually represent smaller returns on resources expended. Development and maintenance costs for water and other utilities will likewise increase in terms of return on investment and asset utilization. Does that mean Ayala Land should avoid the low-end segment? Maybe, but let's first examine the compelling argument for segment diversification.

As the Asian financial crisis winds down and the estimated 80 percent of the Philippine population that is "poor" begins to enjoy the benefits of increased prosperity, massive demand for low-cost housing will emerge. Economists Jeffrey G. Williamson and David E. Bloom of the Harvard Institute of International Development suggest that the Philippines is posed to enter a bonus phase of demographic transition as its dependency ratio declines and "the working-age population grows faster than the nonworking-age population," which means there will be "few mouths to feed per worker and [that] the size of [the] working population is growing" (Goad, 1998, p. 1).

With a population of somewhere in the vicinity of sixty-five million, at least ten million Filipino families presently fall within the 80 percent of the population that cannot afford to own a home. If just one-half of one percent of those families each year are able to obtain the jobs necessary to qualify for government-subsidized low-income housing loans, 50,000 new homes a year will be required. Many of the families that obtain this housing will be relative newcomers to the workforce, and therefore relatively well-educated.

Indeed, "'South Asia should see a 0.8- to 1.4-percentage-point increase in its growth rate as it leaves the burden stage of the demographic transition and enters the gift stage,' say the [Harvard] economists. 'The biggest gainer will be the Philippines while the biggest losers will be Malaysia and Thailand'" (Goad, 1998, p. 1). Providing the government doesn't stumble too badly and this GDP boost is realized, despite low margins, it is clear that the prospects for high growth in low-income housing are great. That in itself offers potential for developers, which is admittedly hard to pass up, even for adherents to

Porter's argument that the contrast between segment demands bodes ill for companies that attempt demographic diversification.

But an even more intriguing question is how many of these increasingly prosperous families, as they trade up, will elect to stick with the developer, who built their first houses? And that's not an easy question to answer either.

It depends on any number of variables, including perception of prestige, which is one of Ayala Land's clear strengths, before it actually enters the segment in a meaningful way. But for purposes here, the important variables will be customer satisfaction or delight in his first home-owning experience, the nature of the after-sale relationship with the developer, and the incentive offered to encourage trading up.

There's very little data anywhere, and especially in Southeast Asia, that suggests that home ownership provokes any reasonable degree of loyalty toward developers. In fact, that is not the nature of the business, although like with any other industry there are prestige perception benefits that are important. However, the perception of prestige does not represent a high barrier to entry for other developers. Thus, there is very little relationship-induced loyalty in the industry.

For Ayala Land to transform itself into a best total solution for the lifetime of home owners, then, the company must truly accomplish something unique in its industry: customer delight. That is the principal long-term challenge for Ayala Land: What mix of services, support, and incentives will be sufficient to encourage customers to make a lifetime commitment to the company?

DISCIPLINE CONCENTRATION

Now that we've had a chance to look at and think about how the three disciplines—best quality, best cost, and best total solution—work in one Asian company, let's go back and look at where some of the previously mentioned companies stand. More important, it is interesting to examine where many of them seem to want and need to go in response to crisis, globalization, and liberalization. It becomes evident that many companies are moving toward best total solution, while safeguarding and building on quality and productivity gains.

BS-CBN Broadcasting

ABS-CBN is part of a very large Philippine conglomerate that has interests in energy generation and retail, water and transportation infrastructure, telecommunications, banking, and broadcasting. Chairman and CEO Eugenio Lopez III is the oldest son and the reigning patriarch of the family. The Lopez family was essentially thrown out of the Philippines—and its businesses—during the Marcos administration. After the People Power Revolution in 1986, the family reentered Philippine business, recovering control of Manila's principal power distribution source, the Manila Electric Company, and other companies such as ABS-CBN, which quickly prospered.

Quality programming was sadly and sorely absent from the Philippine broadcast industry during the Marcos years. ABS-CBN believed that viewers were craving innovative programming, and that advertisers would be willing to pay a substantial premium for the enhanced viewership expected to follow. They were right, and ABS-CBN shot to the number-one position in most timeslots and stayed there.

Although the Philippine constitution prohibits foreign ownership of media, the broadcast industry is extremely competitive. This is primarily because unlike most of Asia, the Philippine press is not controlled by the government and hasn't been since the overthrow of Marcos. As noted earlier, after the resignation of Suharto, the Indonesian press changed dramatically when heavy-handed government controls were lifted. Likewise, the Thai media has been mostly free of government intervention as democratic institutions have strengthened. But this is certainly not the case in Singapore, Malaysia, and Asia's other developing economies. Even among the region's leading economies, it is rare to see the independence in media that is taken for granted in Manila.

There are six major television broadcasters in the Philippines. Although ABS-CBN dominates the industry, there is at least one real competitive threat, GMA, which led the industry during the Marcos years. The rivalry between the stations has been fierce. Talent and production staff under contract to one broadcaster are prohibited from working for another. If a producer comes up with a good idea, he does not have the right to sell it to another broadcaster, as independent producers are able to do in the United States, for instance. ABS-CBN has looked at quality of homegrown productions as a major source of competitiveness. As a result of that emphasis, the corporation has successfully syndicated some of its programs outside the Philippines. Its own broadcasts are received by satellite in neighboring countries, and its newscasts are a source of reliable news.

Eventually, in response to increasing competition in the industry for talent, ABS-CBN began to think about its business model. The inspiration came from hitting a quality wall that presented a major dilemma to Lopez. Although the company had made great strides in improving quality, Lopez felt that productions were not moving into the world-class range fast enough.

Ultimately, it became clear that ABS-CBN was a victim of its own success. It had led the market for so many years by such a substantial margin that the pressure to perform wasn't there any more. The company needed a way to rekindle the fire of innovation and imagination. Lopez realized that one reason production quality was so high in other countries was that producers were independent. They had to come up with ideas that they could sell to competing studios. And they had to follow through on their ideas to get top dollar for their productions the next time around.

The dilemma for Lopez was that in the Philippines, like the original American movie studios, talent was closely guarded. No actor or producer was allowed to work for another studio. Lopez wondered if the quest for quality and creativity meant giving up control over these resources, control that formed an important part of the competitiveness of his company. Finally, he decided that it might be possible to enjoy the best of both worlds.

Instead of paying handsome salaries to actors and producers, Lopez decided to pay fairly basic wages. The real money would come when actors "sold" themselves to producers, and for producers, when they produced a hit that would bring in top-dollar advertising revenues. But everyone was still under contract with ABS-CBN and couldn't go to work for the competition. As a result, nonperformers were more quickly identified and left on their own, while solid performers— especially in the economic sense—were potentially unlimited in terms of the returns they could generate for themselves. For Lopez, ABS-CBN was once again moving incrementally up in quality levels to that point where he could justifiably proclaim his productions world-class. He calls this a "free market system within the ABS-CBN system."

Still, Lopez understands that his business model and its resultant quality can be emulated quickly and easily. Ultimately, the choice will be to live with the pressure of consistently coming up with major hits, or to live with increasingly thinner margins as rivals compete for advertising revenues, or to find other ways to capture new audiences throughout more of the viewing day. Once again, demographic data tells Lopez that he will have an increasingly productive market to please. As Wiersema warns, the audience and consumers will change as time patterns, family structure, and interests adjust to new circumstances.

Those adjustments are already becoming apparent, most visibly in motion pictures, rather than television productions. In the past few years, despite more subjects being taught in the Tagalog vernacular and a general decline in English competency, English-language movies have begun outshining Tagalog movies at the theaters. The problem, according to Lopez, is quality. Filipinos are demanding better movies, and because they are not getting them from local production outfits, they are switching to big-budget, English-language films produced with the global market in mind.

Quality is not so much a problem of budget, according to Lopez, but rather where the budget goes. Thirty percent goes to the government in the form of an entertainment tax. Then there is another 10 percent in value-added tax. "That means a film that costs ₱20 million to make has to bring in ₱40 million to break even," Lopez, a graduate of the Harvard Business School, explains. "And I don't know of any movie that makes ₱40 million these days." Lopez says he's left with about thirty centavos out of every peso to cover costs and pay more tax, this time on the income.

Lopez knows this is a problem of quality, and not language, because his Tagalog productions do not demonstrate the same pattern. But because he can't increase the share of customers through quality motion pictures, what does he do? The answer to that question, Lopez says, lies in working with government, which he admits, "scares me." But he is encouraged because the president is a former actor and "understands the problem."

If he is successful in getting the entertainment taxes removed or reduced, will Lopez have transformed his business model from quality discipline centric to best total solution? Strictly speaking, no. He will have changed it back. The company has always made movies, but was forced to concentrate on television production for two reasons: 1) low returns on motion pictures due to excess taxation; and, 2) television production became the battleground for the industry, and forced the chief beneficiary of ABS-CBN's decision to compete on the basis of quality. Ironically, to improve his business model, Lopez must go back to the past for inspiration. He'll need a lot of inspiration to get government off the back of the entertainment industry, even if it is run by a former movie star. However that episode turns out, it's a safe bet that conditions in the marketplace will continue to change rapidly, and with them, Lopez's business model.

Cycle & Carriage

The Asian automobile industry is one of the principal targets of the Asian financial crisis. Several years ago, Cycle & Carriage finance director James Riley accepted the third in a series of awards on behalf of the firm for management excellence. One would have expected him to be ebullient. Instead, he was almost sullen, explaining that winning awards was dangerous because it made people complacent. That attitude may have been another good reason why the company deserved an award.

Cycle & Carriage retails automobiles principally in Singapore although the company sells cars throughout Asia. It holds the franchises for Mercedes-Benz, Mitsubishi, and Malaysia's national car, the Proton. Although the Asian financial crisis badly dented sales— down 80 percent in Malaysia in 1998, for instance—Riley believes that it will not be the crisis that drives business model development in his industry, but the industry itself—specifically, technology and the manufacturer-dealer relationship.

Technology is changing the nature of this relationship because it makes the manufacturer less dependent on the dealer to sell cars. Thanks to the Internet, buyers can quickly canvas dealer prices and negotiate an aggressive deal. But even more direct to the point, the buyer can conceivably connect direct to the retailer, obtaining the factory price, specifying what options and modifications he or she desires, and indicating to which dealer the car should be delivered. The dealer would then receive a nominal fee—perhaps half of its normal markup—to prepare the car for final delivery and provide warranty servicing.

Does that mean that car retail is now a commodity business, albeit a mass customized one? Yes, it probably does. Does that remove the element of service as a competitive advantage? No. "We are a service business," Riley explains. "We have an in-between role," he says, that makes quality of service—customer delight—the principal source of competitiveness in an industry renown for its big-name luxury players and quality throughout its product lines. Cycle & Carriage goes up against competition Riley characterizes as the world's toughest. Along with technology that competition has increasingly made customer relationships the deciding factor in new-car sales.

At another level, competition includes other dealers. With buyers empowered by the Internet, quality and consistency of service will become the principal determinants of success. Buyers will know exactly what they are paying the dealer for, and they will expect to be delighted in return for the privilege of selling him or her an automobile. It's unlikely that dealers will disappear in Asia, but those that survive will learn how to astound their customers with service.

Singapore Airlines

Singapore Airlines (SIA) is practicing its own brand of market intimacy. When this icon of Asian service was learning to dominate the Asian airways, it focused on maintaining a young fleet of impeccably serviced aircraft and superior service in the air. Only after it had done these things did the airline realize that it had undermined its impact on the customer by not providing comparable service on the ground. Ground service was "the weak link" in SIA's chain of quality, according to spokesman Rick Clements.

Now, the company is working on both air and ground services, continually searching for ways to boost customer satisfaction on Asia's most successful airline, even during the crisis. Instead of postponing approximately US$300 million to overhaul and upgrade aircraft and airport facilities during the Asian financial crisis, Singapore Airlines not only pushed through with the enhancements, but undertook a major marketing blitz to announce them while the rest of the industry was hemorrhaging. The effect: "No other airline in Asia can compete with an investment of this size," one analyst said. "When the economy turns around, they will be able to charge more" (Lipper, 1998, p. 3).

Being able to charge more for service is a distinction the airline shares with Cycle & Carriage. And what service! Business and first-class passengers check in at special lounges in Singapore, similar to procedures for regular clients at five-star hotels. On newly refurbished 747s, "the number of leather-trimmed seats in first class has been reduced from sixteen to twelve, allowing passengers up to 1.9 meters to sleep flat on their backs. Each passenger in the wood-appointed section has his or her own 36-centimeter video screen—the largest on any international airline—to watch video channels. Meals are delivered upon request" (Lipper, 1998, p. 3), rather than according to arbitrary schedules.

Even economy-class passengers share in the delight. They are offered free champagne and better seats. Like in first class, the number of business-class seats has been decreased "and adjustable reading lamps and privacy screens have been added"(Lipper, 1998, p. 3).

Analysts believe that the airline is making the upgrades—while delaying orders of new aircraft to save on costs—to remain competitive with North American and European airlines. But SIA seeks more than parity; it wants customers to feel right about spending a premium to fly on a phenomenal airline. Although revenues for the airline were down sharply during the Asian financial crisis, it remained profitable, something its most important competitors in Asia weren't able to accomplish. While there may be other reasons for that than the degree of customer satisfaction the airline achieves, satisfaction remains a big part of the equation. This equation is based on the capacity of the airline to convince more people to travel with SIA even when other, more cost-effective alternatives are available. Customer satisfaction is built on perception of value, not lowest cost. SIA is becoming expert not just at providing the value, but communicating it, too.

THE MIGRATION TO
BEST TOTAL SOLUTION

Each of these cases indicates a migration to best total solution discipline in response to shifting profit zones, increasing competition, and new rules of competition within industries (see Table 8.4). This is a strategy for expanding relationships with profitable customers. For Ayala Land, traditional markets are more competitive and near saturation, at least for the time being. It needs to find new, younger customers, and keep them all their lives as they develop and prosper.

ABS-CBN raised the quality bar in Philippine—and Asian—broadcast production and journalism. But as democracy and liberalization

Shifting Profit Zones	Traditional sources of competitiveness, such as quality and productivity, have been emulated
Increasing Competition	Consumers have more choices due to technology and the Internet
New Rules of Competition	New business models prioritize share of customer over market share

Table 8.4.   Reasons for the Shift to Best Total Solution.

spread across the region and provoke increased competition in media, competitors will benchmark global industry leaders the same way ABS-CBN does. To offset that competition, Lopez is trying to catalyze an innovative cultural transformation that will produce programming across a broad spectrum spanning news to entertainment. He is also working to boost returns on the production of motion pictures by lobbying for reductions in clearly onerous taxes, further expanding the opportunities for ABS-CBN to capture a greater share of customer.

For Cycle & Carriage, the competition is world-class—comparable in quality and reliability. Margins are getting thinner, and buyers are becoming more powerful. James Riley's response is to seduce his customers with a level of service that becomes a key variable in subsequent purchases. Customer satisfaction results from intangible yet off-the-chart customer care. Riley knows clients are willing to pay to be pampered.

Riley predicts another first for Asia and Cycle & Carriage. Clients will purchase their automobiles right off the Internet, including picking the color, options, and delivery date. If a car in stock can be modified to fit the order, it is delivered immediately. If not, a factory at a strategic location is alerted automatically and the particular automobile is built to order.

Singapore Airlines knows, too. To make the alternatives to flying SIA less appealing, the airline has introduced—despite incredibly challenging economic times—a level of service that rivals the best five-star hotels in the world. The difference is between boarding an airplane and stepping onto an executive jet—but with loads more space. The company's focus is on most profitable customers, those who can travel in style. But even in economy class, the emphasis is on value, not cost.

As previously discussed, many companies have dramatically rebuilt their business models in response to new conditions. Others have merely adjusted their business models to reflect new priorities. Excel Machine Tools, like Cycle & Carriage and SIA, is a service business that, incidentally, makes some of the best precision tools in the world. On the other hand, Hong Kong's fast food company Café de Coral has shifted priorities from store or branch expansion to increasing the volume of business it does with its regular customers. The solution was simple—and contradictory—to fast food philosophy: Rotate the menu three times a week. Important innovations come from simple ideas, like using a computer to type, a network of computers to shop, and a smart computer to tell you who your most important customers are.

The signs that best quality and best cost are on their way out as priority disciplines for value-added companies in Asia are everywhere. But as companies begin to shift priority to best total solution and sustained relationships with clients, the challenge for many companies will not be discovering who the most valuable customer is, but realizing that each of these customers is unique and expects something special.

St. Luke's Hospital in Manila is proud to have developed a corporate culture that caters to the demands of high-achieving CEOs, for instance, who stay in the hospital's state-of-the-art internetworked suites. In terms of medical services, an array of executive check-up packages is provided that covers most imaginable combinations of medical inquiry. But any package can be further customized to reflect the executive's— or his or her company's—concerns. As noted earlier, Jose Ledesma is determined to create a culture in which no service request—within legal and ethical boundaries—is too off-the-wall for the hospital. To fulfill those requests, he has created a concierge function that operates exactly as a concierge at a five-star hotel—only better. Executives may choose their meals from a menu, and eat when they like.

Even in an industry as mundane as consumer foods, companies like RFM, while sticking to the core business, diversify across product lines to grow revenues. But how does a company that produces canned meat and fish, for example, develop a sense of customer intimacy? For RFM, relationships are built on popular moods. Although RFM is a well-established Philippine conglomerate, it created for itself an image of an upstart, entrepreneurial Filipino firm taking on the big boys— Coke and Nestle—and winning. Consumers were not just proud of RFM, they were proud of their country.

IN SUMMARY

Finally, one of the most remarkable companies examined here is, unbelievably, a privatized oil company. Once again, this is an example of resourceful thinking in the Philippines, at significantly state-owned Petron Oil Corporation. During the Ramos administration, 40 percent of the company was sold to Saudi-Aramco and 20 percent to small investors. The remaining 40 percent is expected to be sold to a second strategic partner.

Petron is the largest oil company in the Philippines. Its principal competitors are Shell and Caltex. As an indication of how well-operated the company is now, consider this. Several months into the Asian financial crisis, the oil industry liberalization law was declared unconstitutional by the Philippine Supreme Court. As a result, the oil companies were not allowed to raise oil prices following the steep devaluation of the peso. In the middle of a presidential election, the companies found themselves selling thousands of barrels of petroleum products at a loss.

Because it could do nothing about the pricing and couldn't withhold the product from the marketplace, Petron focused on operational efficiency. It did such a good job at tightening up operations that when the three oil companies announced 1997 losses, Petron, the largest of the three, had the smallest loss. This and other changes at Petron prompted the country manager of a multinational competitor to remark that Petron was now on his radar screen, whereas under government ownership, Petron was not even considered a serious competitor.

The Saudi-Aramco partnership has worked well for Petron. One of the reasons why is the company's overriding concern about competitiveness and the future. Because it is impossible to distinguish its commodity products from the competition in terms of price or quality (although some marketers persist at trying), Petron, a very large oil company in an industry known for not taking very good care of its customers, identified seven competencies that it would strengthen. They are as follows:

1. Entrepreneurial spirit

2. Critical thinking

3. Commitment to excellence

4. Team orientation

5. Empowerment

6. Adaptability

7. Customer intimacy

Petron says that ethics provides the anchor for these seven competencies. Of the seven, customer intimacy stands out. In an age of super stations where fuel is pumped into the automobiles, trucks, and utility vehicles of thousands of faceless customers, why is an oil company thinking about customer intimacy? First of all, a number of major oil companies have tried to learn how to take better care of their customers, and all have generally failed. This includes Shell, which is considered an enlightened competitor with deep intellectual underpinnings. The company has produced many respected strategic and human resource thinkers. And in Southeast Asia, Shell has a reputation for effectively developing its employees into world-class workers and technicians who function extremely well in teams. But most customers probably haven't noticed.

They are beginning to notice at Petron. And so are bigger customers such as dealers, large corporate accounts, and distributors. Suddenly, Petron cares about them. "Innovation is the only way to survive," president and CEO Ali A. Al-Ajmi says, and customer intimacy is definitely an innovative approach to business in the oil industry. One of the signs of the level of innovation is the introduction of gasoline stations that resemble a small town square, a first in the Philippines. New stations provide banking services, fast food outlets, a convenience store—and gasoline, of course. Even air-conditioned toilet facilities.

Funny? Yes. Important to customers? *Yes.* When Shell executives came to check out the new station, Petron managers say they spent an unusual amount of time in those toilets and were overheard talking about them on their way back out to the car. Once again, customer intimacy doesn't always require big decisions—it just requires attention to customers. For proof, just ask any parent how important a clean, air-conditioned restroom is after being stuck in a car full of tired kids on the way back from vacation.

But like quality and productivity, customer intimacy is constantly benchmarked, as the visit of the Shell executives demonstrated. As author and consultant Frederick Reichheld found, it translates immediately into increased profitability. Continual enhancement of the corporation's capacity to satisfy customers by providing services and products that demonstrate a concern for them and their individual needs is more than basic good sense. As Al-Ajmi says, it's the only way to survive.

PART FOUR

Pressing Asian Realities

CHAPTER NINE

Training and Education: The Innovation Factor

~~~

It's clear now that the Asian economic crisis was a financial panic that grew into an enterprise crisis. The International Monetary Fund—and dithering by United States president Bill Clinton when his leadership was urgently required—helped promote the crisis by trying to cure something it didn't understand with remedies it did. But as was the case in previous financial crises in South America, Mexico, the United States, and Japan, Asia was ultimately responsible for its problems.

The Asian values euphoria helped convince government officials and corporate chieftains alike that they could have growth without responsibility. In other words, there was no need to pay a price for the benefits of globalization. It was a free lunch. But of course, there are no free lunches. Abusing the benefits of globalization exacerbated the effects of the trade-offs.

Has Asia been irresponsible in other areas? And will there be a price to pay? The answer to those two questions is yes. The next big crisis for Asia will be a people crisis, which will evolve from an inadequate supply of trained and educated managers, engineers, technicians, scientists, and programmers. In the same way that Asian governments and companies assumed that growth had no price or risks, they ignored the need to develop the competencies required to transition from assembly and contract manufacturing to high value-added businesses. The only way to increase value-added is to apply knowledge to products in the form of innovative technology, processes, and systems.

Asia will struggle with this transition not because multinationals hesitate to transfer technology, but because Asian governments, for the most part, have not provided the educational infrastructure necessary to produce the people who will add value. Unlike the economic crisis, curing the educational crisis is not a matter of reform and restructuring to restore confidence, nor is it a matter of recapitalizing troubled institutions. It is a matter of substantial long-term investment to create institutions, acquire equipment, and recruit faculty.

THE ROLE OF INTELLECTUAL CAPITAL IN ECONOMIC DEVELOPMENT

"The research facilities of our universities," United States Federal Reserve chairman Alan Greenspan said in a 1999 talk, "are envied throughout the world. The payoffs [from investment in higher education]—in terms of the flow of expertise, new products, and startup companies, for example—have been impressive. Here, perhaps the most frequently cited measures of our success have been the emergence of significant centers of commercial innovation and entrepreneurship—Silicon Valley, the Research Triangle, and the clustering of biotech enterprises in the Northeast corridor—where creative ideas flow freely between local academic scholars and those in industry" (prepresentation remarks at Dallas Ambassadors Forum, Dallas, Tex., April 16, 1999).

The importance Greenspan, as the money manager for the world's number-one economy, places on the contribution of education to economic well-being suggests that education—and the quality of education—is every bit as important to emerging economies as the quality of their infrastructure, the competitiveness of their investment incentives, and the stability of their governments.

The connection between investment and education, according to Greenspan, shows up in gross domestic product gains over the past century, which have averaged around 3 percent per year. "Only a small fraction of that represents growth in the tonnage of physical materials—oil, coal, ores, wood, raw chemicals, for example. The remainder represents new insights into how to rearrange those physical materials to better serve human needs" (Dallas Ambassadors Forum, Dallas 1999). The incidence of such insight, Greenspan and others argue, is proportional to public and private sector investment in education, training, and research. "The history of education in the United States traces a path heavily influenced by the need for a workforce with the skills required to interact productively with the evolving economic infrastructure."

Likewise, writing in the February 25 issue of the *Far Eastern Economic Review,* Harvard University economist and director of the Harvard International Institute of Development Jeffrey Sachs said that Southeast Asia must, for the sake of longterm prosperity, make significant investments in education. "East Asia will restore its competitiveness in world markets only if the investments in social software are now given their due priority," he argued. "Most of Southeast Asia is deficient in higher education, science, and technology."

Like Greenspan, Sachs believes that investment in social software must keep pace with investment in hardware and equipment to realize real and meaningful returns. Those returns are ultimately dependent not on the hard resources—increasingly available to anyone—but, as Greenspan implies, on how those resources are used. Their use, ultimately, comes down to local brainpower, or indigenous intellectual capital. "FDI [foreign direct investment] can't substitute for local scientific talent," Sachs warns.

Neither Greenspan nor Sachs are the first to argue that a sound economy and economic resurgence are so highly dependent on the quality of education. Neither is Sachs the first to say that the gap in social software investment in Southeast Asia is perilous. Research by the International Institute for Management Development and the

United Nations Development Program shows that in terms of research and development as a percentage of gross national product and numbers of scientists and technicians per one thousand persons, investment in education in Southeast Asia is dwarfed by advanced economies (see Figure 9.1).

That's not an excuse for low levels of investment for the Philippines, Malaysia, Indonesia, and Thailand. Both India and Pakistan perform substantially better in both categories. So does the People's Republic of China. Even Singapore performs only slightly better than India. Inci-

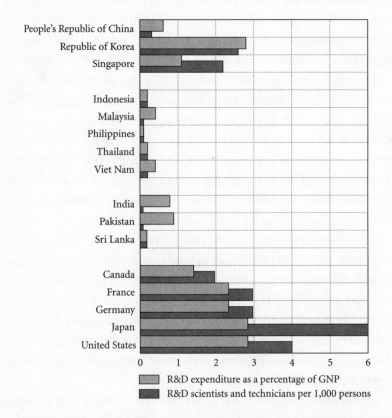

Figure 9.1.   The Status of Research and Development Capabilities, Selected Countries and Years.

Sources: International Institute for Management Development (1996) and United Nations Development Programme (1997).

dentally, South Korea leads the region, and Japan leads the world, a good indicator of the eventual resurgence of both those economies.

It was noted earlier that despite Southeast Asia's humble investment in education, the products of that investment—bright, young Southeast Asians—are being heavily recruited by companies in developed economies. This is because there are an estimated 190,000 unfilled jobs in the United States technology sector alone. Despite huge investments in education and research, the vibrant United States economy must also absorb much of Southeast Asia's meager intellectual capital base to sustain growth. This growth is the product of innovative resource utilization.

There are benefits to losing intellectual resources to developed economies for Southeast Asian economies. For example, the value-added of the intellectual resource increases as Southeast Asians go to work in many of the world's leading enterprises. If Southeast Asia succeeds in creating new opportunities for these individuals, it is likely that they will bring that value-added back home, as many of Taiwan's scientists and engineers have. Another benefit is that a significant portion of the earnings of these knowledge workers is repatriated back to their home countries to support family. Those earnings—along with the wages of domestic and labor workers scattered around the world—were critical to the integrity of the Philippines' financial markets during the height of the Asian financial crisis.

But as consultant Richard Farson argues, those strengths can also become weaknesses, or excuses, that handicap prospects for long-term prosperity and the attainment of economic potential. Even massive recruitment of Southeast Asian graduates by developed economy firms—bringing about the great irony of emerging economies in a sense underwriting developed economies—cannot be an excuse for failure to adequately invest in local educational infrastructure.

Investment in education creates opportunity at home. First, investment in education increases the attractiveness of the work force and demonstrates to investors that the Philippine workforce has the capacity to take on higher value-added work than traditional low-tech assembly and manufacture. Companies do look ahead to determine where the talent will be. Bodies alone count less. They must be knowledgeable and trained workers.

Second, investment in education contributes to the development of what we call competency zones. The "significant centers of commercial innovation and entrepreneurship" that Greenspan refers to may be the product of creative capitalist zeal, but that zeal is fostered—or capitalized by—effective higher learning. "If we are to remain preeminent in transforming knowledge into economic value," Greenspan said, "America's system of higher education must remain the world's leader in generating scientific and technological breakthroughs and in meeting the challenge to educate workers." Every major industrial cluster is accompanied by an educational infrastructure that supplies a steady stream of research and a pool of charged-up knowledge workers anxious to achieve something phenomenal.

Third, investment in education develops a national propensity for taking calculated risks, or a willingness to test individual limits. By doing this, those limits are continually stretched. Each of these cases demonstrates the qualities of leadership. To deny investment in education, which is a vital strategic priority, is to hobble future prospects for playing a significant role in the regional economy.

To justify investment in education in an emerging economy with many profound social needs, it is critical that national leadership effectively communicates the value of knowledge creation. As economies struggle toward prosperity, it is difficult to attach economic value to such things as "the most conceptual and impalpable of all new major products—software," as Greenspan says. Software is an impalpable but significant step from education, where the notion of conceptual value ultimately resides.

Communicating the priority education should have is not just the government's job. It is also the private sector's responsibility. "Education is increasingly becoming a lifelong activity," Greenspan noted. "Businesses are now looking for employees who are prepared to continue learning and who recognize that maintaining their human capital will require persistent hard work and flexibility." Education and training is not a cost to the private sector; it is an investment.

Executives in Asia frequently complain that they invest significant sums in education only to have key employees leave. But the choice not to educate is the choice to remain embryonic in a global marketplace. As any industry-leading company will attest, that's no decision at all. In fact, training and retaining the very best is a requisite of global competitiveness that is constantly gaining vital importance.

Next, top executives must set the example themselves. It's easy to criticize the charlatans among the world's gurus and consultants and say that they all write the same things. But the fact is that this is usually an excuse for not taking the time or spending the money to enhance the executive's own knowledge bank, or those of the people who work for the company. As a result, everyone loses.

It comes down to this: If we expect to use input more wisely and creatively, we have to learn how. Education precedes competitiveness.

THE NEED FOR EDUCATIONAL INFRASTRUCTURE

Despite the ferocious character of the Asian economic crisis, few predicted that recovery would require more than two to three years, even at the height of the crisis. Two to three years of hardship pales in comparison to the decade, if not more, it will take to develop the foundation for the educational infrastructure most of Asia—particularly Southeast Asia—sorely needs. Ironically, for inspiration, Asia needs to look no further than Taiwan. The tiny island government has established "seventy-five universities that educate more than eight thousand engineers annually. There are currently forty-three research scientists and engineers for every ten thousand people in Taiwan, compared with thirty-three in South Korea and twenty-eight in Singapore.[1] Government research institutes accumulate know-how

---

[1] The National Science and Technology Board of Singapore statistics show that in 1994 the nation had approximately the same number of research scientists and engineers as Taiwan. *Asian Development Outlook 1998* shows slightly over two "scientists and technicians per 1,000 persons."

for exploiting future products, such as devices for conducting Internet commerce, and sell it to local companies" (Kraar, 1998, p. 39). South Korea also followed this approach.

"In 1966 the government established the Korean Institute of Science and Technology to undertake applied research for industry. In the 1970s, the government set up other specialized research institutes in a number of fields. By the end of the 1970s, Korea had sixteen R&D institutions" (*Asian Development Outlook,* 1998, pp. 218–219). Although South Korea has severe yet unrelated problems in its financial and corporate sectors, the investment in technology generation capacity has paid off. "In the early 1970s, the government accounted for nearly three-quarters of the national R&D expenditures, but by the early 1990s, 80 percent were borne by the private sector. Note, however, that because R&D is lumpy and often risky, R&D expenditures are highly concentrated. Estimates indicate that in 1995, twenty *chaebols* accounted for 80 percent of total private R&D in Korea" (*Asian Development Outlook,* 1998), which supports the argument that government plays an important role in helping companies increase value-added.

The research institutes are a method for leapfrogging the educational infrastructure bottleneck, as well as for making technology available at manageable costs. By concentrating limited human resources in dedicated research institutes where their work supports an array of export-oriented manufacturers, particularly technology companies, Taiwan was able to make indigenous technology available to priority sectors relatively early in its march toward industrialization. Instead of a researcher being dedicated to a particular company, he could dedicate himself to a particular industry or related industries, substantially multiplying the effect of his work. This also resulted in high absorption of the results of his work across industries. A single employer would likely pick and choose which part of the researcher's work was appropriate, resulting in much lower absorption rates.

This has been the case with Malaysia's SIRIM Berhad. In fact, the Asian economic crisis has highlighted the importance of the state corporation's contribution to small- and medium-size, or mid-market, industrial sector (SMEs). According to vice president Chong Chok Ngee, SIRIM conducts research into three "strategic technology" areas: advanced materials, process technology, and advanced manufacturing technology.

SIRIM has made important contributions to some of Malaysia's largest firms, but it has also made contributions to smaller firms, due in large part to the fact that "government is generous in funding capital expansion," according to Chong, which makes it possible for SIRIM to offer reduced fees for services for contract research services. In addition to its capital investment in SIRIM, the government also offers grants-in-kind for research undertaken by mid-market enterprises. This means that two-thirds of the cost of research is borne by the government, although the "long-term goal is to reduce reliance on government support," according to Chong.

SIRIM has done some interesting work for mid-market enterprises, according to Chong. For instance, the institute recently developed a new glue adhesive from palm oil. Once developed, the new product was promoted to mid-market enterprises, and the technology licensed to a qualified applicant for M$250,000 plus 2 percent of sales for the first two years. In the third year, the royalty jumps to 5 percent.

The other half of the research and development equation is cost, or investment. To put investment into perspective, it is useful to consider that despite Japan's leadership position in many technologically advanced industries, only in the last few years has it begun to try to match and then exceed the United States in research and development investment. Both countries spend close to 3 percent of gross national product on research and development. Japan now spends more on research, but how far it has to go to achieve a return shows up in the Relative Citation Impact (RCI) index,[2] which measures scientific

---

[2]Like virtually all indexes measuring scientific and research output, RCI has a clear language bias favoring English-speaking countries and English-language journals. However, as most serious research is published in English in international journals for a variety of reasons, the relevance of the index cannot be disputed.

productivity. The index shows that the United States achieved a ratio of 1.42, Japan 0.78. Singapore, the Philippines, Thailand, and Malaysia had RCIs averaging about 0.4 (Bulls, 1998). It's interesting to note that while the RCIs of Singapore, the Philippines, and Thailand have recently been on the upswing, Malaysia's has been decreasing. This suggests that while research institutions like SIRIM are important in introducing technology to mid-market enterprises, they do not address the need for the basic research that creates new products and industries. Malaysia is addressing needs today without investing in the future. The country is not alone in this.

Part of the problem is the capacity to retain the best and the brightest. Frederick B. Kintanar, manager of software design engineering for NEC Technologies Philippines, likes to explain that before the Philippine economy contracted in the early 1980s, the country had approximately 12,000 Ph.D.s engaged in scientific inquiry. By the 1990s, more than half had either left the country or moved on to other jobs. Demonstrating just how hard it is to create that kind of intellectual core, Kintanar says he is skeptical that when a new survey is published in the early 2000s, the Philippines will have replenished its ranks of productive Ph.D.s.

The effect of inadequate investment in educational infrastructure is shown in Figure 9.2. Despite significantly more schooling in the Philippines, for example, economic value-added per employee is much lower than in Singapore. This suggests that either Filipinos are underutilized by the private sector, or that Filipinos have not been provided the skills required to undertake high value-added work. This is probably right on both counts. Filipinos are underutilized because value-added foreign direct investment has not been as successfully recruited in the Philippines as in Singapore, in part because Filipinos haven't been developed to compete in knowledge industries. However, surveys of expatriate managers generally show that workplace productivity of Philippine workers is on par with those in Singapore.

Low RCIs in Singapore and Malaysia, where scientific productivity is actually decreasing, do not signal much confidence in their high-profile race to become Asia's Silicon Valley. It is a serious matter that

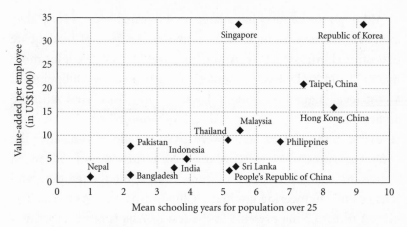

Figure 9.2.　Value-Added per Employee in Relation to Mean Years of Schooling, Manufacturing Sector, Selected Asian Countries, 1990.

Source: Asian Development Outlook based on UNIDO Industrial Statistics Database 1994 & Barro & Lee.

despite spending more than 1 percent of GNP on research and development and a significantly higher number of scientists and technicians than either Malaysia or the Philippines, scientific productivity in Singapore is essentially on par with those two countries. But Singapore is determined to change this.

The Philippines shares the ambition of Malaysia and Singapore to become Asia's Silicon Valley, but likewise has difficulty demonstrating distinctive competitive advantages in the crowded sprint for "Valleydom." For instance, in 1997, the Bureau of Export Promotion estimated that software exports from the Philippines reached the paltry value of US$250 million. If an informal rule of thumb for service industries is applied and that total multiplied by three to US$750 million, it would provide a rough approximation of the equivalent value of hardware exports. That's more impressive, but the Philippines exported more than US$6 billion in electronics in the first half of 1998, mostly low value-added components. Software—technology's ultimate high value-added dreamland—has a way to go to catch up. Joseph Lacson, a Filipino executive in Microsoft's headquarters, doesn't believe that the Philippines has the intellectual infrastructure to become a software center.

Although the country has a large pool of capable engineers, "they aren't suited for very high-value activities" because of inadequate educational infrastructure. And China and India "have a lot more master's- and Ph.D.-level computer scientists than the Philippines at a cost level that's even lower," Lacson notes (interview with the author, May 16, 1998). Not only that, fifty thousand Chinese students studying in the United States were given indefinite visas after the 1989 Tiananmen Massacre. Many have returned with advanced degrees to lead new research ventures comprising the ten thousand science and engineering graduates China turns out every year. The biggest threat China presents to the rest of Asia is not competition for cheap export markets, but its educational infrastructure.

"The Philippines is competing not only with United States cities but with India, China, Singapore, Malaysia, and Eastern Europe. Every plus that may indicate that the Philippines will be a technological hub is shared by a dozen other countries," Lacson says. He should know. Part of his responsibility at Microsoft has been conducting a global competitive evaluation. It will thus be crucial that Asian countries refine their development focus to hi-tech niches they can dominate. Lacson believes that the speed of innovation and huge costs also make it absolutely critical to focus on specific niches of the software industry.

That's advice that Hong Kong, Singapore, and Malaysia—and every other Silicon Valley aspirant—should take to heart.

INVESTING IN EDUCATIONAL INFRASTRUCTURE

People, not economies, develop countries. It is easy to forget that economies are one important part among other parts of what makes a country a nation. The quality of people—and their education, creativity, tolerance, responsibility, knowledge—determine the quality of the state. If investment in people is neglected, the state's growth is stunted. In important respects, Asia's growth has been stunted not just by the Asian economic crisis, but by the failure to provide a development pathway beyond mobilization of capital and labor. This pathway is provided by developing people's capacity to think with originality, and to rely on their thinking to produce innovative approaches to product and business process development.

Competition for Asian knowledge workers urgently requires that Asia make the substantial investment necessary to produce a larger talent pool. Singapore has approached this objective with some degree of ferocity, establishing new institutions and equipping them with Ph.D.s with the same degree of resoluteness it approached development following its separation from the Malaysian Federation.

It is also experimenting with the character of institutions, in a bid to boost the capacity of innovative thinking. Professor Chin Tiong Tan, formerly on the business administration faculty of the National University of Singapore, has been named the deputy provost of a new university, Singapore Management University. Professor Tan says that "the Singapore government has decided that it's time to set up a third university for Singapore." SMU will be a private university and will be United States-based rather than repeating the Oxbridge model of the existing two universities. In a speech given in Singapore in February 1998, Deputy Prime Minister Tony Tan says, "The establishment of SMU will be a milestone in Singapore's university education. SMU's private status will allow for more room for innovation and the testing of new ideas which, if found suitable, can be applied to NUS and NTU," two existing government universities.

When SMU is fully developed, Tan says, "it will have 13,000 undergraduate and 3,000 graduate students. It will be in the city and will offer business-related courses for a start. Wharton has been signed up as our partner." Establishing the Singapore Management University shows that like private enterprise, filling the educational infrastructure gap can be hastened by recruiting outside resources. Singapore also heavily lobbied the University of Chicago Graduate School to set up a permanent campus in Singapore, a partnership that was announced in January 1999. Nanyang Technological University is working with Carnegie Mellon University to offer a postgraduate degree in financial reengineering. This makes sense for both Asia and United States universities and business schools.

Declining population growth in the United States makes identification of new sources of revenue an important goal. Western schools have established a variety of mostly short-term alliances in Asia over the past decade to help meet demand for training and management development. Asia's depreciated currencies also make it harder for Asians to study in the United States. With foreign student contingents running up to 44 percent in top United States B-schools, the implications are serious. "Today, 269,000 Asians—defined as citizens from China, Japan, Korea, Taiwan, and the nations of the subcontinent and Southeast Asia—are getting graduate degrees in the United States. Of these, 16 percent are enrolled in business courses" (Kahn, 1998, p. 39). Those implications are not just directed toward United States institutions. Although the United States economy swallows up huge numbers of Asia's best and brightest, Asia itself is less capable of training its young people than at the world's best schools. The Singapore Management University-Wharton model will have to be molded for other disciplines as well.

Outside of management, there are few instances of collaboration, although Johns Hopkins University will set up a medical school with the Singapore government and "has a joint program with the National University of Singapore" (Borsuk, 1999, p. 6). MIT's Media Lab has collaborated with the Singapore government in the same way that the lab collaborates with private-sector companies with mixed results. The Singapore Digital Media Consortium (SDMC) links the National Science and Technology Board with the Media Lab. But SDMC is merely financing two projects, one a "peer-to-peer communication model for the interchange of digital media," and the other a mass of "several new and promising research areas" ("NSTB: Spearheading Technopreneurship and Capability Development," 1998). That's typical for short-term collaborations, and hazy alliances in general in the private sector, as previously discussed. For better results, it is worth considering a transition from educational alliances to the realm of joint ventures.

Like all joint ventures, someone must be in control. This could be a messy argument when it comes to educating the young generation.

SMU is enlisting Wharton to help, but not to manage or run the new school. Instead, the local, private-sector Singapore Institute of Management will form a new foundation to manage itself and the new university. But at the level of basic research, they will not so much be educating the younger generation as developing a new tradition of research excellence. The choice is clear, particularly for most of Asia, which is significantly less well-heeled than Singapore: educational nationalism or world-class educational infrastructure supporting private enterprise. Like most clear choices, this is no choice at all.

A good number of Western B-schools are following the Wharton example. "Faculty from such universities as Stanford, Northwestern, and INSEAD are taking up residence at campuses across Asia, or running crash courses on finance in corporate conference rooms. Other schools are offering long-distance learning programs over the Internet. The result is that Asians now have more options than ever for pursuing Western-style management education close to home" (Thornton, 1998, p. 78).

But like corporate management, B-school managers are beginning to chaff at the limitations of such partnerships. As a result, "France's INSEAD will invest US$36 million on a school in Singapore similar in size to its Fontainebleau program. Wharton and Northwestern's J. L. Kellogg School are joining forces to found the Indian School of Business" (Thornton, 1998, p. 78). The University of Western Ontario already has a Hong Kong campus.

Other disciplines have yet to receive the attention of the glitzy B-schools, but are no less important. Because Asia has little tradition or experience in the conduct of world-class research, educational joint ventures will provide an invaluable mentoring advantage. Because the joint venture will be designed to develop researchers as well as to conduct research, the programs should be managed by established, respected faculty. The beauty of this is that many of the most prominent research faculty in major research institutions in the United States are Asian, many of whom were part of China's tens of thousands of former students educated in the United States. Educational joint ventures will accelerate the process of bringing this talent back to Asia.

For example, Jose Ledesma's hospital, St. Luke's in Manila, has shown that a medical facility on par with American facilities can effectively woo Asia's best and brightest back home. The same will be true for other institutions.

CREATING COMPETENCY ZONES

Competency zones in high value-added industrial sectors tend to be located near major educational institutions. For instance, the high-technology clusters in California, Texas, and Massachusetts are all located near the world's most respected research facilities. Efforts in Asia to develop similar clusters have lacked such facilities. The key here is that the research facility must come first, not the cluster.

Clearly, for Asia to seriously attack the problem of productivity and innovation through development of educational infrastructure, it must do more than just create institutions staffed with Ph.D.s. It must create institutions staffed with some of the best Ph.D.s in the world. The only way to attract that kind of talent is to do it by wooing the institutions that serve as repositories of the world's most important intellectual capital.

A third beauty to this proposal of forming educational joint ventures is that it will rapidly speed the development of educational infrastructure by leapfrogging the decade required to create the research leaders. Instead of creating the first wave of serious researchers, Asia will in effect import them. Remember, the most important factor in the educational infrastructure equation is people. The fastest, most direct route to gaining qualified people in this instance is the educational and research joint venture.

Given the earlier discussion on the nature of alliances and joint ventures, let's briefly examine the most important principles that would govern our educational joint ventures.

REALISTIC VALUATION. Where does the value of the joint venture lie? In the market? Or in the intellectual talent? The objective for government is to increase productivity and foster innovation to attain high value-added output of manufacturers and services. Future growth and prosperity for the nation depends on creating the capacity for real knowledge input into the economy, whether that input is coursed through multinational or domestic corporations. In other words, Asian governments must domesticate multinational corporations not by nationalizing them but by supplying them with developed national talent.

Sovereignty will evolve not from who controls corporations, but who accounts for their worth. The objective is to make local talent input account for an increasing percentage of that worth. Therefore, Asian governments have a lot riding on creating the institutions that will nurture industrial clusters reliant on a continuous stream of innovative input from the educational institutions.

On the other hand, Asia has the market United States educational institutions need to sustain growth. But there's a problem with that need. The *best* United States institutions don't really need the Asian market, although it is likely that they would have to lower admission requirements in the event of a substantial decrease in foreign applications to maintain student body size. Still, it is the second- and third-tier organizations that will increasingly rely on the Asian market to fill up classrooms and labs. Yet these are not the institutions that Asia will want to enlist in its strategic partnerships.

What price, then, is Asia willing to pay to enter into educational joint ventures with the best research institutions in the world? Again, the choice is clear.

OPERATIONAL CONTROL. If education is seen as a national strategic interest, does it make sense to have foreigners in control? It is likely that over just the short-term, this issue will become irrelevant, in part because of the repatriation of talent and in part because of the development of talent. In fact, the danger lies in the failure to maintain diversity, a situation which can foster debate and distillation of the strongest ideas and research proposals. As in the best Western schools, advancement must evolve from performance, not ethnic heritage.

WHERE DOES THE OUTPUT GO? Ultimately, the output of research must be commercialized if it is to have the desired effect on economic development. In the quest to develop globally competitive Asian companies, should there be a preference for selling or giving away the results of research to Asian companies? Will Asian companies be willing to buy the output? Will they be *able* to buy the output?

There are at least two ways to approach this question. The first is through commissioned research. Whoever commissions the research owns it. But the problem here is that even very large companies are unwilling to put all their research eggs into one basket. It is far better to own part of a globally profitable idea than all of one that had promise—and little else. This means that Asian companies will have the chance to join consortia of funders. It is likely that these consortia will be made up entirely of competing firms in a single industry.

That's fine. The real test for these somewhat uneasy collaborations will be in how the commissioned output is transformed into a marketable product, and how fast this happens. Although Asian corporations may not always have the same deep pockets as their consortia partners, there will be finances for them to participate in reasoned, strategic investment in research initiatives commissioned by the consortia. And of course the institutions themselves will frequently have their own ideas about which direction their research should take, and will seek to build consortia in the private sector to support those initiatives.

What is the second approach to the question of who owns the output. Again, the happy answer is that whomever buys into the project owns a piece of the output. But what of mid-market firms and entrepreneurial start-ups? That brings us to the industrial cluster.

DEVELOPING THE INDUSTRIAL CLUSTER

As we suggested earlier, efforts to develop high value-added industrial clusters in the technology sector in Singapore, for instance, have had notably mixed results. In one instance, a firm run by Singaporeans in Silicon Valley was given a government grant to set up a research facility in Singapore. It didn't work out because the founders felt Singapore was too far away from the racing innovation taking place in the United

States, and closed the facility. It later reopened an office in Singapore; however, it was not for the purpose of doing value-added research, but for programming because of the shortage of programmers in Silicon Valley. But the thinking and value-added innovation was still happening there.

Mark Andreesen, the inventor of the Mosaic and Netscape browsers, and Jeff Hawkins, creator of the PalmPilot, are two good examples of the impact of educational institutions and value-added corporate research on the development of industrial clusters. Andreesen's case is well known. He invented the first browser in college and refined it into Netscape as one of two principal, high-profile founders of the eponymous company. The rules of the technology industry—hardware and software—were changed virtually overnight, giving Microsoft founder Bill Gates the fright of his life.

In Hawkins's case, he invented what at the time was the most popular hand-held computer/organizer. Afterwards, Hawkins decided it would be a lot more fun to create new things in a corporate environment where the financial returns were greater—his own company. His former employer, Hewlett-Packard, knew two things: that there was no hope of retaining Hawkins, and that he represented a hugely formidable threat, especially if HP's competitors became involved in his new company. So they did the sensible thing: They became his partner.

These examples show again that the first priority is providing the basic requisites for value-added research, meaning the educational institutions. The institutions themselves will produce entrepreneurial talent that will attract meaningful financial support. The institutions will also create the kind of talent that Hawkins demonstrated for his employer. As in his case, success will create not just new products, but new companies which are, again, capable of attracting meaningful levels of investor interest.

Everything evolves from infrastructure. The most important investment Asian governments can make now is not to recapitalize bankrupt banks and corporations with taxpayer money, but to put those funds into productive, critical investments like education. If Asia is to ever truly transition to high value-added manufacturing, those investments must be made. And the sooner, the better.

MANAGEMENT AND
THE CORPORATE SECTOR

As the old adage goes, advertising and training are the first to go in times of trouble. That was certainly the case after the advent of the Asian financial crisis. In an orgy of cost cutting, plump corporate advertising budgets rapidly dehydrated. Training and education were no longer investments in the future but unnecessary costs. There were exceptions. For example, for a time it was popular in Malaysia to send employees off to training so that they would not sit around wringing their hands and wondering how much longer they would keep their jobs. Morale was in a chasm, and the rank-and-file needed to keep their minds busy.

The National Productivity Corporation—a government training institution—put a nice spin on this development, suggesting that companies could "take advantage of the prevalent economic downturn to train their workers in productivity development programs. This is because the companies are now slowing down their activities while focusing more on their restructuring processes," said Ismail Adam, the head of the corporation ("Good Time to Train," 1998).

Still, Ismail noted that local companies had cut back. But this was not so for multinational corporations. "The multinational corporations are doing alright, but unfortunately our firms are having problems," he said ("Good Time . . . ," 1998). Ismail also noted that about 50 percent of his agency's business came from the multinational sector in good times. Tough times increased reliance on multinationals.

Multinationals also persevered with advertising, with many of them apparently believing that the disappearance of local competition from the airwaves and newspapers presented a good opportunity to increase market share, despite increasing pressure on margins due to the crisis. This was particularly good for consumer products companies, whose revenues remained fairly static or even grew during the crisis.

People still had to eat, babies had to be diapered, and most felt they still had to bathe.

Multinational technology companies frequently saw that with the good times winding down, Asian companies would have to become more efficient and productive to continue growth and sustain competitiveness. Getting focused and reengineering business processes would be key to achieving these goals, both of which depend on technology. So while local firms were cutting back on both training and advertising, they were making strategic capital investments in technology.

They were also making investments in people, as shown in Figure 9.3, which displays estimated and forecast increases in salaries for 1997 and 1998, respectively. While low value-added workers and middle management in inefficient domestic corporations were losing jobs, multinational corporations and profitable domestic companies were paying higher wages for quality people.

"The tougher economic times in Asia 'may require a different kind of leader,' said Michael Bekins, who heads Korn/Ferry's Asian operations. Many of the multinationals for whom Korn/Ferry conducts searches 'would rather make the change now, especially if the economies aren't going to get better for a while,' he added. Companies are now looking for leaders with experience in an ailing economy or experience turning around a company, Mr. Bekins said. This is a switch from the marketing and brand-management skills that were in demand in years past" (Western, 1998, p. 10). It also signals, as Michael Porter and others predicted, that the era of managing by remote control, mistake, and good fortune in Asia is over. Now, it takes brains, like any truly competitive market. "Asian firms are now considerably more ambivalent about Asian values and are willing to follow best practices, wherever they come from" (Kahn, 1998, p. 40).

Korn/Ferry's research also shows where executives were in demand, and that was in Asia's most troubled sectors, as shown in Figure 9.4. Manufacturing and chemicals and consumer products—fields particularly susceptible to competition—were investing heavily in talent. The demand for executives in the financial sector also remained strong, despite widespread bank failures, mergers, and acquisitions.

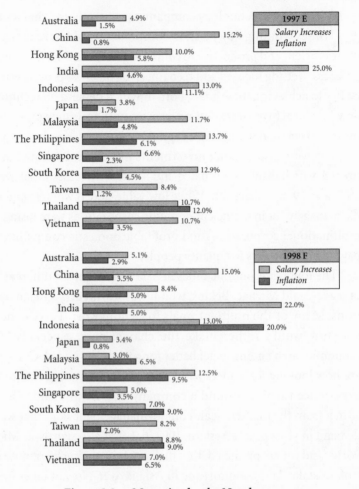

Percentage increase in salaries and inflation in Asia.
1997 numbers are estimates, 1998 numbers are forecasts.

Figure 9.3.   Managing by the Numbers.
Source: CRG Asia/Pacific GDP, Inflation, and
Salary Increase Bulletin.

What this means for corporate Asia in general is that it will see more highly qualified, better-trained executives in top positions than in the past. It also means that, as noted, there will be ferocious competition for the best and the brightest minds. When *BusinessWeek* published its famous list of the best B-schools, it noted, "Wharton may

Where executives are in demand

Share of total hirings in Asia in the second quarter

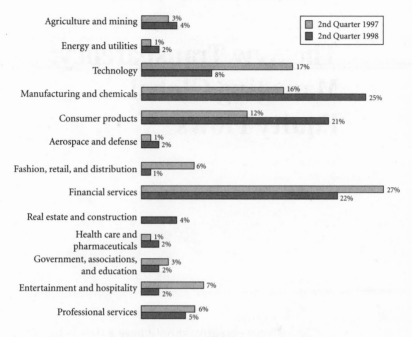

Figure 9.4. Managing by the Numbers.

Source: Korn/Ferry International, Executive Demand Index.

be tops—again—but this year, every grad is golden" ("The Best B-Schools," 1998). In the Asian context, the financial crisis meant that not only every MBA, but every scientist, technician, engineer, and programmer was golden. The shortage of all of them meant that the most important investment Asia would make in its future would be in its people.

CHAPTER TEN

The New Transparency: Managing Global Equity Flows

—⁓— "Every executive should have a sign in his office that says, 'I will never get fat again,'" chairman and chief executive of Giordano International, Peter Lau, says to explain one of the most important lessons of the Asian financial crisis (Goad, 1998, p. 1). Like "good" cholesterol and "bad" cholesterol, there were three kinds of fat that proliferated during the Asian miracle years, all bad.

The first had to do with the proclivity of Asian conglomerates to swallow up a huge variety of businesses that not only provided little synergy, but reduced or more frequently destroyed any capacity for agility. This was briefly discussed earlier. The second kind of bad fat had to do with bloated operations in uncompetitive markets because companies didn't have to think seriously about productivity and efficiency issues, also covered here previously. The third kind of fat was the exuberant acquisition of debt—not just any old debt, but debt collateralized with stock inflated by the investment mania of international investors who were enamored with the idea of making a killing in Asian equities. That fat is one that has yet to be covered here.

This "bad" fat is a product of what various analysts and economists have called volatile or "virtual" money. At the onset of the Asian financial crisis, virtual money quickly evacuated Asian equity markets. The rapid evacuation stimulated serious and endless debate on the irresponsibility of international fund managers, the perils of globalization and unfettered capital flows, and the difficulty financial institutions and the corporate sector alike have in restraining their unbridled optimism during boom cycles, thus setting themselves up for withering falls.

It isn't certain, however, that volatile money is as bad as its critics argue. Some even say that blaming portfolio investors for the Asian financial crisis is a case of attacking the symptom of crisis, and not the crisis itself. There's a third part of this argument as well, and that is that Asia cannot afford to do without volatile money if it expects to raise more than two billion people out of poverty in the first quarter of the twentieth century. Asia had too much of a good thing, but recoiling by limiting portfolio investment as Malaysia did, will definitely succeed in limiting volatile flows of capital, but at the price of the speed of capital formation necessary to stimulate economies. Long-term foreign direct investment (FDI) is not enough to lift economies out of crisis. In fact, FDI directly stimulates an increase in productive capacity. Excess capacity is one of the principal products of the Asian euphoria that led to conditions which created crisis. Unless economies are stimulated to utilize that capacity, they will not exit from recession.

The availability of portfolio money did not trigger the Asian financial crisis. In fact, it was a security blanket. "Extraordinary results can lull investors into forgetting the dangers. And regulators aren't any smarter," Nobel laureate Gary S. Becker wrote recently (1998, p. 18). Becker wasn't writing about the de-fanged Asian equities markets, but about the Long-Term Capital debacle, which found the world's chief exponent of free-market capital flows—the United States Treasury—putting together a bailout that prompted MIT's Paul Krugman to ask, "Did somebody say, 'crony capitalism?'" Krugman believes that investors took big risks in Long-Term Capital because the government would bail them out if there was trouble. Long-Term Capital is the giant hedge fund that came alarmingly close to wreaking more chaos on the global financial system than even the Asian financial crisis. Founded by former Salomon Brothers whiz John Meriwether, the fund was preeminent in part because it was run by Ph.D.s—rather than investment bankers—including two Nobel Prize winners, Myron Scholes and Robert Merton. But in the first half of 1998, the fund lost 50 percent of its capital. By September, it was almost all gone. The fund was rescued because it owed fourteen banks and brokerage firms around US$100 billion. This is precisely the same reason Krugman and other economists say that Asian financial institutions and investors made hugely unwise bets in Asian real estate and other unproductive investments: the government safety net. And government let it happen because of the IMF safety net.

So it is not really lack of regulation that caused the virtual money to blast out of Asia. It was the realization that Asian governments, corporations, and financial institutions had overplayed their hands. And as scripted, government and the IMF stepped in to play out their roles in the drama, looking for ways to bail-out banks and save influential corporations. In Indonesia, IMF loans intended to recapitalize financial institutions were redirected to failing enterprises owned by the same tycoons who owned the banks, and only the change in administration provided the prospect of any of those funds being recovered. After Indonesia, the IMF turned around and did exactly the same thing for Russia's decrepit banks, and Mafiosi bankers hustled the IMF funds right out of the country to the tune of billions of dollars.

But the interesting part of this equation is not just human avarice, but that avarice always begins on the local level, particularly when bankers think that government will bail them out. And investors were foolish—a nicer word than greedy—not to understand, or belatedly profess not to understand, the utter riskiness of investing in companies that did not present an accurate picture of the financial health in terms of profit, cash flow, and asset base. But the bankers and top management of these companies were naïve to think that the party would never end. Even still more naïve were Asian governments, like Western and South American governments before them, that talked themselves into believing that the corporate growth they were seeing was real. In other words, the problem was not virtual money, but virtual growth and profit. And maybe virtual brains.

World Bank economist Tara Vishwanath says, "The financial crisis in East Asia is a stark reminder of the severity of information problems and the need to develop institutions to deal with them. . . . [p]art of the heavy outflow of foreign funds in the region was 'inadequate information.' Depositors, unable to distinguish good banks from bad ones, withdrew their money from all banks. Investors, unable to distinguish viable firms from bankrupt ones, dumped the share of all companies" (Villamor, 1998, p. 1). That's a very polite way of saying that investors really had no idea of what was going on, no real understanding of the quality of their investment, and nowhere near an adequate understanding of Asia and its growth, but they had been enjoying the bandwagon. When it slowed, they bailed.

But it is still naïve to suggest that either increased transparency or greater levels of regulation would have prevented the Asian financial crisis. What would have prevented the crisis is this: a sense of financial responsibility, and commitment to shareholder value. Neither government nor the private sector can instill that responsibility and commitment. That depends on investors.

THE ROLE OF VOLATILE MONEY

It is interesting that the debate on how to cure the Asian crisis generally orbited around recapitalizing poorly run banks, stabilizing currencies (at any cost), and restoring foreign direct investment. It is interesting because the financial crisis rapidly evolved into an enterprise crisis that would ultimately put the global economy at risk, and yet the crisis resolution debate remained anchored on economic issues—as if banks and financial institutions could actually generate wealth or investor confidence.

One reason—aside from economic myopia—that enterprise issues went ignored is that no one wanted to think about how to recapitalize enterprise, although around US$2 trillion in equity had "vaporized" since the onset of the crisis (Goad, 1998, p. 1). No one wanted to think about recapitalizing the corporate sector because it required politically incorrect volatile money. That was bad, because the recovery equation wouldn't work without volatile money. Leaving it out of the equation meant that the principal indicator of investor confidence went ignored. And therefore, Asia's fragile (but once booming) equity markets remained decimated.

Vishwanath is of course correct to suggest that inadequate financial information—full disclosure and transparency—contributed to worsening and prolonging the effect of the crisis on equity markets. Indeed, the reluctance to remedy the information "shortflow" contributed in a mighty way to the perception that "Asian Inc." was a façade. Amazingly, virtually nothing was done to manage perception that communicated another reality: No one was really in control of managing the crisis. Not the government, nor the IMF or World Bank, nor the private sector.

None of these sectors did anything to improve matters by screaming about volatile money, and how undesirable, at worst, and unreliable, at best, it is. The rapidity with which the contribution of portfolio money to Asian growth was forgotten was staggering. Instead of government leaders trying to woo it back, Malaysia's Mahathir, one of the principal beneficiaries of global fund flows, seemed determined to make sure it didn't rescue his deflating economy and continued to insist that controls remain in place when by mid-1999 it was obvious that neighboring economies were recovering rapidly without controls. Other governments and preeminent economists—notably Jeffery Sachs and Paul Krugman—fret about unfettered fund flows. One effect of this ambivalence has been that the panic encompassed foreign direct investment. This significantly exacerbated the crisis in the minds of investors and left governments little recourse to IMF dictates to obtain funds that would also quickly vaporize under the tight money policy regimes the IMF loves (and never stopped arguing were "curing" the crisis).

Let's take a look at a few of the reasons portfolio investments are important for an economy and why it is unthinkable to have development without it. Figure 10.1 shows how dramatically private invest-

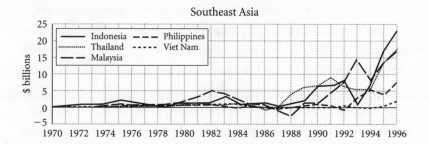

**Figure 10.1.   Net Private Capital Flows: Selected Asian Economies
1970–1996.**
Source: Asian Development Bank.

ment helped finance Asia's miracle. First, portfolio money provides
the economic fuel required by every economy's engine of growth—
mid-market enterprises. There are very few truly large companies in
Asia, or anywhere else, in relative terms to the size of its economies
and populations. Most enterprise activity takes place in the mid-
market sector. But mid-market companies are important for more
than their number and their collective contribution to the economy.
Mid-market companies are the principal drivers of entrepreneurial
innovation and creativity. At the end of the first quarter of the next
century, Asia's most inspiring success stories will be those of mid-
market enterprises that redefined competition in their industries in
Asia and elsewhere.

Mid-market enterprises are also the biggest generators of jobs and,
in their frequent capacity as supplier to larger domestic and multinational firms, they are the end result of the multiplier effect of large-
scale corporate activity on job generation and economic activity.
Therefore, development of equity markets should be aggressively pur-
sued to assure adequate capacity for capital formation in this sector.
More than in any other sector, mid-level enterprises are responsible
for providing economic opportunity to the majority of Asia's poor.
Support for mid-market enterprise is an important contribution to
national prosperity.

A second reason why portfolio investments are important to an
economy is that they throw off liquidity to individual investors who

are more willing to spend equities earnings than more conservative investments and savings. This liquidity, combined with mid-market enterprise job generators, helps absorb the output of excess capacity in the industrial sector, and it contributes to the development of local enterprise focused on local economies.

It must not be forgotten that the largest cash flows into Asia during the miracle years were not foreign direct investment, but equity investment in Asian enterprises. More than any other source of capital, portfolio investment has contributed to the growth of Asian economies. For example, in 1996, Malaysia received approximately US$5.3 billion in direct foreign investment. But US$23 billion entered the economy in the form of net capital inflows. What economy really wants to go without the difference?

But as already mentioned, there are no free lunches. If an economy wants to enjoy the benefits of US$23 billion in investment, it must be prepared to do what it takes, within reason, to make that investment pay off, particularly if it wants to sustain inflows, and what economy doesn't? Despite examples in the United States, South America, and Japan, investors, bankers, and corporate managers alike all forgot—in an orgy of irrational, financial exuberance—that there must be a pay-off to sustain investor interest, meaning that the funds must be put to good use. Incredibly, the major multinational financial institutions involved in previous debacles—Japanese, European, and United States banks—oversaw and even contributed to Asia's crisis. So it must be true that you can't teach an old dog new tricks. At some point, the dog should be put to sleep!

So what went wrong with portfolio investment and the Asian miracle? What went wrong tells us what shouldn't happen again.

INFLATED STOCK AS COLLATERAL. Rather than collateralizing loans with hard assets or cash, domestic Asian firms got into the nasty habit of putting up stock as collateral at inflated market values, rather than at discounted values that provided for volatility. As economist Gary Becker says, people forget the risk when they are used to long-term, extraordinary results. The lesson here is not to forget. Thai Farmers

Bank's Lamsam Banthoon won't. He's through lending to large corporations with grandiose dreams. So is every other Asian banker that survives the crisis—that is, until he forgets again.

HIGH DEBT TO EQUITY RATIOS. Some Asian corporations just couldn't grow fast enough, it seems, and so with government support—even encouragement—they assumed unrealistic levels of debt in order to undertake large infrastructure projects, to develop nonproductive enterprises such as very tall towers, national cars, and digital cities, and on occasion to fund foreign acquisitions and investments with low returns. In the end, such economic activity taken on in the name of nation building imperiled the nation in ways that had been unimaginable. The best thing corporate citizens can do for their nations—and their shareholders—is to manage themselves responsibly, and to evaluate legitimate opportunity on the basis of financial rather than political returns.

LACK OF TRANSPARENCY. Risky projects, investments, and loans were kept well-hidden by corporations and banks alike because they remained majority controlled by influential Asian tycoons. One of the most obvious examples is the Alphatec Group, founded by Charn Uswachoke. Charn not only kept his books to himself, he lied about the profitability of the core company while spiriting loans and payoffs to other corporations and corporate directors. Had Charn done this in the United States where he went to college and learned the ropes of the semiconductor business, he would be in jail. One doesn't have to look far to find plenty of other examples replete with overt government support of erring top management, but those have been well-documented elsewhere. The important point here is that investors must pass on companies that are not up front with their financial information, or suffer the consequences when things fall apart.

ASIAN VALUES EUPHORIA. The PriceWaterhouseCoopers survey "found broad agreement among CEOs in Asia for the proposition that

'Western companies have a lot to learn from the attitudes, practices, and philosophies of leading Asian companies.' As Klaus Schwab, president of the World Economic Forum, points out, 'Too often there is a tendency on the part of global business leaders to perceive a one-way street in terms of importing Western management methods to the East'" ("Inside the Mind of the CEO," 1998).

Schwab seems to have forgotten that Asia's problems are not uniquely Asian problems. As repeatedly pointed out within this work, irresponsible management in the banking, investment banking, and corporate sectors—as recently as in 1998 in the case of Long-Term Capital—contributed to crises in Mexico, South America, the United States, and Japan. All of these crises clearly show that the principles of responsible management and fiscal integrity are universal. Whether a company or bank is located in South America, the United States, or Asia is irrelevant. If they forget the basic principles of sound management—efficiency, productivity, value-added, financial prudence and risk management, return to shareholders—they will be in trouble.

Before the crisis, the arrogance in Asia evolving from the pride associated with rapid, profound, and historic growth of nations and domestic corporations was a clear danger sign that success was being taken for granted. The arrogance of Western managers after the crisis began was comparable only to the irritation of Asian managers who were eating crow and in many instances trying to hold on to their family businesses. No doubt this cycle will come full circle again at some point, with Asia resurgent and enjoying its role in the global economy once again. That's human nature. And that's history.

But the truly important point here, besides universal principles of corporate responsibility, is another finding of the PriceWaterhouse-Coopers survey. This was that the capacity to manage multicultural teams was the quality most valued among Asian CEOs. While there will always be particular cultural realities that managers in Asia must respect in leading their teams, Asia is a cosmopolitan, cultural melting pot that recruits—and attracts—the best minds regardless of cultural heritage, Asian or otherwise.

Like all regions, governments, and corporations, Asia must learn, as Intel Chairman Andrew S. Grove says, that inflection points— radical change—frequently but unpredictably take place everywhere. For this reason, Grove says that it pays to be paranoid, regardless of how well things are going; in fact, the better they're going, the more prepared one should be. Crises usually strike when managers and corporations are at the top of the cycle, not the bottom. That's certainly the case in Asia. Put more simply, Asia must keep its feet on the ground next time around in order to recognize the danger signals.

RELIANCE ON PORTFOLIO INVESTMENT

As Peter Drucker has said, "There's one thing securities analysts will never understand, and that's business, because they believe that money is real. Securities analysts believe that companies make money. Companies make shoes" (Schlender, 1998, p. 113). The inability of analysts to understand business leads to pressure to perform in the short-term, but Drucker argues that both short-term and long-term measures of performance are needed. An over-focus on the short-term acts to the detriment of long-term strategic decision making, by implication.

Is this a downside to portfolio investment? Probably. However, it can also be said that management that doesn't have to worry about the short-term interests of shareholders, such as Asia's large conglomerates during the miracle years, may as a result have far too long to mismanage the company strategically before it becomes clear that something must be done. So the question is: Which is worse— short-term pressure or having to put long-term faith in a manager to grow shareholder value? In most instances, even investors who understand business, or think that they do, will want the regular feedback.

As Asia enters recovery, equity financing will become increasingly important to companies that can no longer afford to finance development with debt, but that must enhance operations and speed development in a much more competitive, liberalized environment. Equity markets will develop rapidly as a result, as will an international-standards regulatory framework. However, the framework will be less effective in actually regulating equities markets than it will be in boosting investor confidence, which is the key to bringing trillions of dollars in portfolio investment back to Asia.

Whether or not corporations should rely on portfolio investment is not the important question. They will *have* to rely on portfolio investment. The important question is, will they be able to create the perception of transparency and excellence in management that investors will require? That is, will they adopt Western standards of financial reporting and accept the preoccupation of Western markets on quarterly earnings or not? They will.

Accepting those standards will put the same pressure for financial responsibility and solid strategy development that Western firms must endure in the lap of Asia's corporations. Because many of the large corporations will eventually have taken on strategic Western partners, this will be a change that they would have had to make anyway, in the interests of their partners' shareholders. So standards of evaluation for large cap firms will fairly quickly become globally universal. The real challenge to develop will be on those important mid-market firms that will be the critical engines of Asian recovery and growth. But they will have no choice but to be up to the challenge as well.

REGULATING GLOBAL CAPITAL FLOWS

In a 1998 essay, Harvard's Jeffrey Sachs argued that we "now need an international equivalent" of "government-mandated deposit insurance." Sachs notes that Nobel Prize-winning economist Martin Friedman "argued that banking panic, unattended by the Fed, created the Great Depression. So this free-marketeer has long championed deposit insurance as a protection against bank runs" (Sachs, 1998, p. 20).

The problem with this point of view is that the Asian financial crisis was not unattended, but that it was attended to ineptly. The ineptness of the IMF was made worse by the United States administration's initial disinterest in the crisis (caused by distraction due to the investigation of President Clinton's relationship with a young White House intern), and later when the crisis's impact on the American economy became apparent. As Sachs himself argues, billions of dollars in IMF insurance wound up in the pockets of currency speculators and corrupt politicians and businessmen—and not only in Asia. He also makes the point that Friedman, another Nobel laureate, argues that the IMF be dissolved, underlining just how inappropriate government-mandated insurance, in the form of the IMF, has been for Asia and other financially troubled economies. That's what the IMF has been: insurance against irresponsible banking and corporate practices and bad government.

Sachs continues to argue, nevertheless, that "the best idea around is that developing countries should impose their own supervisory controls on short-term international borrowing by domestic financial institutions. To avoid panicky capital outflows, it is best to prevent banks from exposing themselves to excess short-term indebtedness in the first place. Chile does this by taxing short-term flows" (Sachs, 1998, p. 20). This is an indirect means of preventing banks from biting off more than they can chew. It punishes the investor for taking money out of the banks, not for putting too much in.

So the question here, then, is what's the difference between this and what Malaysia did to restrict investments in securities? And the answer is: very little. Malaysia forced the money to remain in the economy for a year; Chile merely punished it for leaving. But the bigger question is, "Is penalizing the investor the best way to control or regulate international fund flows?" Aren't these countries trying to turn portfolio investors into foreign direct investors? And the answer to that is yes. This is assuming that fund flows should be regulated at all.

In a truly happy world, investment decisions and returns would be based on best practices. But in an imperfect world, short-term portfolio investments are frequently based on simple greed. In a perfect world, therefore, there would be no need for regulation. Because the world is imperfect with an imperfect capitalist global economy, are an international regulatory body, a Global Securities and Exchange Commission, or a Global Central Bank really necessary?

For the answer to that question, let's return briefly to Long-Term Capital. There are two points. First, as Gary Becker notes, "Is there much reason to believe that regulators, who are monitoring not their own but other people's money, are more immune to this optimism," demonstrated by "bankers and investors after several years of growth"? (Becker, 1998, p. 16.) The obvious answer is no. Regulation has never stopped a financial crisis, and it should not be confused with Friedman's safety net in the form of deposit insurance, meant to protect small investors from bad banking practices that regulatory authorities *failed* to spot or remedy. There is little comfort to be taken in the notion that regulators will insulate the world from financial crisis.

Second, Paul Krugman believes that Long-Term Capital and the bankers and investors got as crazy as they did because they knew that the government would always bail them out for the sake of the financial system. And they were obviously right. So the safety net actually contributes to the problem of bad management and decision making because no matter what, there is a light at the end of the tunnel. Krugman has not entirely rejected the idea of some sort of global regulatory framework. "Capital markets are global, but the institutions that support and regulate them—that allow them to work—remain national" (Krugman, 1998, p. 27).

The distinction between what Sachs is arguing and what Krugman implies is that Sachs believes some order can be brought to financial and equities markets by instituting some sort of internal regulatory framework in individual countries, while Krugman suggests that it be figured out how to provide the same sort of regulation the United States. The Securities and Exchange Commission, for instance, provides domestically, on a global scale. "It's hard to imagine how truly global institutions could come into existence—how we could, for example, prosecute American traders working in London for manipulating some market in China. But until we figure it out, it's going to be a very tough ride" (Krugman, 1998, p. 27).

In fact, the framework probably already exists. The World Trade Organization already oversees international trade of goods and services. The same technology that makes it possible to send funds around the world provides the mechanism to monitor them as well. And in the same way that brokerages and financial institutions in the

United States are required to exercise a degree of self-regulatory behavior, institutions trading overseas can be required to observe rules of "fair play." Again, the distinction from straightforward regulation here is that no one is relying on regulators to be less human and emotionally euphoric than private-sector investors, but to have the common sense to make sure that everyone is playing by the same rules, whether they are bears or bulls. In the same way that it is illegal to artificially manipulate the value of an equity in the United States, it can be illegal to manipulate currencies and equities on a global scale when such attempts are obvious efforts to distort market forces.

Such a regulatory framework would have the additional benefit of instituting universal standards of financial reporting, at least for economies that want to avail of the protection such a regulatory framework would provide. Likewise, it will put increased pressure on organizations not just to be transparent, but to regularly—as in four times a year—demonstrate that they are acting in the best interests of all shareholders. And then if investors—and managers—get too euphoric, they have no one else to blame. But to temper their enthusiasm, it should be clear that no potential for bailout is available.

Sachs, Friedman, and others believe that the IMF has passed its prime, and that for developing economies particularly, it acts as a safety net rather than a builder of strong economies. Because of this, the IMF is in the curious position of undermining its own mandate. That needs to be fixed. An international regulatory framework on the order described will assure that players in financial and equities markets play fair, or disappear. Understanding the seriousness of the penalties for breaking the rules of the game will do two things: 1) assure level playing fields reliant on market fundamentals; and, 2) rid the global marketplace of rogues. Well, at least a good many of them.

PART FIVE

What Comes Next?

CHAPTER ELEVEN

Asia in the Next Century

W hen business and government leaders gathered in October 1998 for a World Economic Forum (WEF) meeting in Singapore, despite the gloom that hovered over the presentations, CEOs professed that they were by and large "optimistic that their businesses will experience growth. And, most say, Asia itself is where the opportunity for growth is greatest." WEF president Klaus Schwab said, "Clearly, CEOs in Asia see cross-border growth within Asia as a priority before expanding into global markets" ("CEOs in Asia . . . ," 1998, Internet edition).

The survey—and the WEF—that captured this optimism about the future were indications of big business opinion in Asia, and hardly represented a cross-section of Asian business in general. But these rainmakers did reveal an underlying sentiment that persisted throughout the crisis: Ultimately, Asia would not only deal with the crisis, but recover much of its wounded pride as well. But while pride could be restored, the Asia that would emerge from crisis would be very different from the one that it took by surprise in the summer of 1997.

There was another undercurrent as well, provoked by Japan's fumbling attempts to right its own economy. Would Asia struggle in the same way trying to figure out how to get back on its feet? That was, in many respects, a good question to ask in 1998, as Asian nations struggled not only with their profound economic, enterprise, and political problems, but increasingly with their tolerance for each other. Most of Asia blamed Japan for its insistence on maintaining uncompetitive productive capacity despite its duplication around ASEAN, which kept imports into Japan low, as well as its reluctance to undertake financial and government reforms required to meaningfully stimulate its economy. But Japan's relations with the rest of Asia have never been warm, despite massive investment. Criticism of Asia's dominant economy wasn't surprising.

What was surprising was the way ASEAN was beginning to argue with itself. Occasional cannon-blasts between Singapore and Malaysia were expected, given their rocky marriage and subsequent divorce, but when senior minister Lee Kuan Yew accused neighboring governments of causing the financial crisis, the gloves came off, forcing a protracted series of spats. Later in the year, Thailand proposed that ASEAN's policy of noninterference be reviewed, largely out of frustration with dealing with Burmese refugees fleeing Myanmar's corrupt military dictatorship. The biggest surprise however, came when Indonesia's president B. J. Habibie and the Philippines' president Joseph Estrada publicly voiced concern over the treatment of former Malaysian deputy prime minister Anwar Ibrahim. Estrada "met with the daughter of the former deputy prime minister and said he supported Datuk Seri Anwar's program of reforming what the Malaysian says is high-level corruption" (McDermott, 1998, p. 1), just following the WEF meeting. Virtually all of Asia had gone to considerable pain to clarify that other regional economies would not follow Malaysia's example of imposing currency controls.

But rather than a sign of disintegrating regional cooperation, the disputes were a better indication of the evolution of ASEAN relationships. "'If ASEAN is going to survive as a grouping at all, it needs a new kind of personality and leadership,' says Surin Pitsuwan, Thailand's foreign minister" (McDermott, 1998, p.1). And indeed, conscious ignorance of one neighbor's affairs may be said to have worked well during a simpler time when ASEAN's economies—and its people—were popular destinations for foreign capital with few alternatives and inefficient means for moving international fund flows. But no more.

ASEAN—and Asia as a whole—are complimentary only within a very narrow, low-value band of trade, although before the Asian financial crisis, intra-regional trade accounted for about half of total trade in ASEAN. As pressure continues to improve the value-added of exports within the grouping, particularly with new members like Vietnam and Laos cornering the labor-intensive foreign direct investment sector, ASEAN will increasingly find its members competing with each other for opportunity, trade, and all kinds of investment. Technology will continue to heighten the pace of that competition, as ASEAN's members take on each other face-to-face in the race for capital. The square-off between Malaysia and Singapore in separate, well-publicized efforts to create high technology industrial clusters is but one example.

Competition from without will further complicate Asia's business model. "In the past we had the whole [export] market to ourselves," economist Manu Bhaskaran of SG Securities said by way of explaining the more complex world within which Asia's recovery will emerge. "We just had to get our act together and everything else would fall into place. Now we're competing with Eastern Europe and their fantastic human capital. Mexico, with its access to the United States market. And China of course.

"Definitely, Southeast Asia is losing [export] market share," he warned ("Asia Needs to Be Smarter . . . ," 1998).

Competition will increase the chances for disputes, even as global trade pressures push for increased economic integration within the region. This will create conditions conducive to disagreement, even when good times do eventually return. Conflict will become the norm, as it was becoming in 1998, and not the exception. It is therefore important that ASEAN learns how to manage conflict and how to get through it without coming to blows. For that reason, the disagreements occurring in 1998 were healthy opportunities for heads of state to learn to disagree, and to do so publicly for the first time.

What some observers saw as a crumbling veneer of solidarity was actually a strengthening, a sign of maturing societies that were beginning to understand the importance of disagreeing when looking the other way could mean not just tolerating a neighbor, but suffering as a result. ASEAN's members have suffered in the name of solidarity, from enduring the haze from Indonesian forest fires to Thailand's irresponsible nurturing of its bubble economy to Malaysia's continual rages against international currency traders and fund managers. Each of these incidents led to substantial economic damage to neighboring countries. Because it was supposed to be ignored in the name of solidarity, the incidents continued.

Tearing down the barriers to intraregional debate presents a new form of peer pressure for regional governments. Integrity will evolve not from ignoring the transgressions of one's neighbors, but from making sure that one's nation does not transgress against another. That is why Asia's bickerings were a sign of growing maturity and responsibilty.

AN ASIAN FATE

Apparently in the belief that Asia must export its way out of crisis, economists and analysts at the WEF argued that despite signs of the crisis bottoming out, recovery would be dependent on the global economy's capacity to boost demand for Asian goods. While a healthy global economy would of course be a considerable help in speeding Asia's recovery, it depended on Asia, not the United States, Japan, or Europe. Indeed, sustaining the global economy's principal engine— the United States—depended in large part on restoring the capacity of Asia's to buy American exports.

While there is little to debate with respect to the interdependence of national economies in the global market, Asia owned its crisis, and the ineffectiveness of the remedies and indifference in Japan and the United States helped it spread. But principally it spread because Asia, like others before it in similar circumstances, couldn't cure itself for a long while. Only when it became clear that Asia in fact could not export its way out of recession, did meaningful reform begin, stimulating the first early signs of resurgence. This is why "Thailand's beleaguered banking system may be the first in Asia to recover from the region's crisis" ("Thai Banks May Be First . . . ," 1998), as Thomson Bankwatch-Asia's president Philippe Delhaise predicted. Thailand was the first regional government to work up the political will to force reform in its banking sector despite damaging powerful vested interests.

Fifteen months after his early-crisis visit to Thailand, *New York Times* columnist Thomas Friedman gushed, "[A]ll I can say is: What a difference a year makes!"

"Thailand is still not out of the woods financially, but the situation has stabilized and the country is on a growth path again. What is most striking, though, is the degree to which Thai political reformers, who were hit hard by the economic crisis, now view it as an enormously useful turning point for their country" (1998, Internet edition).

A curious blend of humility and optimism has helped Asia begin to turn the corner, without much truly constructive help from its would-be rescuers. While much is made of the fact that good management is universal, it should also be acknowledged that for all the wrong-headedness that was associated with the notion of Asian values, the region's rich cultural heritage and tradition has been a strength in times of crisis. It is not easy to accept change, or the responsibility for mistakes, in any culture. And it is regrettable that real change so frequently must be preceded by debacles on the scale of the Asian financial crisis. But for all the tycoons who clung to their family businesses, there were thousands of managers who understood and accepted that Asian euphoria—as Japanese and United States euphoria before it, within the second half of the nineteenth century—had caused a whole region to lose touch with reality, only to be consumed by it when the reckoning came.

Not many stood by mourning for long. Determined to get to the head of a new line of Asian success stories, governments and the private sector shook off the lethargy of shock, stared the future in the face, and raced for it. And so Asia emerged stronger from its debacle, wizened but renewed, trimmer but stronger, wiser and ready. Ultimately it would be seen that the Asian financial crisis not only had to happen, it happened almost too late. And it helped make Asia better.

THE NEW ASIAN CORPORATION

RFM's Joey Concepcion has been busy. Recently, he's taken on a global strategic partner, Unilever, that will strengthen RFM's Selecta Ice Cream brand. He's taken on a subsidiary private, and is well into preparations for the second, increasing the value of his company, as well as increasing interest among other potential partners. Meanwhile, he is focused solidly on building his core businesses and is scouting for a strategic partner for the group.

Concepcion, like his father and grandfather before him, wants to build a market-dominating company. But unlike his predecessors, he's building in a competitive environment, with new rules. And he's playing by those rules.

Banthoon Lamsam still needs more money to fully recapitalize the bank. But he knows that he's turned the corner. Thai Farmers Bank will emerge from the Asian financial crisis still at number two, but with a significant investment in "fantastic human capital" and technology that is pushing the industry envelope in Asia. Still, he won't be satisfied until the benchmark he uses is global.

Criticized when it wasn't in fashion to be farsighted, Banthoon can't relax but he can take comfort in the knowledge that he was right to press early for productivity-enhancing reengineering, promoting the best and the brightest in his organization, and making expensive investments in technology that seemed to be evolving hourly by leaps and bounds. But now, everyone knows his secret, and so he's well on the way to developing more.

Across town, Roger Mollerstuen is still struggling, learning how to break-in Thailand's new bankruptcy law so that he can recreate the firm he started building a decade earlier. Not a very exciting way to enjoy the pinnacle of one's career, if it can be called that. But it's necessary. It's necessary for the people he brought into the venture, for the people who believed in him, and for himself.

It is probable that Mollerstuen will be one of Asia's most fascinating success stories. He's not only bringing modern technology—and modern management—to Thailand, he is steadfastly determined to resuscitate a company and mission he believes in and bring corporate law in Thailand into the twentieth century. In the meantime, his customers are counting on him, and by mid-1999 Alphatec was again building new production facilities.

Hotelier John Segreti didn't make his goal with reopening the Shangri-La. Instead of moping about it, he decided to send out an announcement. Above an obviously aging case of fine wine is the caption, "Sometimes, the Finer Things In Life Take a Little Longer."

Segreti had to wait until December 1998 to open his newly refurbished Tower Wing, but he is the first professional hotelier to recreate an Asian hotel—not just the building, but its functionality, the productivity of the people who run it, and the improved business model that will restore it to the ranks of the most profitable and elegant hotels anywhere.

Wee Yue Chew is still hiring three of every four bodies he needs to create and manufacture new machines—and factories. Despite the crisis, he's as hyper as ever, setting the pace, and dreaming up new ways to Excel.

As Asia emerges from the financial crisis, Wee will be incredibly busy. This is not just because of his penchant for productivity and quality, but because he's helped keep his customers in business. And they will remember.

Michael Chan is thinking about the next wave of reengineering at Café de Coral, and where the recovery will lead his business model. In the meantime, he's built up a war chest—his stock has even been in play—from booming sales. Will recovery be as good?

Chan is lucky, and he's smart. While his revenues were growing during the Asian financial crisis because executives were eating down, he realized that good times never last. Therefore, he madly pushed new productivity and cost-reduction initiatives. Recovery will present whole new conditions though, and to keep growing the business, store expansion will once again be in the cards.

Tony Tan Caktiong understands. Since visiting Jollibee, the fast-growing company has made arrangements for additional stores in California. The Greenwich Pizza chain has captured the number two spot in the fast food industry, pushing McDonald's down to number three, which made history. Now the pressure on Tan is to keep the good times rolling.

To do that, Jollibee continues to experiment with new but related businesses. Some work and some don't. But one thing's for sure—Tan will keep experimenting and finding new synergies.

Wong Hong Meng of TA Securities has had a rollercoaster year. First, he was sending his people out for training because they had nothing to do. Next, securities came home and the market shot up when Malaysia withdrew from the global economy. Then, nothing happened. If ever there were a time for innovation, this is it.

Fortunately for Malaysia—and TA Securities—Malaysia will be pulled out of crisis by the rest of the region. But it won't emerge as fast as it could or should have. That means building investor confidence will be a long haul. The success of the firm rides on creating new relationships with new investors, as well as developing new business outside Malaysia. TA's future is clouded, however, by charges brought against founder Tony Tiah in 1999. The company broke securities laws, according to the government, when Tiah helped fugitive businessman Soh Chee Wen defraud struggling Omega Securities. Amid speculation that the charges were politically motivated—Tiah was identified with former deputy prime minister Anwar Ibrahim—the firm announced that it was conducting business "as usual."

Sime UEP's Dató Mohamed Haji Said will emerge from the Asian financial crisis sitting pretty. But not as pretty as he should have. His country's withdrawal from the global economy means it will take much more time to breathe new life into real estate.

This just goes to show how smart he was in the first place to buy low, stay focused, and conserve resources. When he does emerge from crisis, Mohamed—and Sime UEP—may be the only old boys left in town.

Success stories like these are elusive in Indonesia. Sure, there are tycoons who are back to selling commodities to raise money for other ventures that are going nowhere, but that's luck, not good fortune. That doesn't mean that Indonesia won't come roaring back eventually. It will. But first, the country has to find itself. When it does, it may very well look different from the way it does today, and that's probably a good thing.

Despite the enormous creativity and sensitivity of the Indonesian people, its emergence will take time. It needs to incubate and grow. But when that's done, providing government is enlightened and sees the future the way much of the region does, then Indonesia will have an extremely important role to play in Asia, as will Indonesian enterprise. But nowhere else is Peter Drucker's rule weighing so heavy: No monopoly ever existed more than fifteen years. That means that Indonesia's corporate landscape will emerge virtually unrecognizable from the Asian financial crisis. It will face huge challenges, not the least of which is the people challenge, despite its two-hundred-million-strong population. Sadly, no country has neglected educational infrastructure more than Indonesia.

END WORD

Watch out for the New Asian Corporation. It is battle tested, focused, and determined. Here's what business in Asia will be like in the first quarter of the next century.

First, the opportunity is in Asia. There is competition, but no one can compete with the vast, contrast-filled region the world knows as one massive continent. And get this: The Asia-Pacific Century is real. It will happen. It's still on track. There are those who don't think so, and that's fine. But every major global business will count on Asia not just for growth, but for the majority of its business before the middle of the twenty-first century.

Second, Asia is thinking strategically. Ask most CEOs what takes up their time these days, and they'll say strategy, the business model, and vision. That's the stuff of innovation. And innovation is the key to competitiveness. These are not reactionaries, they are managers who are changing the way their industries compete. Don't think so? Take your chances.

Third, there's a new way of doing business, and it is value-driven. Don't expect the best Asian corporations to commoditize their product or service. Instead, they'll keep adding value.

Fourth, the New Asian Corporation is a learning organization. Along with Asian governments, it will increasingly invest substantial resources in education and research and development. It's often said that training and organization won the Second World War. Education and research will win the next century.

Fifth, no monopoly lasts more than fifteen years. This means that the New Asian Corporation will keep reinventing itself. It understands that the reason the American companies examined in Thomas Peters's *In Search of Excellence* didn't stay excellent. They forgot to recreate. Asia won't do that again despite fear of complacency and short memories. It may forget the Asian financial crisis, in time, but it won't forget that there's no tomorrow unless it's created.

It's a new Asia.

~~~ References

"America's Most Admired Companies." *Fortune,* Mar. 2, 1998, p. 38.

"Analysis: Government Investor Rift Over Malaysia Deepens." Reuters, Mar. 16, 1999, CNN, Internet edition.

"APEC Ministers Trip Liberalization Expectations." Reuters, June 23, 1998.

"Asia Must Address Productivity: Political and Economic Risk Consultancy." Reuters, Sept. 3, 1998.

"Asia Needs to Be Smarter in More Competitive World." *The Asian Wall Street Journal,* Oct. 13, 1998, p. 8.

Asian Development Outlook 1998. Oxford, U.K.: Asian Development Bank, 1998, pp. 218, 219.

"Bank Calls Productivity Key to Hong Kong Competitiveness." Xinhua, Aug. 30, 1998, Internet edition.

Baum, J. "Be Prepared." *Far Eastern Economic Review,* Jan. 29, 1998, p. 44–45.

Becker, G. S. "You Want High Returns? Brace Yourself for High Risk." *BusinessWeek,* Oct. 19, 1998, p. 16, 18.

Berfield, S. "Robert Chua—Unplugged." *Asiaweek,* Aug. 10, 1998, Internet edition.

Boey, D. "Sim Wong Hoo Wins Top Business Award Again." *Business Times,* Mar. 28, 1998, Internet edition.

Borsuk, R. "Chicago Business School Picks Singapore." *The Asian Wall Street Journal,* Jan. 25, 1999, p. 6.

Borsuk, R. "For Creative Technology, Share Woes Are in the Cards." *The Asian Wall Street Journal,* Feb. 9, 1999, p. 13.

Bulls, D. "Why Malaysia's MSC and Singapore One Are Missing the Market." *Asia Pacific Economic Review,* vol. V, no. II, Internet edition.

Byrne, J. A. "Jack: A Close-up Look at How America's #1 Manager Runs GE." *BusinessWeek,* June 8, 1998, p. 47.

"CEOs in Asia Upbeat About Growth Prospects, Survey Shows." Survey from PriceWaterhouseCoopers, Oct. 12, 1998, Internet edition.

Chan, A. "As in Chess, Strategic Planning Is a Good Move." *Business Times,* Nov. 19, 1997, Internet edition.

"Charn Resigns From Alphatec After Audit." *The Asian Wall Street Journal,* July 29, 1997, p. 1.

Chen, M. Y. "Borders' Bookstore Formula Is a Hit With Singaporeans." *The Asian Wall Street Journal,* Aug. 5, 1998, p. 8.

Chowdhury, N. "Asia Logs On." *Fortune,* Apr. 17, 1998, p. 33.

Cohan, P. S. *Net Profit: How to Invest and Compete in the Real World of Internet Business.* San Francisco: Jossey-Bass, 1999.

Cohan, P. S. *The Technology Leaders: How America's Most Profitable High-Tech Companies Innovate Their Ways to Success.* San Francisco: Jossey-Bass, 1997.

Collins, J. C. and J. I. Porras. *Built to Last: Successful Habits of Visionary Companies.* New York: Harper Business, 1994.

Cumming-Bruce, N. "Alphatec Restructuring Gets Go Ahead." *The Asian Wall Street Journal,* Feb. 3, 1999, p. 1.

Delhaise, P. F. *Asia in Crisis: The Implosion of the Banking and Finance Systems.* Singapore: John H. Wiley, 1998.

"Entrepreneurs the Engine for HK's Economic Revivial—Tung." *AFP,* Aug. 10, 1998, Internet edition.

Evans, P. B. and T. S. Wurster. "Strategy and the New Economics of Information." *Harvard Business Review,* Sept.–Oct. 1997, p. 71–72.

Farson, R. *Management of the Absurd.* New York: Touchstone, 1996.

Fortune 500 Index for 1998. April 27, 1998, Internet edition.

Freidman, T. L. "Foreign Affairs: The Thai Bind." *The New York Times,* Dec. 11, 1997, Internet edition.

Friedman, T. L. "The Reverse Domino." *The New York Times,* Mar. 19, 1999, Internet edition.

Fuller, T. "Asian Crisis: More Than Just Crony Capitalism." *International Herald Tribune,* Aug. 14, 1998, p. 1.

Gearing, J. "Bite the Bullet." *Asiaweek,* July 31, 1998, p. 47.

Gilley, B. "Buying Binge." *Far Eastern Economic Review,* Aug. 20, 1998, p. 43.

Gilley, B. "Looking Homeward: Tiananmen Exiles Lead Way into China's High-Tech Future." *Far Eastern Economic Review,* Mar. 11, 1999, Internet edition.

Goad, G. P. "Study Cites Demographics for Asia's Rapid Growth." *The Asian Wall Street Journal,* July 27, 1998, p. 1.

"Gold Peak, Ltd." [www.irasia.com/listco/hk/goldpeak/profile.htm]. April 14, 1999.

Goodfellow, R. "Understanding RI Business Culture." *The Jakaarta Post,* Apr. 30, 1998, Internet edition.

"Good Time to Train Workers, Says Malaysian Skill Agency." *Bernama,* June 10, 1998, Internet edition.

Granitsas, A. "Back in Fashion: Hong Kong's Leading Garment Makers Are Going Global—Learning to Add Value and High Technology." *Far Eastern Economic Review,* May 21, 1998, p. 52, 53.

Grove, A. S. *Only the Paranoid Survive: How to Exploit the Crisis Points that Challenge Every Company and Career.* New York: Currency, 1996.

Hamel, G. and C. K. Prahalad. *Competing for the Future: Breakthrough Strategies for Seizing Control of Your Industry and Creating the Markets of Tomorrow.* Cambridge, Mass.: Harvard Business School Press, 1994.

Hamlin, M. A. *Asia's Best: The Myth and Reality of Asia's Most Successful Companies.* Singapore: Prentice-Hall, 1998.

Hamlin, M. A. "Marching Across Asia." *BusinessWorld,* May 8–9, 1998, p. 27.

Hamlin, M. A. "Reengineering Singapore." *Manila Bulletin,* Feb. 8, 1999, p. C-2.

Hamlin, M. A. "The New Competitiveness." *Business World,* Oct. 2–3, 1998, p. 29.

Hiebert, M. "Megabyte Heaven: New Disk Drive Puts Malaysian Manufacturer Into Orbit." *Far Eastern Economic Review,* Aug. 27, 1998, p. 55–56.

Hilsenrath, J. E. "Thai Farmers Recapitalizes; Shares Decouple." *The Asian Wall Street Journal,* Mar. 18, 1998, p. 3.

"How Dare You Say These Things!" *Time,* June 15, 1998, p. 30.

"How Mahathir Wrecked His Tech Dream." *BusinessWeek,* March 22, 1999, Internet edition (editorials).

"IMF Sees Thailand on Verge of Recovery." Reuters, Aug. 16, 1998.

"Inside the Mind of the CEO: A Survey of Asian Chief Executives." *BusinessWeek,* Oct. 12, 1998.

"Internet Thrills: Tough Times Get a Singapore Techie Going." *Asiaweek,* Oct. 16, 1998, p. 82.

Ismail, N. "Reduced Forecast Sinks Creative's Shares." *The Asian Wall Street Journal,* Aug. 10, 1998, p. 6.

Jamaludin, F. "Mission to Explain True Situation." *The Star,* Aug. 16, 1998, Internet edition.

Kahn, J. "Where Asia's Best & Brightest Get Their MBAs." *Fortune,* Oct. 12, 1998, p. 39.

Karlgaard, R. "It's the Software, Stupid." *Forbes*, Aug. 10, 1998, Internet edition.

Kraar, L. "Taiwan Does It Right." *Fortune*, Aug. 17, 1998, pp. 39, 42.

Kristof, N. D. and E. Wyatt. "Who Sank, or Swam, in Choppy Currents of a World Cash Ocean." *The New York Times*, Feb. 15, 1999, Internet edition.

Krugman, P. "Krugman Part 2: Hong Kong's Hard Lesson." *Fortune*, Sept. 28, 1998, p. 27.

Krugman, P. "Saving Asia: It's Time to Get Radical." *Fortune*, Sept. 7, 1998, p. 33.

Krugman, P. "The Myth of Asia's Miracle." *Foreign Affairs*, Nov.–Dec., 1994, pp. 62–78.

Krugman, P. "The Return of Depression Economics." *Foreign Affairs*, Jan.–Feb. 1999, pp. 70–71.

Krugman, P. "What Happened to Asia?" Jan. 1998, http://www.mit.edu/krugman/www/DISINTER.html.

Lian, Y. "An Economic Roundup of Post-Handover Hong Kong." *Hong Kong: The Challenges of Change*. New York: The Asia Society, May 1998, p. 14.

Lipper, H. "Singapore Airlines Will Upgrade Services, Boost Passenger Comfort." *The Asian Wall Street Journal*, Sept. 14, 1998, p. 3.

Lo, A. "The Cyberport Is the Latest Hope for a Brains-Based Economy: But Will It Fulfill Expectations?" *South China Morning Post*, Mar. 14, 1999, p. 11.

Lo, A. "Steps On High-Tech Route." *South China Morning Post*, Mar. 1999, Internet edition.

Lynch, C. "Southeast Asia Still Seen As Solid Investment." *The Boston Globe*, Mar. 19, 1998, Internet edition.

"Making a Bundle in the Rag Trade." *BusinessWeek*, June 29, 1998, p. 53.

"Managing in Asia: A Study of Business Practices and Corporate Images in Asia." *Far Eastern Economic Review*, June, 1997, p. 32.

"Malaysia Bans Government Subscriptions to Three Publications." CNN, Feb. 18, 1999, Internet edition.

"Managing Asia." Interview on CNBC, March 1999.

McDermott, D. "ASEAN Struggles to Regain Its Balance." *The Asian Wall Street Journal*, Oct. 16–17, 1998, p. 1.

"Microsoft Tops All High-Tech Donors." *Computerworld*, June 29, 1998, Internet edition.

Moore, J. F. *The Death of Competition: Leadership & Strategy in the Age of Business Ecosystems*. New York: Harper Business, 1996.

Munk, N. "The New Organization Man." *Fortune*, Mar. 16, 1998, Internet edition.

Nivatpumin, C. and B. Sivasomboon. "The Power of a Good Idea." *Bangkok Post*, June 4, 1998, p. 1.

"NSTB: Spearheading Technopreneurship and Capacity Development." [http://www.nstb.gov.sg/rdn/corsotia/sdmc/ index.html] 1998.

"Oversea-Chinese Banking's Net Profit Falls 27%." *The Asian Wall Street Journal*, Mar. 2, 1999, p. 4.

"Pay and Productivity: The Need to Boost Competitiveness Is Changing the Workplace." *Asiaweek*, Apr. 10, 1998, p. 15.

Pereira, B. "KL Team Counters 'Negative' Reports." *The Straits Times*, Aug. 13, 1998, Internet edition.

Plotz, David. "The Queen of Spin Is Spun." *Slate*, June 6, 1998, Internet edition.

Porter, M. E. Taken from public presentations in Malaysia, Philippines, and Singapore in 1996.

Porter, M. E. "What Is Strategy?" *On Competition*. Boston: Harvard Business School Press, 1988.

Pratap, P. "Don't Rush Into Arms of Cash-Rich Businessmen from West." *Business Times* (Malaysia), Apr. 24, 1998, p. 6.

"PR Blitz to Explain the Measures." *Bangkok Post*, Aug. 14, 1998, FT Asia Intelligence Wire.

Ramos, F. V. "Nationalism in the Age of Globalism." *Asiaweek*, June 12, 1998, Internet edition.

Reichheld, F. F. "The Forces of Loyalty versus Chaos." A special essay for Leigh Bureau, 1998, Internet edition.

Reyes, R. "Expense Doesn't Tarnish Ayala Land and Its Parent." *The Asian Wall Street Journal*, Mar. 30, 1998, p. 13.

Rohwer, J. "Asia's M&A Explosion: What's Holding It Back." *Fortune*, July 6, 1998, p. 82.

Sachs, J. "Global Capitalism: Making It Work." *The Economist*, Sept. 12, 1998, p. 20.

Sachs, J. "Missing Pieces." *Far Eastern Economic Review*, Feb. 25, 1999, p. 11.

Schlender, B. "Peter Drucker Takes the Long View." *Fortune*, Sept. 28, 1998, p. 113.

Shankar, J. "Public Relations Should Be Constantly Stressed." *New Straits Times*, July 27, 1998, Internet edition.

Sherer, P. M. "Bangkok to Unveil Bank-Rescue Plan." *The Asian Wall Street Journal*, Aug. 14, 1998, p. 1.

"Singapore Seeks to Curtail Foreign TV Reporting of Elections." Associated Press, Mar. 13, 1999, Internet edition.

Sirower, M. L. *The Synergy Trap: How Companies Lose the Acquisition Game.* New York: Free Press, 1997.

Sirower, M. L. "What Acquiring Minds Need to Know." *The Asian Wall Street Journal,* Mar. 1, 1999, p. 8.

Slywotzky, A. and D. J. Morrison. *The Profit Zone: How Strategic Business Design Will Lead You to Tomorrow's Profits.* New York: Times Business, 1997.

Smith, Craig S. "Yuan Devaluation Reference Spooks Markets." *The Asian Wall Street Journal,* Jan. 26, 1999, p. 1.

"Survey Says Korean Corporate Executives Highly Aware of IT's Impact on Business." FT Asia Intelligence Wire, May 12, 1998.

SyCip, W. "The Managerial Challenge and Response to the 1997/1998 ASEAN Economic Crisis." Tunku Abdul Rahman Lecture, Kuala Lumpur, Malaysia, June 23, 1998.

Taylor, A. III. "Is Jack Smith the Man to Fix GM?" *Fortune,* Aug. 3, 1998, Internet edition.

"Thai Banks May Be First to Recover—Bankwatch," Reuters, Oct. 16, 1998.

"Thai Government in Public Relations Blitz for Reforms." Reuters, Dec. 9, 1998, Internet edition.

"Thailand: Banking Chaos." *BusinessWeek,* Aug. 17, 1998, Internet edition.

"The Bill & Warren Show." *Fortune,* July 20, 1998, p. 41.

"The Best B-Schools." *BusinessWeek,* Oct. 19, 1998, Internet edition.

"The Economy is in a Shambles." *BusinessWeek,* Aug. 17, 1998, p. 30.

"The Stars of Asia." *BusinessWeek,* June 29, 1998, p. 59, 62.

Thornton, E. "Pursuing Western MBAs—Without Leaving Home." *BusinessWeek,* Oct. 19, 1998, p. 78.

Thurow, L. *Head to Head.* William Morrow and Company, 1992.

Tichy, N. M., and E. Cohen. *The Leadership Engine: How Winning Companies Build Leaders at Every Level.* New York: Harper Business, 1997.

Tiglao, R. "Swimming Upstream: Philippine Tycoon Gokongwei Expands in Tough Times." *Far Eastern Economic Review,* Aug. 20, 1998, p. 46.

Tripathi, S. "A Different World: But Few of Asia's Big-Business Groups Are Adapting to It." *Far Eastern Economic Review,* Aug. 13, 1998, pp. 49–50.

Villamor, R. J. "Inadequate Financial Data Seen Behind Lingering Crisis." *BusinessWorld,* Oct. 12, 1998, p. 1.

Vittachi, N. *Doctor Doom: Riding the Millennial Storm.* Singapore: John H. Wiley, 1998.

Wain, B. "Creating a New ASEAN Way." *The Asian Wall Street Journal,* Aug. 14, 1998, p. 8.

Walker, T. "U.S. Buys $8 Billion of Asian Business." *Financial Times,* June 15, 1998, p. 5.

Weisbert, J. "Dear Microsoft: A Political Correspondent's Advice to His Politically Embattled Employer." *Slate,* Jan. 1, 1998, Internet edition.

Western, L. "Multinational Concerns in Asia Focus on Hiring Top Executives." *The Asian Wall Street Journal,* Sept. 22, 1998, p. 10.

Wiersema, F. *Customer Intimacy: Pick Your Partners, Shape Your Culture, Win Together.* Santa Monica, Calif.: Knowledge Exchange, 1996.

Wong, D.S.Y. "Henderson Land Offers Buyers Incentive." *The Asian Wall Street Journal,* Sept. 2, 1998, p. 3.

Wong, J. "Asia's Middle Class Defies Definitions," *The Asian Wall Street Journal,* vol. XX, no. 85, Dec. 30, 1995, p. 1.

Wysocki Jr., B. "American's Spending Urge Helps Asia-Crisis Victims." *The Asian Wall Street Journal,* Aug. 12, 1998, p. 1.

~~~ Index

ABS-CBN Broadcasting, 29,
    208–11, 214–15
accountability, 26–27
Acer, 32
ACL Consultants, 103
acquisitions: of Asian businesses,
    110–13; and the New Asian
    Corporation, 103–25; pros
    and cons, 113–17;
    reconciling corporate
    cultures after, 121–22. See
    also mergers
added value. See value-added
advertising, versus corporate
    communications, 143–45
affirmative action, 28
Al-Ajmi, Ali A., 218
Alphatec Electronics Group,
    19–20, 25–26, 108–10, 253
Altruda, Vin, 82
Andreesen, Mark, 241
anti-virus software, 88
Anwar Ibrahim, 133, 134, 188,
    264
APEC (Asian Pacific Economic
    Cooperation), and
    liberalization, 56–58
ASEAN (Association of
    Southeast Asian Nations),
    15, 264–66
Asia: affected by prospective
    devaluation of the yuan,
    72–77; business schools in,
    235–37; decline of
    conglomerates in, 30–36;
    defining, 15; importance of
    investing in innovation in,
    197; in the next century,
    14–15, 263–72; net private
    capital flows in, 251;
    productivity in, 177;
    recovery from crisis, 266–68;
    relations between countries
    in, 264–66; reputation versus
    profitability in, 140–41;
    research and development
    in, 226; similarities and
    differences of countries in,
    46–49; understanding of by
    Asians and others, 82–83;

use of Western marketing
    strategies in, 83; and younger
    generation, 28, 95–97,
    101–2. See also Asian
    financial crisis; New Asia;
    New Asian Corporation;
    Southeast Asia; individual
    countries
Asia in Crisis: The Implosion of
    the Banking and Financial
    Systems, 4
Asia Leadership Forum Survey,
    98, 99, 105, 128–29
Asia's Best: The Myth & Reality
    of Asia's Most Successful
    Companies, 50, 95
Asian financial crisis, 1–7, 38–39,
    48, 223–24, 256–57;
    acknowledging, 81–82; after
    one year, 37; analyses of, 3–7;
    and banks, 39–40; as catalyst
    for change, 159–60;
    conglomerates affected by,
    30–36; continued foreign
    investment despite, 7;
    corporate strategy and
    structure during, 91–92; and
    currency trading, 3–4; effect
    on guanxi (connections),
    103–6; effect of on middle
    class, 49–50; factors, 246–49;
    implementing lessons
    learned from, 13–14; and
    investment in management,
    242–45; learning from,
    81–102; and move to strategic
    planning, 156; opportunities
    seen in, 61–62, 86–91;
    overcoming, 81–102; positive
    effect on Asian businesses, 19;
    recovery from, 266–68;
    reforms brought about by,
    59; seen as panic, 3–4
Asian Leadership Forum Survey,
    84–85, 92
Asian miracle, 48–49
Asian Pacific Economic
    Cooperation. See APEC
Asian success, overvaluing,
    253–55

asset building, 87
Association of Southeast Asian
    Nations. See ASEAN
Au Siu-Kee, Alex, 185–86
Australia, seen as innovative,
    189
Ayala Land, 201–3, 205–7, 214
Aziz, Rafidah, 127

Bangkok Bank, 39, 129–30
banking systems, reforming,
    71–72
banks, and the Asian financial
    crisis, 39–40
Banthoon Lamsam, 20, 59, 67,
    72, 93–94, 97, 105, 253, 268
Batavia, 5
Becker, Gary S., 247, 252,
    257–58
Bekins, Michael, 243
benchmarking, 176, 193–94
best cost, 199, 200, 202–3. See
    also best total solution
best price, 199. See also best total
    solution
best quality, 198–99, 200, 202–3.
    See also best total solution
best total solution, 200, 202–3,
    205; as corporate strategy,
    200, 201–19; reasons for
    shifting to, 214–16. See also
    total solution leadership
Black, Sam, 136
Bloom, David E., 48, 206
Bluebird Taxi, 190
Booz Annlen & Hamilton, 31
Borders Books, 82–83
Botly, 23
Boulas, Chipper, 31
brand image, building, 142–43
Braxton Business Model, 91–92
Brown, Tina, 125
Built to Last: Successful Habits of
    Visionary Companies, 157
buses, 122
business ecosystem, 42–43
business schools, 235–37
buzz, 125. See also corporate
    communications; public
    relations; spin

Café de Coral, 22, 86–87, 93, 215–16, 270; and added value, 181
Cahn, Rosanne M., 113
Calcutta, 5
Canton (Guang-zhou), 5
case studies: ABS-CBN Broadcasting, 208–11; Ayala Land, 201–3, 205–7; Café de Coral, 181; Cycle & Carriage, 211–12; Gold Peak Industries, 173–74; Henderson Land, 195–96; Overseas Chinese Banking Corporation (OCBC), 184–86; RFM Group, 164–71; St. Luke's Hospital, 190; Shangri-La, 181–84; Singapore Airlines, 213–14; SM Supermarket, 186–88; TAL Apparel, 196; Trans Capital Holding, 171–73
cash flows, global, 246–59
Cathay Pacific, 143–44
chaebols (conglomerates), 9. See also conglomerates
Champy, Jim, 40
Chan, Michael Yue Kwong, 21–22, 29, 86–87, 91, 93, 181, 270
Chang, Steve, 87–88, 102
Charn Uswachoke, 19–20, 108, 253
China, 179; developing competency zones in, 68; educational infrastructure, 234; family corporations in, 9; foreign investment in, 69; government and public perception, 132; Internet in, 101; and prospective devaluation of the yuan, 72–77; workforce in, 54. See also Canton; Hong Kong; Shanghai; Taiwan
Chin Tiong Tan, 235
Chong Chok Ngee, 231
Chua, Robert, 104
Chuan Leekpai, 129, 130
Citibank, 148
Clarke, Christopher J., 112
Clements, Rick, 213
Coca-Cola, 96
Cohan, Peter S. , 95, 173
collateral, inflated stock used as, 252–53
Collins, James C., 157, 164
competency zones, 62–67, 228; creating, 238–40; developing, 68–71
competitiveness: through best price, 199; through best quality, 198–99, 200, 202–3; through best total solution, 200, 201–19; innovation as a

source of, 189–97; market/customer intimacy as a source of, 198–219; productivity as a source of, 176–89
Concepcion, Jose A. III, 156, 165–66, 168, 169, 268
conglomerates: as acquisition targets, 112–13; decline of, 30–36; effect of globalization on, 34–35; effect of liberalization on, 34; international consolidation of, 35–36; lack of focus and discipline, 32; liberalization's effect on, 161–62; management professionalized, 35. See also chaebols; RFM Group connections, versus strategy, 155–56. See also guanxi; networking
consolidation, international, 35–36
Consumer Bank, 169
Cooperman, Leon, 115–16
corporate communications, 135–36; comprehensive and long-term, 146, 150–51; controlling the dialogue, 145, 146–48; everything communicates, 145, 148–49; principles of, 145–52; publicity, 145, 146; reaching target constituencies, 146, 149–50; using new technologies, 146, 151–52; versus advertising, 143–45. See also buzz; public relations; spin
corporate culture, 25–28, 36–38; at Excel Machine Tools, 117–22; reconciling in mergers, 121–22
corporate identity, building, 125–52
corporate sector, and management, 242–45
corporate strategy: best price, 199, 200, 202–3; best quality, 198–99, 200, 202–3; best total solution, 200, 201–19; examples, 202–3; Gold Peak Industries, 173–74; RFM Group, 164–71; Smart Communications, 191; Trans Capital Holding, 171–73. See also strategy
corporations: principles of successful corporations, 8; reputation versus performance, 136–43; and response to change, 8–9. See also family businesses; New Asian Corporation

Cosmos, 165–66
cost. See best price
Creative Technology, 163–64
Cspel, 117, 121–22
cultural change, and New Asian Corporation, 27
currency: devaluation, effect on Asia, 179–80; trading, and Asian financial crisis, 3–4
Customer Intimacy, 162
customer intimacy, as a source of competitiveness, 198–219
customer retention, and profitability, 162–63
customer service, importance of, 193–94
customer support, 118–19
customers, importance of, 30, 41
Cycle & Carriage, 211–12, 215
de la Rosa, Raffy, 89–90
debt: acquisition, 246; financing, 26
debt to equity ratio, 253
decision making, during transition, 92–95
Delhaise, Philippe F., 4, 267
Dell, 91
devaluation: effect on Asia, 179–80; of the yuan, 72–77
developing country, defining, 51
developing economy, transition from, 50–55
development strategies, 62–67
discipline concentration, 207–14
Doctor Doom: Riding the Millennial Storm, 4
Dornbusch, Rudi, 58
Drucker, Peter, 50, 58, 76, 255, 271
e-commerce, 99–101, 123. See also Internet
economic development, role of education in, 224–29
education: available in the United States, 236–38; benefits of investing in, 227–29; cooperation between Asian and U.S. universities, 235–37; effects of inadequate investment in, 232–34; infrastructure, 229–34, 238; infrastructure, investing in, 234–38, 241–42; innovation through, 223–45; joint ventures, 235–37, 238–40; and value-added per employee, 233
electronic commerce. See e-commerce
emerging economies: defining, 51; importance of workforce in, 54–55; systems and

processes, 53–54; transition
to, 50–55
employees. *See* knowledge
workers; workforce
enterprise resource planning
(ERP), 187–88
equity financing, 26, 255–56
equity flows, global, 246–59
ERP. *See* enterprise resource
planning (ERP)
Estrada, Joseph Ejercito, 53,
131–32, 264
Evans, Philip B., 101
Excel Machine Tools, 21,
117–22, 215, 269; and best
total solution, 200; CAPS,
119–20
expansion, into new markets, 30
exports: Asian, 113; direction
of, 65
extended value chains, 42–43
Exxon, 140

Faber, Marc, 4–5
family businesses, 26; Chinese,
9; Japanese, 9; Korean, 9. *See
also* Gold Peak Industries;
RFM Group
Farson, Richard, 72, 227
fertility rate, effect of on Asian
economy, 49
financing: debt financing, 26;
equity financing, 26
foreign direct investment
(FDI), 247
foreign investment, 69
Fortune Top Ten, 137–39
Fraser, Scott, 91–92
Friedman, Martin, 256, 257
Friedman, Thomas L., 81
Fung, Andrew, 103–4
Fung, Victor, 65–66

garment manufacturing, 124,
196; as an example of
extended value chains, 42–43
Gates, Bill, 52, 123, 134, 164
GE. *See* General Electric
GE Capital, 114–16
General Electric(GE), 30;
corporate strategy, 40–42;
reputation versus
profitability, 140
General Motors, 137–38
Generation X, in Asia, 28,
95–97, 101–2
global capital flows, regulating,
256–59
global equity flows, managing,
246–59
globalization, 2, 9, 38–39;
and Asian corporate
restructuring, 160; of
communications, 152;
effect of, 77; effect of

on conglomerates,
34–35
Gokongwei, John, 32
gold-collar workers, 95–97
Gold Peak Industries, 9, 35;
corporate strategy, 173–74
Goodfellow, Rob, 106
governments, and public
perception, 126–34
Great Giant Pineapple
Company, 190
Greenspan, Alan, 58, 224–25,
228
Greenwich Pizza, 22
Grove, Andrew S. , 163, 255
Guang-zhou (Canton), 5
guanxi (connections), 9: and the
New Asian Corporation,
103–25; pros and cons,
108–10; versus strategy,
155–56. *See also* connections;
networking
Gutierrez, Iva, 203
Gyohten, Toyoo, 83–84

Habibie, B. J., 134, 264
Hamel, Gary, 45, 49, 77, 158,
162
Hammer, Michael, 40
hardware, 45, 77, 84
Hawkins, Jeff, 241
Head to Head, 14
hedge funds, and Asian financial
crisis, 4, 6
Heinecke, Bill, 87
Henderson Land, and
innovative financing, 195–96
Hewlett-Packard, 138–39
Hong Kong, 47, 48, 50, 64, 66,
102, 179–81; developing
competency zones in, 68;
development strategies,
52–53; foreign investment
in, 69; garment industry,
196; political leadership in,
60; property values in,
195–96; and prospective
devaluation of the yuann, 76;
Special Autonomous Region,
76, 102; transformation of
companies in, 21–22;
workforce in, 54. *See also*
Gold Peak Industries
*Hong Kong: The Challenges of
Change,* 180
Hongkong Bank, 143–45
House, Karen Elliott, 127,
147–48
HSBC (formerly Hongkong
Bank), 144–45

Iftikar, Syed, 172
IMF. *See* International Monetary
Fund (IMF)
Indonesia, 15, 46, 47, 48, 64, 188,

271; direction of exports, 65;
foreign investment in, 69;
government and public
perception, 129; growth in
value-added industries,
62; *guanxi* declining in,
106; political leadership in,
60; response to Asian
financial crisis, 2; seen as
innovative, 189–90;
structural reforms in, 72;
workforce in, 54
industrial clusters, developing,
240–42
inflation, and salaries, 244
influence, building, 125–52
information technology (IT),
97–101
infrastructure: economic, 71–72;
educational, 229–38, 241–42;
privatization of, 55–56
innovation: creating
environment for, 192; by
local versus multinational
companies, 189; as a source
of competitiveness, 176–89;
through training and
education, 223–45
Intel, 162–63; promotion of
brand image, 141–42
International Monetary Fund
(IMF), 1, 5, 81, 130, 248,
256–57, 259
Internet, 99–101, 123, 152, 199.
See also e-commerce
investment: in education,
241–42; in educational
infrastructure, 234–38;
foreign, 69; in management,
242–45; portfolio, 250–52,
255–56, 257; in research and
development, 231–32; in
technology, 38
Ismail Adam, 242
IT. *See* information technology
(IT)

Japan, 47, 63; and Asian financial
crisis, 3; corporations in, 9; as
development model, 70–71;
Internet in, 101; investment
in research and development,
231–32; relations with other
Asian countries, 264; Relative
Citation Impact (RCI) index,
232; seen as innovative, 190
JG Summit, 32, 33
joint ventures, educational,
235–37, 238–40
Jollibee, 22, 89, 30, 270
J. P. Morgan, 4

Kang Yong Electric Company,
106
Karlgaard, Rich, 45, 49

Kelly, Philip, 91
Kenichi Ohmae, 58
Kintanar, Frederick B., 232
knowledge workers, 95–97, 101–2
Kopp, Russell, 94
Korea. *See* South Korea
Kristof, Nicholas D., 4
Krugman, Paul, 1, 4, 5–6, 14, 49, 58, 176–78, 191, 247, 250, 258
Kuan, Robert, 190

Lacson, Joseph, 233–34
Lau, Peter, 246
leadership, total solution, 201–7. *See also* best total solution
Ledesma, Jose F. G., 176, 190, 192–94
Lee Kuan Yew, 177, 264
Lehner, Urban C., 60
Leong, K. C., 126
Li & Fung, 9
liberalization, 2, 9, 26, 30, 38–39, 56–58; conglomerates affected by, 34, 161–62; effects of, 77
localizing products, 89
Lo Chung Wing, Victor, 35, 173–74
Long-Term Capital hedge fund, 247–48, 257–58
Lopez, Albert, 123
Lopez, Eugenio III, 208–11, 215
Lopez, Ramon M., 168–69
Loyalty Effect, The, 162

Macao, 5
Mahathir, Mirzan, 127
Mahathir, Mohamad, 61, 68, 111, 127, 132–33, 134, 188
Malaysia, 15, 47, 57, 59, 64, 111, 188, 264, 270; developing competency zones in, 68; development strategies, 52–53; direction of exports, 65; foreign investment in, 69; government and public perception, 126–28, 131, 132–33, 134; growth in value-added industries, 62; lending to private sector, 6; media in, 148; political leadership in, 61; privatization in, 56; productivity in, 177; regulation of capital flows, 257; Relative Citation Impact (RCI) index, 232–33; research institutes in, 230–31; response to Asian financial crisis, 2; structural reforms in, 72; transformation of companies in, 23–24; workforce in, 54.

See also Trans Capital Holding
management: and the corporate sector, 241–45; culture, 25–28, 36–38; of New Asian Corporation, 86–91; principles, 118; professionalization of, 35; training programs, 103–4
Management of the Absurd, 72
Manila, 5. *See also* Philippines
Manotok, Rufino Luis, 199
Manu Bhaskaran, 265
Marcos, Ferdinand, 132
market intimacy, as a source of competitiveness, 198–219
market niches: finding and filling, 87–88; importance of, 163
Marstellar, Burson, 148
media, changes in, 147–48
mergers: and the New Asian Corporation, 103–25; 117–21; pros and cons, 113–17; reconciling corporate cultures in, 121–22; with Western businesses, 110–13. *See also* acquisitions
Meriwether, John, 248
Merton, Robert, 248
Microsoft, 95, 134–35, 136, 162–63, 233–34
middle class, affected by Asian financial crisis, 49–50
Minor Group, 87
Mohamed, Dató Haji Said, 23–24, 270–71
Mollerstuen, Richard, 19–20, 28, 108–10, 269
Mondonca, Lenny, 96
Moore, James F. , 42, 157
Morrison, David J., 39, 40, 41, 64, 96, 158, 174–75, 198
Mudd, Dan, 115
Munk, Nina, 95–97
Murdoch, Rupert, 104
Murray, Simon, 112
Myanmar, government and public perception, 133–34. *See also* Rangoon
"Myth of Asia's Miracle, The," 4

National Economic Action Council (NEAC), 126
networking, pros and cons, 108–10. *See also* connections; *guanxi*
New Asia, 11, 17–77; attempts to attract investment in, 68–71; competency zones in, 62–67; development strategies, 62–67; evolution of, 77; foreign investment in, 69; liberalization in, 56–58; new

model for economic development, 61–62; political leadership in, 59–61; privatization in, 55–56; regulatory environment, 58–59; structural reforms in, 71–72; transition to emerging economies in, 50–55. *See also* Asia; New Asian Corporation; *individual countries*
New Asian Corporation, 7–10, 11–12, 24–28, 43–44, 79–152; and acquisitions, 103–25; and affirmative action, 28; emergence of, 1–2; approach to acquisitions and mergers, 117–21; changes driven by need for enhanced productivity, 188–89; characteristics of, 7, 90–91, 162–64; and consumers, 30; and corporate communications, 135–36; corporate strategy, 12–13, 28–29, 38–42, 91–92, 159–62; and cultural change, 27; decision making during transition, 92–95; expansion into new markets, 30; in the future, 268–71, 271–72; and Generation X, 95–97, 101–2; and *guanxi* (connections), 103–25; and information technology, 97–101; management and corporate culture of, 25–28, 36–38, 86–91; and mergers, 103–25; and opportunity, 29–30, 42–43; overcoming Asian financial crisis, 81–102; ownership and accountability, 26–27; profit zones, 29; and public perception, 135–36; responsibility during transition, 92–95; revitalization and innovation, 29; signs of evolving strategy, 162; and social contract, 27–28; structure of, 91–92; superiority of to predecessors, 24–30; transition to, 36; transition of to younger management, 28
NGO (nongovernmental organization) movement, 133–34
niches: finding and filling, 87–88; importance of, 163
Nimmanahaeminda, Tarrin, 94
nongovernmental organization (NGO) movement, 133–34

OCBC. *See* Overseas Chinese Banking Corporation
Ohmae, Kenichi, 58
opportunities: in Asian financial crisis, 61–62, 86–91; creating, 122–24; and New Asian Corporation, 29–30, 42–43
Overseas Chinese Banking Corporation (OCBC), performance and productivity, 184–86
ownership, 26–27

partnerships: joint educational, 235–37, 238–40; strategic, 26–27
Pask, Stephen, 144
Pelayo, Antonio G., 144
People Power, 132
Petron Oil Corporation, 22–23, 143–44, 217–19
Philippines, 47, 48, 49, 64, 65, 123, 206, 208; attracting investors to, 70; desire to be Asia's Silicon Valley, 233–34; developing competency zones in, 69–70; direction of exports, 65; foreign investment in, 69; government and public perception, 131–32, 134; growth in value-added industries, 62; innovation in, 191; lack of development strategies, 53, 54; political leadership in, 60; privatization in, 55–56; Relative Citation Impact (RCI) index, 232–33; reputation versus profitability in, 141; seen as innovative, 189–90; structural reforms in, 72; transformation of companies in, 22–23; workforce in, 54. *See also* ABS-CBN Broadcasting; Ayala Land; Manila; Philippine Townships; RFM Group; St. Luke's Hospital
Philippine Townships, 167–68
Phutrakul, Teera, 81
Plotz, David, 125
Poranunt Company, 88–89
Porras, Jerry I., 157, 164
Porter, Michael E., 31, 45, 63, 124, 156, 162, 179, 203–4, 205, 243
portfolio investment, 250–52; reliance on, 255–56
Prahalad, C. K., 105, 158, 162
Prapad Phodivorakhun, 106–8
private sector, and public perception, 134–36

privatization, 55–56; Petron Corporation, 143
process engineering, 40
productivity, as a source of competitiveness, 176–89
Profit Zone, The, 64
Profit Zone: How Strategic Business Design Will Lead You to Tomorrow's Profits, 39
profit zones, shifting, 29
profitability: and customer retention, 162–63; increasing, 86–87, 96–97; versus reputation, 136–43
PSI, 168–69
public perception: and the private sector, 134–36; shaping, 126–34. *See also* reputation
public relations, 148–49; for the private sector, 134–36; in the public sector, 126–34. *See also* corporate communications; publicity
public sector, public relations in, 126–34
Pulitzer, Joseph, 145

Ramos, Fidel V. , 56, 64
Rangoon, 5. *See also* Myanmar
RCI (Relative Citation Impact) index, 231–32
real estate, 195–96
reforms, structural, 71–72
regulatory environment, 58–59
Reichheld, Frederick F., 162, 163, 219
reimaging, 143–45
Relative Citation Impact (RCI) index, 231–32
Renful Asset Protection, 103–4
reputation, 136–43. *See also* public perception
research and development: in Asia, 177, 226; importance of, 196; investment in, 231–32
research institutes, in Asia, 230–31
responsibility, during transition, 92–95
Review 200 companies, 140–41
RFM Group, 216, 268; corporate strategy, 164–71; strategic lessons, 170–71
Riley, James, 211–12, 215
risk taking, role of education in, 228
Rohwer, Jim, 112–13, 114–15
Romer, Paul, 45, 49, 77

Sachs, Jeffrey, 3, 5, 225, 250, 256, 257, 258
Saigon, 5

St. Luke's Hospital, 190, 216; productivity and innovation, 192–94
San Juan, Roberto D., 186–87
Scholes, Myron, 248
Schwab, Klaus, 254, 263
Segreti, John, 20–21, 28, 182–84, 269
Selecta, 166
Shanghai, 5
Shangri-La Hotel, 20, 27, 269; and Singapore labor situation, 181–84
Shih, Stan, 32, 102
Siam Commercial Bank, 130
SilkRoute, 123
Sime UEP Properties, 23–24, 270–71
Sim Wong Hoo, 102
Singapore, 47, 50, 64, 117, 179, 240–41, 264; and Borders Books, 82–83; and joint programs with U.S. universities, 235–37; developing competency zones in, 69; development strategies, 52–53; direction of exports, 65; foreign investment in, 69; government and public perception, 133; growth in value-added industries, 62; Internet in, 101; labor situation, 181–84; media in, 148; productivity and growth in, 177–78; proportion of scientists and engineers in population, 229; Relative Citation Impact (RCI) index, 232–33; seen as innovative, 190; transformation of companies in, 20; universities, 235–37; workforce in, 54. *See also* Shangri-La
Singapore Airlines, 213–14, 215
Singapore Digital Media Consortium (SDMC), 236
Singapore Management University (SMU), 235–37
Singh, Anoop, 130
SIRIM Berhad, 230–31
Sirower, Mark L., 114, 115–16
Slywotzky, Adrian, 39, 40, 41, 64, 96, 158, 162, 174–75, 198
Smart Communications, corporate strategy, 191
SM Supermarket, technology and productivity, 186–88
SMU. *See* Singapore Management University
social contract, 27–28
software, 45, 49, 77, 84
Southeast Asia, 15; and Asian financial crisis, 3–7. *See also*

Southeast Asia (*continued*)
Asia; New Asia; *individual countries*
South Korea, 63; corporations in, 9; lending to private sector, 6; political leadership in, 60; proportion of scientists and engineers in population, 229; research institutes in, 230; structural reforms in, 72
Southwest Airlines, corporate strategy, 203–4
Special Autonomous Region, 76, 102. *See also* Hong Kong
spin, 125, 146–47; by the private sector, 134–36; by the public sector, 126–34. *See also* buzz; corporate communications; public relations
Stiglitz, Joseph, 126
stock, used as collateral, 252–53
strategic planning, shifting to, 155–77
strategy, 38–42; acquisition and merger, 117–21; brand image, 142–43; corporate, 91–92; corporate communications, 143–45; defining, 164; development, 62–67; evolving, 162; and focus, 28–29; General Electric (GE), 40–42; importance of, 10, 40, 159; mergers and acquisitions, 114–15; in successful companies, 8; strategic lessons, 170–71; for transition from developing to emerging economy, 51–53. *See also* corporate strategy; strategic planning
structural reforms, 71–72
Suharto, 129, 188
Sunonwealth Electric Machine Industry Company, 123–24
Sunthorn Arunanondchai, 110
Surin Pitsuwan, 265
surveys: of countries with innovative companies, 189; on effect of government policies, 128–29; on importance of *guanxi* (connections), 105; on information technology, 97–99; on reaction to Asian financial crisis, 61–62; on trends in Asian business, 84–86
SyCip, Washington, 155
synergy, achieving, 122

TA Enterprises/Securities, 23, 92–93
taipan, definition of, 32
Taiwan, 47, 48, 64, 87–88; productivity in, 177; proportion of scientists and engineers in population, 229; research institutes in, 230; workforce in, 54
TAL Apparel, investment in research and development, 196
Tan Caktiong, Tony, 22, 29, 30, 89, 190, 235, 270
Tanmantiong, Ernesto, 89–90
Tan Say Choon, 172
Tarrin Nimmanahaeminda, 129, 130
technology: importing, 192–94; improving, 88–89; investing in, 38; younger workforce in, 95–97
Teera Phutrakul, 81
Thai Farmers Bank, 20, 93–94, 129–30, 268
Thailand, 50, 55–56, 64, 81, 87, 88–89, 111, 264; and Asian financial crisis, 3–4; banking in, 93–94; bankruptcy law, 19, 26, 109–10, 269; banks in, 129–30; direction of exports, 65; foreign investment in, 69; government and public perception, 128, 130–31; growth in value-added industries, 62; lending to private sector, 6; political leadership in, 59, 60; recovery from Asian financial crisis, 267; Relative Citation Impact (RCI) index, 232; response to Asian financial crisis, 2; structural reforms in, 72; transformation of companies in, 19–20; workforce in, 54
Thai Military Bank, 130
Thurow, Lester, 14, 129
Tiah Thee Kian, Tony, 23, 92–93
Tiananmen Square, 132
Tichy, Noel, 138
total solution leadership, 201–7. *See also* best total solution
trade regulations, reforming, 71–72
training, innovation through, 223–45. *See also* education
Trans Capital Holding, corporate strategy, 171–73
transition, decision making and responsibility during, 92–95
transparency, lack of, 253
Treacy, Michael, 198

Trend Micro, 87–88
Tung Chee-hwa, 102, 180
Tyler, Glenn, 88–89

United States: Asians educated in, 236–38; Relative Citation Impact (RCI) index, 232
universities: cooperation between Asian and U.S., 235–37

value added, 180–81; industries, growth rate of, 62; transition to, 224
value chains, 42–43
Vishwanath, Tara, 249, 250
Vittachi, Nury, 4–5
volatile money, 247; role of, 249–55

Wain, Barry, 134
wealth creation, 45–46
Wee Yue Chew, 21, 118–22, 200, 269
WEF. *See* World Economic Forum
Weisberg, Jacob, 134–35
Welch, Jack, 30, 40–41, 115
Wen-Tzen Lim, 111
wetware, 45, 77, 83–84
Wiersema, Fred, 162, 198, 200
Williamson, Jeffrey G., 48, 206
Wong, Eddie, 74
Wong Hong Meng, 23, 92, 97, 270
Woo, Gordon, 55–56
workforce: competition for, 101–2; and corporate cultural changes, 27; recruiting, 95–97; role in transition from developing to emerging economy, 54–55; and social contract, 27–28; training and education, 13. *See also* education
Work-Out, 40–41
World Economic Forum (WEF), 263, 266
World Port, 123
World Trade Organization, 258
Wurster, Thomas S., 101
Wyatt, Edward, 4

Yang, Marjorie, 124
Yip, Paul Kwok Wah, 104
yuan, prospective devaluation of, 72–77

Zhang Yan, 73
Zhu Rongji, 73